TRUSTING IN REASON:
MARTIN HOLLIS AND
THE PHILOSOPHY OF SOCIAL ACTION

Books of Related Interest

PLURALISM AND LIBERAL NEUTRALITY
edited by Richard Bellamy and Martin Hollis

THE PHILOSOPHY OF UTOPIA
edited by Barbara Goodwin

THE IDEOLOGY OF ORDER
by Preston King

TOLERATION
by Preston King

THINKING PAST A PROBLEM
by Preston King

HUMAN RIGHTS AND GLOBAL DIVERSITY
edited by Simon Caney and Peter Jones

Trusting in Reason: Martin Hollis and The Philosophy of Social Action

edited by
PRESTON KING
Emory University and Morehouse College

Routledge
Taylor & Francis Group

LONDON AND NEW YORK

First Published in 2003 by
FRANK CASS PUBLISHERS

This edition published 2014 by Routledge
2 Park Square, Milton Park, Abingdon, Oxon OX14 4RN

Simultaneously published in the USA and Canada by Routledge
711 Third Avenue, New York, NY 10017

Routledge is an imprint of the Taylor & Francis Group, an informa business

British Library Cataloguing in Publication Data
Trusting in reason: Martin Hollis and the philosophy of social
action
1. Hollis, Martin – Influence 2. Social action – Philosophy
I. King, Preston, 1936– II. Hollis, Martin
361.2'01

ISBN 0-7146-5500-7 (cloth)
ISBN 0-7146-8400-7 (paper)

Library of Congress Cataloging-in-Publication Data
Trusting in reason: Martin Hollis and the philosophy of
of social action / edited by Preston King.
p. cm.
Includes bibliographical references and index.
ISBN 0-7146-5500-7 – ISBN 0-7146-8400-7 (pbk)
1. Hollis, Martin. 2. Ethics. 3. Social action. 4. Practical
reason. I. King, Preston T., 1936– II. Title.
B1646.H754T78 2003
192–dc21

2003004499

This group of studies first appeared as a special issue of *Critical Review of
International Social and Political Philosophy*, ISSN 1369-8230, Vol.4, No.4
(Winter 2001) published by Frank Cass and Co. Ltd.

Contents

Preface   vi

Trusting in Reason   *Preston King*   1

Liberalism for the Liberals, Cannibalism
for the Cannibals   *Steven Lukes*   35

Hollis, Rousseau and Gyges' Ring   *Timothy O'Hagan*   55

Trust and Political Constitutions   *Albert Weale*   69

Trust, Choice and Routines: Putting the
Consumer on Trial   *Roberta Sassatelli*   84

Whose Dirty Hands? How to Prevent
Buck-Passing   *Barbara Goodwin*   106

Many (Dirty) Hands Make Light Work:
Martin Hollis's Account of Social Action   *Steve Smith*   123

The Bond of Society: Reason or Sentiment?   *Robert Sugden*   149

Collective Reasoning: A Critique of
Martin Hollis's Position   *Nicholas Bardsley*   171

A Quick Peek into the Abyss:
The Game of Social Life in Martin Hollis's
Trust Within Reason   *Alan Scott*   193

Rational Choice and Trust   *Keith Dowding*   207

The Rule of Law and the Rule of Persons   *Richard Bellamy*   221

Abstracts   252

Notes on Contributors   257

Index   260

Preface

I

The object of this volume is to commemorate the work of Martin Hollis (1938–1998), an exceptionally gifted philosopher, Professor at The University of East Anglia from 1981, Fellow of the British Academy, author of a string of excellent, probing, versatile works – among them, *Models of Man: Philosophical Thoughts on Social Action* (1977), *Invitation to Philosophy* (1985), *The Cunning of Reason* (1987), *The Philosophy of Social Science: An Introduction* (1994), and *Reason in Action: Essays in the Philosophy of Social Science* (1996). His last book, *Trust Within Reason* (1998), attracted considerable critical attention, as is evident in the essays that follow. Also, Martin Hollis – among other things – was an editor of *CRISPP* (*Critical Review of International Social & Political Philosophy*). He played an active role in the work of this journal, and *CRISPP* remains sorely diminished by his loss.

Martin Hollis had an impressively coherent philosophy of social science and thus of social action, in which he routinely distinguished between 'understanding' and 'explanation', taking the view that the aptest accounts of human interaction would be retrieved via 'understanding'. He focused more upon the (human) *reasons* for, rather than upon the (natural) *causes* of, action. Hollis refused nonetheless to allow his 'insider' or non-causal account to dissolve into either relativism or authoritarianism. The patterns of group behaviour (like those etched by 'laws of supply and demand') were seen more as the convergence or sum of particular reasons, rather than as a naturalistic, non-ethical force field overriding rationality.

Hollis's account is individualistic, in the sense that reasoning constitutes individuality – not in the sense that reasoning is a relativistic or materialistic or arbitrary by-product of individualism. Hollis's view is that social action is grounded in rationality. It is a view in no way subverted by the consideration that error is the companion to all our reasoning. Given rationality, persuasion kicks in as a crucial device for the management of both social change and stability. Hollis's individuals are embedded in and significantly shaped by the existing social structure: the individual is not a self-moved mover. But individuals help to form and re-form social structures through engagement in the public rationality of interpersonal discourse.

Hollis was an individualist, and a respecter of individuals. He met difference at an open door, smiling. Hollis could live with difference. More likely, he could not live without it. But this itself was a manner of constituting a community. For Hollis, individuality was grounded in community. Hollis's individualism was facilitated by British academic culture, and in Hollis's case it took the form of an energetic, but never peevish, rationalism. It may even be true that Hollis's commitment was really more to rationality than to individuality as such. Except for the highly individuated perkiness of the man's mind. Except, too, for the difficulty of securing rationality where an actor has no individual strength of character, strives too little to think for self, and embraces unreflectively what is already circumscribed as the 'known'.

Hollis's primary community was the academy. It was as interesting and challenging and (thus) congenial for him to lecture in China as in Oxford. He was strongly marked by communal allegiance, driven by a desire to understand and to lend a hand – without desiring to be gripped by hand or clapped on shoulder. Thus in Hollis's work one finds not only insight, logic and wit, but also empathy, respect and mutuality, virtues governed by their own enactive and expressive logic. Rationality, wit, mutuality, transparency and service – these qualities can themselves constitute *Gemütlichkeit, Gemeinschaft*, in short the fellow feeling of a community. They did so with Hollis.

Martin Hollis was a triangular personality, in the sense that he had great intellectual penetration, great heart, and a nicely disciplined exuberance. His mind enabled him to grasp important issues, his heart to relate these to social needs, while his sharp and unfailing wit cast matter, which might normally appear somber, under a more striking and playful light. Hollis was a puzzler, problem-solver, gamesman. His analyses are brisk, refreshing, amusing. Even colleagues of a markedly less 'rationalist' or 'foundationalist' bent, unhappy with the substance of the argument, cannot but admire the elegant and pithy style.

The academy is full of edgily counterpoised argument. In the end, it cannot – certainly it should not – be otherwise. No mind ought to subscribe to a train of argument for fear that disagreement may cause offence. Argument defines the academy, and those unduly put off by contestation, would do best, no doubt, to relocate elsewhere – perhaps to berry-picking or to the exercise bike or to solitary consultation with Higher Powers, unseen and unanswerable. To argue without counterargument is like playing tennis without a partner. The complete indisposition to engage with argument, like the stony disposition to argue always for argument's sake, have it in common that they are equally tedious. One discovers little tedium in Hollis.

It is difficult to think that many of the objections raised against 'rationalism', as by Michael Oakeshott, are not really more to do with misplaced judgment than with the inadequacy of reason. For many who are rational enough, still have very poor judgment, and cannot readily tell when to turn rationalization aside. It is much the same as if, making the acquaintance of a splendid, faultless, coloratura soprano, one accompanied her on long walks, waited on her at endless parties, sat with her at dinner upon dinner, throughout all of which she hadn't the good sense to do anything other than sing relentlessly. The fact that judgment must place limits upon all engagements, including reasoning, is not sensibly to be taken as an argument against rationality.

Hollis's individualism was marked, less by the suspicion that rationality could undermine itself, than by the consideration that too much theorizing, along specifically and narrowly individualistic lines, could sap the solidarism and mutuality of community, on which any worthy rational individualism must stand.

II

Hollis's work centrally revolves round the concern to explain social action. In the essays that follow, that work provokes independent reflection and much lively and insightful debate touching on reason, rationalism, relativism, individualism, solidarism, citizenship, consumerism, trust and ethics generally, along with the status of social science method and rational choice theory and questions to do with how all of these relate or not to one another.

The opening essay does no more than brusquely to explore a fundamental presupposition running pretty consciously through all of

Hollis's work and which touches – if less consciously, then no less centrally – all these essays: that reason and rationalism are more implicit in discourse than subject to external proof or disproof, be it reasoned calculation or empirical demonstration.

Lukes amusingly attends to the knotty problem of relativism, upon which Hollis makes unrelenting war, in the manner of Alexander at Gordium.

O'Hagan dilates knowledgably upon the distinctive type of altruistic individualism and expressive rationalism dear to Hollis, under the troubling, passionate and challenging influence of Rousseau.

Weale, from a constitutionalist perspective, spots and queries the unconventional character of Hollis's individualism, given that Hollis's contractualism is based, not strictly on self-advantage, but on a form of social solidarism ('generalised reciprocity'), which pursues the good of future generations and of strangers – without requiring the omission of some good to self.

Sassatelli has sympathy for Hollis's altruistic individualism and expressive rationality, while seeking to redeem the 'consumer'- whom Hollis insinuates is morally inferior to the 'citizen' – along just such lines. For Sassatelli's consumer is as rational as any citizen, steeped in values, bonding with others in and by rituals of consumption.

Goodwin's essay is also situated within the framework of Hollis's individualism, where individuality implies responsibility, and where responsibility too often prompts evasion, or 'buck-passing', which Goodwin's analysis seeks to help us avoid.

Smith, like Goodwin, is concerned with the problem of 'dirty hands'. Carefully and gradually, via recall of Hollis's intellectual stages of the cross, Smith works up a reluctant critique of what he views as Hollis's failure to get us past that problem.

Sugden, like Veale, Smith and Bellamy, is a past Hollis collaborator, and takes the position that a stronger case can be made contra Hollis in defense of an empiricist, as over against a rationalist, social science methodology.

Bardsley takes up Hollis's critique of rationality as commonly used in economics (rational choice theory), endorses Hollis's broad concern with 'collective' reasoning, but concludes that collective reasoning requires a proper account of spontaneous cooperation if it is to work.

Hollis finds a way of combining an expressive, rational individualism with a supportive form of communal solidarity, retaining a healthy suspicion of unhappy extremes of both individualism and solidarism.

Scott accepts the feasibility of some such combination, while (a) regarding Hollis's account of sociology as exaggeratedly solidaristic, and (b) insisting upon transcendence of the individual-group polarity even in such early sociological accounts of social action as furnished by Durkheim and Mauss.

Just as Scott beats back the attacks of Hollis as he finds them to apply to sociology in general, so Dowding excavates a parallel system of earthworks round the pulsing heart of rational choice theory. Just as Sassatelli contends that trust is pervasive even among consumers, so Dowding maintains that trust is trivially incorporated into the behaviours predicated by rational choice theory as a whole.

In the most extended account in the book, Bellamy takes up a key problem emerging from Hollis. Namely, if we accept, with Hollis, that the enlightenment of self-interest does not so much make it more moral, but only more deeply self-interested, how can we establish a fair political order which somehow bypasses the engaged self-interest, hopefully enlightened, upon which 'rule of law' is standardly presumed to rest?

These essays are essential to the exploration of the work of Martin Hollis, and Hollis's work is central to European debates on social science methodology over the past quarter of a century.

My hope is that this book may excite a re-reading of Hollis, as well as a first reading for those who have not yet had that pleasure. This should enable, first, a deeper appreciation of Hollis's gifts. Second, perhaps more importantly, such reading should better anchor appreciation of the role of reason, and the place of trust within it.

Preston King

1

Trusting in Reason

PRESTON KING

This essay is to do with the basic or elemental status of reason in human discourse. The elemental status of reason underpins and runs through the essays of this volume as a whole. Even where I do not directly advert in what follows to particular authors, what I have in mind in developing the overall position – even as deep background – is essentially the work of Martin Hollis and the commentaries on him in this collection.

I

One important aspect of the matter could be framed as follows: are the claims of reason universal? Or perhaps: in what degree are the claims of reason universal? This opens a door onto the question of relativism. Where we ask if the claims of reason are universal, we are likely enquiring whether we can rely upon reason, whether it is not more temptress than friend, and indeed whether there is really any such thing as truth. There is so much dispute among us about 'truth' and 'justice' that we seem forced to ask whether *this* – and, if the two are ultimately distinct, whether *these* – can ever be more than an illusion. Can we show that there is such a 'thing' as truth, or justice? And how can we possibly persist in thinking we might make such a demonstration – in the dank, vaporous mist of dispute that shrouds these matters?

A second aspect may be expressed differently: Are the claims of reason universal for *some* types of thought and not for others? In discussions of reason or rationality, one of the first issues we encounter is whether the concern is more to describe (hence science) or to prescribe (hence ethics). Is it possible that the one type of rationality is universal, and the other not, or less so? Even if they are assigned an equal rationality, there is still the underlying question whether science and ethics involve genuinely distinct types of rationality. The science/ethics divide is a vital matter for Hollis, since 'the science of society' is a human science, raising the question whether we can have a 'human' or 'humane' science that is not at the same time significantly prescriptive.

Michael Oakeshott remarked the distinction between the 'wink' and the 'blink'. If a grasp of the functioning of human society is to be achieved merely causally, then explanations will follow the model of the 'blink'. If we achieve this grasp by reference to intention, then we adopt the model of the 'wink'. In the one case, we are more concerned with what happens *to* humans, consistent with what happens to the rest of creation, allowing no explanatory gap to intrude between human properties and the properties of other beings and things. In the other case, we are more concerned with what is made to happen *by* humans, however frail and even wretched these creatures are, which insinuates a moral breach between beings that are governed by understanding and purpose, and such other beings and things that are not.

It is enough for now to note the claims for divergence within reason between description and prescription, a divergence sometimes grandly inflated (no doubt misleadingly) into a larger clash between 'science' and 'philosophy'. We return to this divergence in the next section. It is best at this stage to concentrate principally on reason taken as a single and united enterprise. The question must be what it means to challenge reason, or the universality of reason. And this must lead to the question whether we intend reason to be dispensable, and whether there may be one or some alternative(s) to 'reason' or 'rationality' in general. In short, can we sidestep the use of reason, whatever our failures and omissions in exercising it?

What inordinate relief there should be in locating an infallible criterion, the last word, the most sacred text – beyond which we need not poke or spy – of Howtoduism. And how understandable it must be, at least for many, to dream of abandoning the tool of reason that serves us so unreliably, the tool that – worse than unreliable – may seem cleanly broken. *Errare humanum est*: true. But suppose it is not just we ordinary mortals who stumble. Suppose it is the wisest of our kind: *aliquando bonus dormitat Homerus*! Suppose moreover it is not just Homer, but Jupiter, or indeed Jehovah himself, who sleeps! What then? What way out is there for the logician with 'a dream deferred'? What exit is there for the philosophical pilgrim who cannot find a way, one who despairs of locating, let alone 'recovering', this Holy Grail? Does reason, *de pire en pire*, just shrivel up, like 'a raisin in the sun'?

If there is some valid and comprehensive criterion of truth, it is at least clear that we do not have it. Coherence theories are less than satisfactory. Our theories may be logically coherent and still have nothing to do with the facts. Correspondence theories are no better placed. Our theories may correspond to some of the facts, but if theory is universal, and mortals are limited, then we can never secure evidence for universality. We may try to combine coherence and correspondence theories, but the effort appears misconceived, since they are genuine alternatives, and combination yields incoherence. Much else may lie on the table, and none of it fails to occasion a certain academic moaning and gnashing of teeth.

We may reach for Karl Popper's 'falsifiability' criterion and be told the criterion is not so precise as appears, and that the 'basic statements' that enable falsification are not reliable. We may go for the less demanding 'research programmes' of an Imre Lakatos and be told that the method is little more than formal admission of an inability to be more incisive. There is no larger theory of truth or justice or beauty that has ever gone without significant challenge. On the 'evidence', which here means inductively, there can be very little reason to think this will change. Who can tell us abstractly and reliably how we do great science, how we attain moral perfection, or what we must do to write a superlative novel or sculpt a breathtaking bust? It seems improbable that the global college of sages shall ever be satisfied by any universal theory or criterion, whatever its merits, that proposes a formula reliably validating or invalidating all possible claims to truth or justice or beauty.

The agent is, of course, always fallible, hence the need for caution, self-correction, openness to criticism and tolerance. The agent will distinguish (or attempt to distinguish) between appearance and reality, illusion and actuality, the true and the false. The agent, alas, is cautious and open precisely with a view to 'getting it right'. And yet that goal, to 'get it right', lies in an icy and slippery zone, and the failure to score excites much despair. It is no wonder that one may be inspired to think of escape from reason altogether in view of the failure and controversy that dogs its use. Or is this aspiration to escape from reason just another twist in the various turns peculiar to reason itself?

However vexed we may be by our failures, and however understandable may be our despair, the question remains: what options are left? How would it be possible, in attempting to reason our way out of the bag of error and misdirection, just somehow to shed the rationality that so disappoints in our attempts to reach the light? How might we escape from the nets of reason, and if not from 'commitment' to it, then at least from engagement in it? However impoverished and unimpressive our attempts at being rational, what would we *have* to do, what would we be *able* to do, to secure release from the clutches of rationality? We are advised that there are options. We are told, for example, that reason is too narrow; emotion has its place; possibility vastly exceeds our imaginings; we must surrender to impulse, to Love, to ecstasy, to God, to gods, to Faith, to Nature, to Nurture, to Tradition, to History, to asceticism and mysticism. We may even be advised, as by the late Paul Feyerabend: 'anything goes!'

We can, of course, be sure of little. But that little excludes 'anything goes!' For if anything does go, then nothing at all is excluded. If nothing is excluded, then the opposite of 'anything goes' is permitted. If 'anything goes' admits its negative, then it admits that 'nothing goes'. But 'nothing goes' cannot be reconciled with 'anything goes'. This injunction is mired in self-contradiction. However much 'goes', we can be sure it will no more be 'anything', than it is 'everything'.

It makes all the sense in the world to attempt to escape narrow constraints, poverty of the imagination, limited education, foolish prejudices, etc. But whatever we turn to – *omne ignotum pro magnifico* – must be presumed to have some rational content, without intending that this makes it correct or right. Wherever we turn – and even when we are 'not for turning' – it is we who are calling the shots. That is to say, it is what we hold or enjoy or submit to as reason – the rationality within us – that opens the door to Biology or Science or Nature or Tradition or History or whatever.

Andy Young, heading up the demonstrations against racially segregated communities in Chicago in 1966, tells the story of an energized colleague, the Reverend Bevel, who breaks in upon him in the early morning, announcing a vision. The vision was of The Lord, sitting atop Bevel's clothes dryer, enjoining this good man to help to end the carnage in Vietnam. Young confesses here and there to his own divinely inspired moves in life, and thus was not well placed to dismiss out of hand the truth of Bevel's account. But it seems unlikely that Young would quite have seen what Bevel saw, even were both simultaneously transfixed by that remarkable machine. Presumably people who are educated to think that there are visions, such as Bevel's, are more likely than not to see them, given 'appropriate' circumstances. What better way can there be to cap a train of reason, in susceptible company, than with a vision? Visions need not be false. The most persuasive of them most likely are not. But reason can be quite devious. And 'envisioning' is not to be ruled out, in the right setting, as one of the more imaginative turns that reason can take. Sigmund Freud drew similar conclusions regarding e.g. the rationale of dreams.

It might be well to abandon 'reason', in the sense of operating in some alternative mode. The only question is, what that mode might be. Intuition is itself a dimension of reason, and the adoption of any distinctive mode of thinking – such as the theological, scientific, traditional, etc. – is again (on reflection) just another way of reasoning. To think in 'alternative' ways may instance good or bad reasoning. What it does not instance is the *abandonment* of reason, and genuine alterity. The cloth being cut here might be called 'the rational perspective'. It assumes the agent is, ever and anon, what the agent is, and, however the agent was made, or however the agent chanced to evolve, that it is the agent's implicit, ratiocinative decision to embrace whatever is embraced. And that embrace is reflective of such reason as agents have, for better or worse.

The knockdown argument for reason or rationalism, then, may merely be that one cannot coherently avoid it, at least when making claims about what is or about what ought to be. This is not so much to recommend it, as to say that recommendation, in such a matter, is superfluous. In so far as we think at all, then in such degree are we rational. There are higher and lower levels of rationality. There are better and worse ways of making use of reason. But all modes of thought – scientific, ethical, aesthetic, etc. – are categorially rational. So, although we can recommend that we improve at this game, we cannot relevantly recommend that we engage or not engage in it. This was the key principle to which Martin Hollis implicitly held.

It is all very well to complain about dogmatism in reason, but the very fact that we can register the complaint suggests that dogmatism cannot be a part of its meaning. It is all very well to postulate that agents are typically disposed to advance (disguise?) as universal those principles that uniquely favour their own peculiar interests; but the fact that the advocate confuses her individual will with 'the general will' does not show there is no general will. That actors and singers (and academics) may be partial to their own performances does not count against the contention that performances are not all of a piece, are better and worse. Public figures, and not astrologers only, commonly profess knowledge of the future. The fact that they most commonly get it wrong does not mean that there is no future, or that far-reaching claims about it are necessarily incorrect. Some histories (The Bible, Marx, Toynbee, inter alia) make claims that are remarkably broad, unsubstantiated and teleological. But the fact that they are broad and unsubstantiated does not, as such, confirm that they are mistaken.

We may complain ad nauseam, and in the most general terms, about error. Yet the persistence of error does not and cannot demonstrate the inaccessibility of truth. To assert the contrary of the proposition, p – that p is false – is to identify (what one takes to be) an error. To identify (what one takes to be) error is no more nor less *in se* than to lay claim to (putative) truth. Any such claim as that there is no truth, or no objectivity, obviously presupposes what it denies. It does not matter whether we are talking science or ethics. One cannot assert p or not-p without presupposing truth. To claim that there is no truth is to claim that this claim at least is true. To claim that there is no objectivity is to say that this at least is objective. There is an old trap here, which one may aptly call 'the trap of truth'.

The assertion of error is not an escape hatch from the category of truth. It is just another move in the self-same game of claim and counter-claim that aims at truth. It becomes futile ever to assert error in such a way as to convey that the error is evidence for categorial denial of possible access to truth. In this we must be careful that our opposition to falsity does not overreach itself, becoming false in turn by overturning the truth-grounds on which assertions of falsity must rest.

What we appear to be left with as unavoidable is the operative assumption that a coherent proposition must be either true or false, whether or not we know that the concrete claim, p, is one or the other. And that would appear to be much the same as assuming there to be a criterion of truth, despite the fact of not actually having one (i.e., one whose reliability has been properly demonstrated). At least it is not self-contradictory to claim that x, y, z is true, or that x, y, z is false – even where one has no altogether coherent methodology for accessing truth, no plainly coherent criterion for identifying falsity. It is perfectly coherent, though not necessarily sound, to make truth claims x, y, z. It is both incoherent and unsound   to derive from falsity-claims the conclusion that these demonstrate the impossibility of truth. In so far as that is a classic expression of relativism, then relativism up-ends itself.

If I claim that the coherent descriptive proposition, p, is either true or false, I am still entitled to make this claim, even if I am ignorant of which it is. (It is true that the Olde Curiosity Shop is still standing or not, however much or little I know of the matter.) If I claim that the descriptive, p, is neither true nor false, I still intend that what I say (in this) is true. (The Olde Curiosity Shop may be neither standing nor the contrary, in the sense that parts of the original may still stand while much of it, equally, may have been replaced or destroyed.) But this only signals the importance of precise quantitative rigging.

To extend the argument provisionally to ethics: if I claim that the ethical proposition, p, is neither right nor wrong, I still mean that what I say (in this) is right. But that means, in this circumstance, that it is somehow in order, morally, for the agent to adopt either of two opposed stances, to do either p or not-p. This may be to marry one spouse (monogamy) or several (polygamy); it may be to drive on the left (in Papua New Guinea) or on the right (in Tahiti). If relativism is self-contradictory, can it be that this is only so in science, and not in ethics or aesthetics? Still provisionally, one may say that one believes in truth no less – just because four may as readily be reached by $1+1+1+1$, as by $2+2$. Still provisionally, one may be said to believe no less in due process, whether to do with trial by a jury of twelve, or trial by trained judicial assessors numbering, say, three. Where we have two quite distinct organs, (a) the jury of twelve, and (b) the three judicial assessors, we are not radically mad to adjudge both to be right or fair or just or simply OK. Does there lurk anywhere in all this a case for moral relativism? The argument of this paper is in the negative.

II

Broadly speaking, both scientific and ethical questions may provoke answers that we label, at least in aspiration, 'true'. If we take rationality in the round, most especially in relation to its scientific and ethical components, we may concede a common and persistent urge to 'get it right'. Equally, we may insist upon a divergence in rationality. It may be argued, on the one hand, that this divergence accommodates ethics as an inferior engagement; on the other, it may be contended that science and ethics, while diverging, are somehow equally 'rational'.

Whether there is equality of rationality as between science and ethics may best be left to one side, for the moment. The more immediate question is whether these modes of rationality actually diverge or not. The most relevant way to answer this question may be to inspect the possibility of reducing the one mode of discourse to the other. Thus first: if description can be reduced to prescription, or (vice versa, and more relevantly) if prescription can be reduced to description, then this argues for the negation of divergence. Thus second: if that reduction cannot be achieved either way, then this must argue for confirmation of divergence. If divergence is confirmed, this still leaves open the matter of equality of rationality as between science and ethics. If, further, equality is established, what still remains open is the need to explore the precise respect(s) in which equality of rationality between these two might obtain.

So, can description be reduced to prescription, or vice versa? (There is reason not to use (a) 'description'/'prescription' and (b) 'is'/'ought' and (c) 'facts' and values' altogether interchangeably, as I shall show below.) To think that prescription is reducible to description is at least plausible, since so many have tried it. Besides, we need only recall that Kant, e.g., supposed time and space to be distinct and irreducible, while Einstein viewed them as a continuum, meaning that one could be translated into the other. May a similar rapport obtain as between 'is' and 'ought'?

I shall advance a conventional, if still not universally accepted, claim – to the effect that reducibility is not an option. I shall hope to present this, in the first instance, fairly economically. To state that 'x is/is not the case' is distinct from contending that 'x ought/ought not to be the case'. Suppose the claim to be (A) that Mexico City *is* more than 7,000 feet high. Suppose a parallel claim to the effect that (B) Mexico City *ought* to lie at more than 7,000 feet. (It is as possible after all – which is not to say as easy – to raise the level of a city, as to raise the height of buildings within a city.) If B can be said, in principle, to have 'validity', then the validity of the ethical claim B is logically unaffected by the truth or falsity of the parallel factual claim A.

Thus one cannot infer any B ('ought') from any parallel A ('is'). I may have climbed Kilimanjaro or not; shot my enemy or not; aborted the child or not; passively endured the discriminatory antics of my government or not; laboured for independence or not; helped to feed thousands starving or not; been pleased with myself or not. But in none of these cases does it follow that the prior fact described (A) allows any directly parallel logical inference (B) regarding what I ought or ought not to do or have done. To say this is not to say that there can be *no* connection of any sort between describing and prescribing, only that there is no strict logical derivability of Bs from parallel As, of 'ought' from 'is'. When I say no Bs from parallel As, the *parallel* requires attending to. I am speaking strictly here, about any bare description, such as that 'Hitler *is* rounding up Jewish people', or 'The Christian militias *are* attacking Shatila', which then becomes converted into the matching or *parallel* claim that 'Hitler *ought* to be rounding up' etc, or that 'The Christian militias *ought* to be attacking' etc.

Perhaps the only reason for the contentiousness of the claim that 'ought' is not derivable from 'is' stems from the common tendency to formulate the claim too loosely. To say that one cannot derive 'ought' from 'is', or (just a touch more loosely) prescription from description, has much the same intent as saying (more loosely still) that one cannot derive a 'value' from a 'fact'. 'Much the same' – but still perhaps not quite. Consider the difficulty. Let us say that I make the banal claim, 'I climbed Kilimanjaro'. The claim in this case is descriptive. But the question is whether this 'fact' (description) is altogether devoid of 'value', at the least of an evaluative component.

If we focus upon the agent who makes this declaration, it will be clear that he could as well have made a million and one other claims – indeed virtually infinitely many of them. The agent was not compelled to declare what he declares. This is far from being the only claim he could have made. He could have said: 'I tied my laces at the foot of Kilimanjaro.' He could have said: 'I saw the dead rhino and the smashed Citroen a moment after they collided on the Mombasa Road.' He could have said: 'I lit a mosquito coil in my tent on the night of 25 December thirty years ago and it caused me to cough and splutter.' And on and on. There can be no need to continue with such a litany of options. We shall readily agree that the possible claims that might be made are without number.

The fact that the agent could have said something other than what was said means that the factual claim, 'I climbed Kilimanjaro', is only one of an unspoken number of possible claims that might be made. The fact does not declare itself. It is declared. The fact does not select itself. It is selected. The fact is never obvious in the sense that it leaps from the page or from the ground or even from heaven, though one who reaches out to catch it may be excused for thinking so. Where a fact is declared, some agent declares it. Though the fact remains a fact 'for all that', it is no longer – of course it never was, strictly speaking – a *value free* fact. For the fact cannot now be taken apart from its *declaration* as a fact. We are always entitled to look at facts, not just as they may be conceived to exist *in se*, but as otherwise evitable claims which someone *chose* to make, which someone thought worth *making*, which someone somehow thought to *matter*. We are entitled always to ask why it was that Anne or Abe chose to say this and not that. It becomes entirely appropriate, consequently, to qualify, not the fact *in se*, but social declaration of it, as a speech act, or an act of speech, or an act through speech. A word may easily substitute for a slap in the face, or a pat on the back, and so much more. Any such act, as by an agent, can be said, or left unsaid. Any such act, as through speech – quite like all those acts that bypass speech – is *prima facie* subject to choice. An act through speech, being subject to choice, to commission or omission, is for that very reason categorially moral – assuming the act to be social. To say that an act is categorially moral is not to say that it is either categorically good or bad, right or wrong, better or worse. But it is to say that it will qualify for possible characterization in one of these terms.

Accordingly, wherever we view facts as being declared – and we shall find it difficult to enunciate any that are not – then we are equally always looking at acts that are subject to choice, and thus also subject to potential commendation or censure. If e.g. I say, 'all Africans are liars' (as the late Lord Salisbury famously did in heated debate over unilateral independence for Rhodesia), then listeners are likely entitled to draw certain conclusions about my character from that remark. Not because I am mistaken: for how probable can it be that one might locate an adult denizen of any clime who has not told a fib? Listeners are likely entitled to make moral inferences because my claim, freely chosen as it is, has a moral tenor. I selected it, I chose it, when I could have done other, and very likely better. Thus from any *statement* of fact, you are entitled to make some valid moral inference, given that the speaker, in a social context, chose to make this claim from among myriad others that could as easily have been made in its place. The minimal inference to be made from anyone's statements of fact is that the speaker places some value upon making those statements. Otherwise there would have been other statements – or indeed none.

Given that we must choose or select 'facts' in order to perceive them, it follows that we can have no facts that are not fished from the sea of theory. This is not the same as saying (with Bishop Berkeley) that facts unperceived do not exist. It is only to say – absent theory, perspective, commitment, interest – that we cannot otherwise know them to exist. The recuperation of facts is unattainable without perspective, engagement, point of view, conditioning, training and so on. Where we posit hypotheses, we may search for those facts only that we think may confirm or disconfirm them. Where we identify, as cleavers or axes or knives, a cache of obsidian stones located along the mountain tributary, that identification is only possible due to our possession of an historical and archeological framework that makes sense of stones in these terms. Where Juliet identifies Romeo as the proper object of her romantic love, she can only make this identification due to the personal and social framework (ideology) of romantic love that is already in place. Where the Church undertakes an Inquisition to ferret out witches, this is done by the grace or malice of a theory that claims bodies can be and are possessed by evil spirits. Where Hollywood so commonly privileges elaborate displays of violence, as among cinematic cowboys, policemen, soldiers, gangsters, space warriors and the like, the thing is incomprehensible absent a persistent Manichean division of society (domestic and international) into 'good guys' and 'bad guys'.

We could recognize no claims as facts had we no theories to hold them together. (That there is a pen on my table is a fact, but had I no general construct of a pen, it is not a fact of which I could make much sense.) So facts do not impose themselves. They are, and can only be, assimilated from some perspective. Attending to facts means choosing them; choosing them means evaluating them; and it is always in this sense that we 'value' them, which is to say either positively or negatively.

The point remains, as established earlier, that (b) we cannot strictly speaking derive 'ought' from 'is', though it should now be plain, as established immediately above, that there is a firm sense in which it might be said that (c) we are able to derive 'values' from 'facts'. The claim (b) does not contradict the claim (c). It is only important not to run them together and mistake them for equivalents. The only utility of this parenthesis – relating to the possible derivation of value from fact – is to play a more sharply focused light on the precise and restrictive character of the claim that 'ought' cannot be derived from 'is'. Because 'no ought from is', may sometimes be read as the strict equivalent of 'no value from fact', we do best to surrender any suggestion of equivalence, thus to sidestep a tired and often misplaced retort. Too often the correct claim that we may, in the sense advised, derive 'value from fact', is implausibly thrown down as a supposed demonstration of the non-derivability of 'ought from is'.

If 'ought' cannot be derived from 'is', it is even easier to show that 'is' cannot be inferred from 'ought'. In this sense: if I argue for the good of B, I am not required to assume the parallel fact of A. Thus if I claim that fire is desirable (here and now), the validity does not logically depend on the fact of my actually being possessed or not of fire. Whether I ought to have it, is unaffected by whether I do have it or not. I may have fire, and this fire may be desirable (it will be used to warm the sailor I have just fished from the sea). I may have fire, and this fire may be undesirable (perhaps I am a pyromaniac). If the fire is desirable, is a good, when I have it, it is presumably just as desirable, no less a good, if I do not have it. Because I ought to have fire it does not follow that I do have fire. Because the children ought to have food, it does not follow that they do have food.

Thus we rule out the derivation of 'is' from 'ought', just as we ruled out the derivation of 'ought' from 'is'. This claim for the non-derivability of 'ought' from 'is' or 'is' from 'ought' is in turn an affirmation of divergence as between science and ethics. This is not to deny that science ought to be subject to ethical direction. Nor is it to deny that ethics ought to be informed regarding the facts to which it seeks to give moral direction. But this leaves unaffected the two claims, that As cannot be logically inferred from Bs, and that Bs are not logically derivable from As.

On the non-derivation of 'ought' from 'is', a final comment. It should be seen that a formal case for the falsity of this claim *can* be made. The case is unsound, but all the more reason to underscore the point. Suppose one were to say, if abbreviatedly, that A *is* the Provost of Emory University, or *is* the President of Iraq, or *is* the Captain of the grounded oil tanker, Exxon Valdez... and therefore *ought* to promote gender equality, or *ought* to attend fairly to the needs of Kurds, or *ought* not casually to put at risk Alaskan wildlife. In any of these cases, it might be asserted, however precipitously, that 'ought', *mirabile dictu*, has been derived from 'is' – directly contradicting all that was painstakingly urged before.

Hopefully, one requires no distinguished professorship in philosophy to see that this supposed derivation of 'ought' from 'is' constitutes no such thing. 'All is not as it seems'; 'appearances are deceiving'; etc.

Which is much the same as saying that Goldilocks is no bear, never mind that she sleeps in a bear's bed; the wolf is not Grandma, despite the uncanny resemblance; no more than the cuckoo, nested among doves, transcends its counterfeit identity. No prescription (where equivalent to 'ought') is logically derivable from a description (here equivalent to 'is').

The positions of provost, president, captain: these are all roles. Roles detail acceptable or excludable forms of conduct. It may well be a 'fact' that A is Provost. But the office of Provost comes with and imposes upon office-holders a set of moral and legal expectations; and so similarly with the presidency (which requires, among other things, an oath of allegiance); and so again with the captaincy. Where we say to the Provost, 'you *are* x and *ought* to do y', we are inferring, from the prior (normative) burden of the office, that she is under a broad obligation to promote the equality of welfare for all students; and we infer from this general principle the particular defence of e.g. gender equality. The appearance of the inference may be from description to prescription, but is actually from a wider to a narrower norm. Though that normative inference takes on a descriptive disguise, the description remains a disguise, and the valid substantive derivation is never from 'is' to 'ought', so that 'ought' is never reduced to 'is'.

Here we find prescriptions being masked as descriptions. A moral claim may be made to appear non-moral. The process of disguise may be innocent or deliberate. Nothing can be more common. The *appearance* of the teacher's rebuke to her class is plainly descriptive, where she admonishes them: 'we do *not* talk during exams!' But they *are* in fact talking. They are talking during the exam. Her object cannot be to point out to them what they *are* or are not doing: this they already know. The *reality* of her concern is to change, rather than to describe, actual conduct. She is not literally stating but is plainly intending to show what desirable action consists in, and to insist that it be deployed. She is conveying, somehow 'against language', how students ought to behave and she is demanding that they do so now. This intent may be lightly veiled, but is nowhere obscured, by her form of words. The words constitute a piece of rhetoric, and the rhetoric makes a pitch for conformity. Her veiled demand is a call for a conformity precisely because it does not now obtain. And she calls for it on the falsely implicit grounds (herewith the rhetoric) that the desired behaviour is already on display. The teacher's speech, read off as an intention, is then less a description than an appeal.

How we explain the proclivity deliberately to disguise prescriptions as descriptions is another matter. Possibly, if we are already persuaded that only facts matter, and that values are wisps of cloud on a parched horizon, then such camouflage and mis-description may be perceived as an effective means of either altering or re-enforcing moral behaviour. This indirect and furtive resort to moral language is a 'persuasive' use, not so much of definitions (an echo of C.L. Stevenson), as of accounts.

We do well, however, not to infer from the distinctiveness of the ethical perspective, a form of argument for mind over matter, or for the triumph of human will over the 'blind forces' of nature. It has nothing to do with such claims as that the human body is (prospectively) entirely subject to the human will. The human will can of course work wonders, wonders even that we might not normally credit. But in the end our capacity consciously to control the body has severe limits, however admirable it often is to seek to impose such control. After all, a fairly conventional object of the human will is to avoid death, as Hobbes claims. Were the will so distinctively powerful, it might be fair to think that very many more of our antecedents – the overwhelming bulk of whom died long since – would be moving among us today. Were the human will stronger than we know, we should expect to meet with a more impressive narrative of survival. Thus the concern here is not with willpower. It is, rather, with how we are to come to grips with the legitimation or delegitimation of intentions and decisions, as distinct from the confirmation or disconfirmation of historical or material or descriptive observations and hypotheses.

III

The general position advanced thus far, with regard to description and prescription, is that each nudges us onto a different path, and that it seems as well to surrender to the divergence. The argument for divergence claims no more than that one cannot come to grips with an ethical point of view by reconfiguring it as an exercise in scientific observation. One may not explain the point of an ethical stance in the terms appropriate to scientific description. One may not suppose that (1) an explanation e.g. of the biological evolution of humans or the social evolution of systems can do the same work as (2) understanding whether it is one direction, D, or some other direction, O, that ought to be taken, given the heavy pressure to act that lies upon this individual or that group *now*. The conclusion is that descriptive and prescriptive claims belong to different categories and that to confound them is a category mistake.

It is now in order to pursue a little further a specific dimension of the divergence between science and ethics, in particular the relation between human nature, on the one hand, and political or social philosophy, on the other. Observers commonly enough attempt to describe human nature, and then, drawing on that description, seek to extract from it some relevant prescription(s) about how we should live or how we should conduct affairs of state. Whether that is a legitimate tactic depends in part on how it is done, how far it is pushed. If, e.g. in conflict resolution, one is to have any prospect of settling disputes, one must learn as much as possible about the facts attending the case: history, economy, culture, etc. One must assimilate the facts of the dispute in order to overcome it. One must be aware of the way in which understanding the underlying facts in a problem situation may contribute to solving the problem posed. But one cannot assume that the facts lie beyond modification and are only to be reified. If it is an historical fact that two peoples have always made war (i.e. for as long as we can remember), it becomes intolerable to conclude that this is an affair that ought to continue (or ineluctably *shall* continue) for that reason. One must be careful in short regarding the line to be drawn, on the one hand, between *relating* pertinent facts to desirable outcomes when making decisions and, on the other, *making* outcomes desirable because they are consistent with what one identifies as the facts.

To propose somehow to derive a political or social philosophy from an account of human nature would be more persuasive if there were general or even universal agreement on what that nature might be. If we are bound by a common nature, nothing can be plainer than our unrelenting disagreement about its character: whether altruistic or egoistic; herd-like or highly individuated; self-improving or slothful, and so on. However, despite so much variation in the description of what is taken to be 'human', we ought not to allow disagreement as such, on this or any issue, to have a final bearing on whether or not the question can be resolved in principle. The last thing that should put a spoke in our wheels is conflicting viewpoints about the nature of wheels.

Even if we cannot agree on what we take to be the content of human nature, we are still entitled to (a) hypothesise that there may/must be something distinctively, descriptively, and objectively 'human' about humans, (b) hypothetically locate this content as specifically x or y or z, and then (c) test, logically and morally, for what might follow from the designation of that content. Do we invariably find that we can make no sound logical transition from (b), a biological or material condition, to (c) a normative or social conclusion? It is not in dispute that the facts of a matter always have some at least loose bearing on the morality or justice of outcomes associated with it. The question rather is whether we can strictly infer from a description of human nature some related political or moral philosophy. The hypothesis embraced here is that there is no exception to the non-derivability of (c) from (b). We find surprisingly many, among them earlier incarnations of John Searle and Alasdair MacIntyre, who kick against these pricks, with the doubtful happiness that follows therefrom.

Suppose we say that all humans are alike in various material – not ideological or philosophical – respects. We may assume them all to have e.g. use of speech, or bipedal motion, or a capacity to use tools, or to think abstractly and to plan, etc. If we claim descriptively that they *are* all distinctively alike in respect to use, say, of speech, then (whether this claim is true or not) it still will not follow that they all *ought* to be treated in the same way (give each a boiled sweet). Nor does it follow that they all *ought not* to be treated in the same ways (boiled sweets to some, carrots to others, nothing for the rest). It is difficult to see, whatever the facts, how anything specifically moral follows, strictly logically, from the 'facts' of human nature. From the fact that humans are bipedal, it no more follows that they ought to have comprehensive, statewide health care, than that they ought to have exclusively private health care. From the fact that humans have speech, it no more follows that they should treat one another with respect, than that they should treat one another with disdain. If they ought to treat one another with respect, the conclusion cannot follow from the fact that they speak: those who do *not* speak presumably ought also to be accorded respect.

If we say with Aristotle that 'man' is by nature a 'social animal' (*zoon politikon*), it does not logically follow either that 'he' ought to be politically active, or not. It does not follow that 'he' ought to seek a 'middle way' (*via media*), or not. If we say with Hobbes that 'man' is by nature solitary and egocentric and proud, it does not follow morally that 'he' ought to be governed along despotic lines, or not. For even if we agree on what human nature 'is', this still will not enable us strictly to infer how it 'ought' to be socially managed. Nature and morality, 'is' and 'ought', are intimately intertwined, but they remain stubbornly distinct. Description always helps, knowledge of prior conditions is immensely helpful, but the fit between these and emergent moral and social principles is not easily made, and certainly not deductively.

The standard concern to evoke evolutionary biology to overleap the divergence between science and ethics has a doomed look about it. It is important to determine how and under what imperatives human society evolved, thus the play of territoriality and other matters will helpfully divert us. But having recovered the territorial or sexual or other imperatives of the capricorn beetle or of the bonobo or even indeed of ourselves, it remains a separate moral question whether or not we are right to strike at Iraq or any other state on anything more than a suspicion that Iraq may wish to strike at us, or indeed may already have done so. Humans are perhaps as much territorial as they are appetitive creatures. But the fact that one does and must occupy territory says absolutely nothing about how and when and on what principles such occupations should be enacted. The fact that humans have been equipped via evolutionary biology with unspeakable appetites for fat and sugar does not allow us to infer that we ought now to gorge ourselves on such substances. A factual history will establish how we have been dealt the hand we hold. But it is for agents in place to determine how that hand should now be played. It is no use saying we are driven by history, by nature, by tradition, by God – since it is ultimately by our will or decision that we say this, and by our will or decision that we implement whatever we infer follows from this.

The only exception to the non-derivability of (c) a normative or social conclusion from (b) a biological or material condition is the obvious one – viz. that (b) itself, supposedly strictly factual, already contains some moral premise, usually disguised. Thus these supposed derivations of 'ought' from 'is' are belied on inspection by the fact that the supposedly completely biological or material premises on which they are predicated are nothing of the sort: they involve from the start a normative evocation of 'nature' transcending dry-as-dust 'descriptions', such as that this supposed nature is 'balanced' or just' or 'ideal' etc., meaning, in all such cases, 'fit to be emulated'.

Herewith an end of this pardonably brief detour into the wood of human nature and social philosophy. We readily enough recognise that the question of 'the nature' of human nature is vexed. But we presumably also recognise that we can put the question of 'nature' aside in as far as it bears on the present concern. We seem unlikely ever to be able logically to derive from it any conclusion regarding what we are entitled or have a duty to do.

IV

Having concluded that rationality bifurcates and displays itself in at least two distinct spheres, the descriptive and the prescriptive, the predominant form of rationality that we now address is to do with ethics. The problem is whether the 'truth' of ethical questions is any more avoidable than that of scientific questions. Can we avoid such questions as: what *ought* I to do? Or: what *must* I do? The problem reaches well beyond determining 'what *can* I do'. Of course 'ought' implies 'can', but mere *possibility* is not here the issue. Having already taken possibility on board, having conceded its plural character, the issue becomes: which of these paths *ought* to be taken? One may imagine this question to apply only to the individual, as in the isolated, pre-Friday circumstances of R. Crusoe. But these are not the circumstances of most people most of the time. Even were the position otherwise, it suffices to note that humans are interrelated and interactive in such degree that they cannot characteristically be read off as isolates.

'What I want to do' is the absorbing concern of the isolate. 'What I ought to do', by contrast, is the distinctive concern of the social animal – which is also to say the moral animal. We may contest, individually and socially, the proper answer to the question: 'what ought I to do?' But it is hard to see how we might escape the question as such – putting death aside. One may duck the idea that there is such a question by mistakenly assuming that 'what I *ought* to do' is another way of asking 'what *do* I do', or 'what do I *want* to do'; but that is not effective evasion of the need to respond.

'What I ought to do' is the province of moral, and by collective extension, of political and social philosophy. It is a large matter, it has many twists and turns, and in no one essay can these be attended to in gross. We must restrict attention to some smaller aspect of the larger debate. A convenient way of exploring the rationality of ethics, understood as a response to the question, 'what ought I to do?', is by enquiring, following Steven Lukes, whether 'there is a single best way for humans to live'. It seems fair to say that Hollis would claim that there is.

Other will be disposed to claim that there is not. Others still will be agnostic on the matter.

We have said enough to suggest that it would appear pretty useless to inspect this plainly moral question ('is there a single best way for humans to live?') from a descriptive perspective, so to treat it as mere matter of fact. We have seen that there is likely little point in trying directly to derive an answer to the question from some set of initial claims regarding what human nature, as a matter of fact, happens to be like. So, first, let us take it that the question is coherent. Second, let us take it that it is moral and not descriptive – that it is concerned with whether we are right to live in some one particular way or following more some complex design. Third, let us take it that the question can be answered 'yes' or 'no'.

It is helpful to enquire what hangs on such a question. On the one hand, if there *is* a single best way (this is some sort of universalism or monism), we presumably have an obligation to seek it out. If, on the other hand, there is *not* a single best way (this is some sort of pluralism), then we presumably have a moral obligation to tolerate practices that diverge from those we preemptively endorse or reflectively approve. It will be clear that neither answer enables us to escape from the sphere of moral discourse – and indeed moral obligation.

Let us now inspect more closely the logic of the notion of 'a *single* way', whether or not that single way is best. With regard to this more limited notion of 'a single way', we are entitled to say that any set is a unity, and yet of itself (usually? always?) embraces plurality. A unity is a combination of otherwise diverse elements. Biologically, dogs will be dogs. Yet they come in many varieties. Each member of the species remains genetically unique with respect to all other members, without relinquishing specific inclusion. Philosophically, at least ethically, what is right is right (sauce for the goose being sauce for the gander, etc.); yet it may be right to keep left in Zanzibar but wrong to keep left in Mali.

It will be clear that 'a single way' need not be secured by simple exclusion of variety. If we now move by extension to the larger notion of 'a single *best* way', we shall see that we need not conclude – should we confirm that there is one best way – that all those creatures bound by it must receive, express or implement it in exactly the same fashion. No rule of behaviour, such as 'love thy neighbour', enjoins that those subject to the rule must enact it in every case in a strictly identical fashion. In this example, love comes in different forms, and is appropriately expressed in different ways, to different agents, on different occasions.

'Single' need not mean identical, invariant, inflexible, etc. Let us suppose for a moment that 'single', as in 'a single best way', adverts to a universal principle. A 'universal principle' is allowed to be 'single', without 'single' necessarily excluding divergent applications, as indeed with virtually all laws. Hence a universal principle such as, 'have regard to the needs of others', accommodates considerable divergence in application, such as the gift of a ball to the child, or a crutch to the arthritic pensioner. A law governing fraud or murder is virtually always variably applied (and rightly so), depending on such factors as age, gender, mental state or capacity, etc. The varying conditions for applicability are a thorn in the side of prospective consistency. That is a problem we cannot dismiss. Yet there seems no reliable way in which the conditions for variability of application could ever be fully spelled out. This is one powerful reason for the discretionary authority of judges (however constrained that discretion).

The argument then is that the notion of a single way, as of a single best way, need not be read off as excluding variety. The universal demand, e.g., for equality of treatment is one of many answers to the question whether there is 'a single best way'. To treat all others equally, where equality of treatment can be read off as a moral universal, does not mean to treat all others, at all times, identically. To treat, say, all pupils equally might mean – where the object is to secure equality of *result*, as in writing and reading, and as in the early years of education – that teachers give more time to the less able, so to bring them up to speed. To treat all students equally, contrariwise, might mean – as with equality of *opportunity* – conferring special incentives (like prizes or awards) upon those who perform better, the object being to select only those from a cohort who are most competent at some critical skill, this being the legitimate concern of such as code-breakers, engineers, and logicians *inter alia*. In short, equality, conceived as a 'single best way', must still be implemented in variable ways, having a more homogenising effect in some cases and a more discriminatory effect in others.

If we say there is a single best way, given the way that unity works, we are not necessarily saying that diversity is excluded. Unity may admit of diversity. Unity may even require diversity. That is the principle which so much American coinage proclaims: *e pluribus unum*. (It will not matter that for some interpreters of this phrase, and possibly for many, the intent is to have unity swallow plurality.) In exploring the notion of 'a single best way', it is fair to conclude that a universal norm may readily admit, if not require, pluralistic theses, in the form of variability of application of the universal. This suggests that we must entertain plurality as an expression of universality, not as an alternative to it.

Much of this sort of discussion is conducted under the rubric of Absolutism (A) v. Relativism (Rm), and in that guise may be ill-conceived. If A and Rm are both moral categories, then any Rm, at the most abstract level, is presumably either self-contradictory or a sub-category of A. If, that is to say, Rm is taken to claim that there is no such thing as moral right or wrong, and if the idea is that this claim is right, then Rm is self-contradictory. If, however, Rm is not self-contradictory, then it is to be assumed that 'Rm' is really no more than a pluralism (pl) – which is to say that it is no more than a sophisticated, supple, flexible, sensitive instance of A. If, at the most abstract level, 'Rm' is really 'pl' – i.e. one of various members of the set A – then 'Rm' qua 'pl' only has the effect of sanctioning a higher degree of variation (there is usually *some* variation) within moral behaviour than may be allowed by some other member(s) of the set A. If this is right, then we seem unable to avoid working with some assumption of universal reason, in morals as elsewhere, even where we are able to recognise, with hindsight, that we were mistaken in some previous judgement x or y or z.

We now take it that the idea of there being 'a single best way' concretely encompasses, either always or at least often, more than one possible application. With that in mind, we can now intrude or underscore (with some risk of confusion) a distinction between absolutism (A) and universalism (U), where A, at least theoretically and at the limit, allows no variability in application. Under this scheme, where A admits no varied applications, it follows that A must oppose U, which allows such variation. This means that A will allow no pl as a member of its set, whereas U does allow pl as a member of its set. If we accept such a thesis, then we must significantly alter received views. First, the notion of absolutism has to be made more rigid; second, the notion of universalism has to be admitted as more supple; third, and most importantly, universality and plurality cannot be seen as mutually contradictory.

The fact that drivers are expected to keep to the right in one country and to the left in another means that there is no *absolute* (here = 'global') rule of the road of the type, 'always keep to the left, no matter when or where', or 'always keep to the right, no matter when or where'. But that does not mean that there is or ought to be *no* universal rule of the road whatsoever. The fact that there is *no* one rule, of one specific sort, that we can see to be universally applicable, along the lines of 'keep to the right, no matter etc.', does not mean that there is not or ought not to be a relevant and universally applicable rule of some broader kind.

In fact, should we enquire more closely, there does appear to be a universal rule of the road that applies. And it might be formulated roughly like this: 'normally keep to *some* one side of the road, whether to the left or the right'. The applicable material conditions are that there be (a) an established path or road, (b) two-way traffic, which is (c) moving at a moderately fast pace. The side that is kept to should presumably be that which is locally agreed or enforced – whichever side that is.

It could be countered of course that this is perhaps to do with law, but nothing to do with morality, since we are concerned in such a matter with prospective behaviours ... that are intrinsically indifferent. But that is not altogether so. We are presumably bound by a rule that we not bring upon others (perhaps also not upon ourselves) unnecessary or unwarranted harm. When we drive, especially when we do so inattentively, we may well endanger the lives of others and of ourselves. Thus, it would appear a legitimate moral norm, when driving, to 'keep to some one side of the road, and to that side which law and common practice prescribe'.

If it is true that some given community, say the UK, should *not* be bound by all the rules that bind some other community, say US, then all that this need signal is an area of legitimate difference. It does not show that there is no relevant higher universal by which both communities are bound. Nor does it show by extension that the negation generates a space for moral relativism or that this relativism enjoys some universal validity. In the example given, the universal claim, 'keep to some one side of the road', seems to work well enough, as a higher claim, and a legitimate one, held in common by all those communities otherwise marked by left/right vehicular cleavage.

We encounter many legal and moral notions of 'a single best way'. The case of 'a single best way' for traffic to circulate is banal. Its very banality, however, may be an aid to clarity. Given the abundance of possible counter-examples, we have all the more reason to attend to so simple a case with care, and to hope for greater clarity from it.

The immediate problem with 'universalism' or 'foundationalism' is the prospect of confusing it with absolutism. If we identify universalism with absolutism, then universalism may be made to appear comprehensively – which is to say mistakenly – oppressive. And the smell of oppression predictably excites revulsion, including a reactive anarchism. We must be got to see clearly that universalism, if sometimes expressed through absolutism, is not coextensive with it.

To delineate the mistake involved in confounding universalism with absolutism, it will suffice to disengage and elaborate on four different types of rule (R):

- R1: universal: e.g. 'drivers should keep in principle to one side of the road, irrespective of country'.
- R2: absolutist universal: e.g. 'drivers should always keep to the left'.
- R3: absolutist universal: e.g. 'drivers should always keep to the right'.
- R4: pluralist universal: e.g. 'drivers should keep to some one side, left or right, which side being subject to local decision'.

Inspecting these four rules, we readily see that R2 and R3 (both universal and absolute) are mutually contradictory.

We also see that R2 and R3 (both universal and absolute) contradict R1 and R4 (both universal but not necessarily absolute).

Finally, we can see that R1 and R4 (both universal but not equally unambiguous) need not be mutually contradictory.

All of these rules, R1 through R4, are to be regarded as universal. But only two of them require to be regarded as absolutist. R4, though universal, is also pluralistic, in that its universality consciously accommodates variant, non-contradictory applications. R1, too, is universal; it is only absolutist if it excludes variant applications; but it is not clear that it achieves such exclusion. For R1, in claiming that drivers should keep to *one* side of the road, does not expressly claim that this side must be always and everywhere the same – by contrast with R2 and R3. It is in this way that the absolutism of rules is commonly ambiguous, which is to say that what seems to be an absolutism may often be no more than an underdeveloped pluralism.

It probably makes sense in the end to allow that R1 – as a universal (U) marked by a certain ambiguity – can accommodate the pluralism (pl) that marks R4. If we do that, then R4 is just a superior formulation of the intent of R1. For that reason we may transit to R4 directly, and conclude that R4 is a U that includes pl (keep to right, keep to left). Since all of the rules R1 through R4 are universals, while only two of the rules,

FIGURE 1: UNIVERSALISM

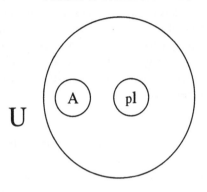

FIGURE 2: PLURALISM

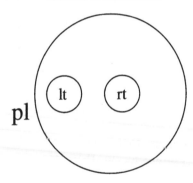

FIGURE 3: ABSOLUTISM

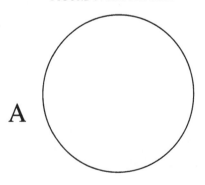

R2 and R3, are absolutist, we are allowed to conclude that the set of universals (U) contains both absolutes (A) and pluralisms (pl). This can be represented most simply by Figure 1: a circle, U, containing as members both absolutism (A) and pluralism (pl). Pluralism in turn is most simply represented by Figure 2: a circle, pl, containing as members both rt and lt (keep to the right, keep to the left)

This means that U is the set-in-chief, and that A and pl are its members. Variability is the condition for pl being inclusive of rt and lt. But variability is equally the condition for U being inclusive of A and pl. Any universal then that accommodates more than one application is to be read off as a form of pluralism. Universalism as such, where it can be read off as containing both A and pl, becomes a pluralism; it is a set with more than one member. Any universal that contains and admits no plural applications can be read off as a form of absolutism.

Absolutism can be an option within pluralism, and thus be a part of pluralism, without itself being pluralistic. For example, the federal union of the USA as at 1860 was sovereign (monistic) containing states that were both free (pluralist) and slave (absolutist). While the *ante bellum* unity of the whole was pluralistic, the statal unity of constituents (such as the eleven states of the South) was absolutist.

An absolutism or despotism, in its turn, can be universal, but not as in Figure 1. It can be universal in the sense of being a set with either an infinite or a closed membership. But it cannot be universal in the sense of admitting varied applications of the rule(s) it instances. Figure 3 represents absolutism in just such terms: it represents a set containing one rule, which admits no variability of application. Absolutism, as portrayed in Figure 3, and as subsumed under Figure 1, can never be pluralist, even if contained within a wider pluralism – not at least if we take R2 and R3 to be absolutist. Absolutism is conceptually feasible, as we can see from the examples R2 and R3, where absolutism is taken as the exclusion of variation in the application of a rule that unites the whole. But whether absolutism is practically feasible is a different matter, given that there are always circumstances that may force abandonment of the rule – the drunk who staggers in front of you, or the truck coming at you on the wrong side of the road, etc. (The feasibility of absolutism cannot be discussed further here, save to say that, what may be most characteristic of it, is a *normative* commitment by some to try to bring it into being – even in the face of its probably absurdity.)

If we take R2 and R3 to be universals, then not all universals can be pluralistic. That only means to say that we are implicitly operating with a second, and a different, conception of universalism. We may then allow two distinct types of universal, one absolute, the other plural. Both express types of unity. They express divergent types of moral and political engagement. But the focus of concern here is the universalism of Figure 1 and Figure 2, each of which features either more than one rule, or one rule with variant applications... or both. In this sense, there are no universals that are not plural, and there can be no pluralisms that are not universal. So universalism is not to be equated with absolutism; pluralism is to be seen as a universal; and pluralism is to be seen as the negative of absolutism.

This exercise does not 'clear up' the general relationship between universalism and absolutism. For we need to look more closely at A, both theoretically and empirically. And we also need to inspect more closely the two different types of meaning we accord to 'universalism', which is not possible here. But some new light at least is played on the relationship between A and U. And it is at least clear from this that universalism is not absolutism.

All four of our rules (R) can be styled universals. Only two of them are absolute. Where R1 (less obviously) and R4 (most obviously) *do* accommodate variant applications, R2 and R3 do *not* (at least not obviously). In this sense, R2 and R3 are both universal and absolute. But when we say that R2 and R3 are universal, we do not mean to say that they are so as in figures 1 and 2, which figures illustrate plural applications of the one rule. Thus if every absolutist claim is universal, it is only so because we admit two different senses of universal, the second of which we cannot now explore. More importantly, and clearly: not every universal claim is absolute. While some claims are universal and absolute (R2 and R3), others are universal and plural (most obviously with R4). The minimal return on all this is that what contradicts pluralism is absolutism, not universalism. Thus universal and absolutist claims are not carelessly to be equated, as though one exhausts the other, with no line to be drawn between them.

Any pluralism can be read off as a negative, as annulling some absolutism. Thus R4: 'drivers should always keep to some one side, left or right, which side being subject to local decision'. R4 can be read off as negating rules R2 and R3. It can be reconfigured to hold: 'the rule, "drivers should always keep to the left", is *not* valid, and the rule, "drivers should keep to the right", is *not* valid'. The idea of annulation too often suggests, misleadingly, annihilation. To say that pluralism historically and logically attacks absolutism is not the same as saying that pluralism attacks the notion of a universal moral order. Any pluralism, in so far as it advances a moral claim, and however negative its form, equally has a positive agenda. More broadly, every negative claim has some positive burden.

Even absolutisms can be rephrased negatively. Thus R2, 'drivers should always keep to the left', is easily rephrased negatively, to read, 'drivers always should not keep to the right'. And in parallel, R3, 'drivers should always keep to the right', is readily rephrased to read, 'drivers should always not keep to the left'. A negative formula has the appearance (possibly the reality) of leaving something open. But if one is told one ought not to enter by the front, it probably means that one should enter by the back. If one is told one ought not to take one's time returning, it probably means that one should hurry. The fact that the negative may actually or apparently 'leave something open' does not mean that it carries no sharp edge or no positive thrust. So negative moral claims, even if looser – and they are not necessarily looser – still betray some concrete, positive thrust. A negative moral claim need not open up more options, though it is only pluralistic where it effectively generates at least two. Pluralistic negative claims will create some sense of more options and of greater openness, but that is not the same as producing boundless options, moral incoherence, or moral relativism. Nor can it be the same as countering universalism.

Let us apply the argument e.g. to federation. Federation is normally viewed as a pluralistic political arrangement. And so it is. But I have sought to delineate elsewhere the effectively sovereign, and therefore residually monistic, shape of federations. The USA, Canada, Switzerland, Germany, *inter alia*, are all crucially sovereign, but they also accommodate diverse statal/provincial/cantonal arrangements. The universal perspective of the centre is sustained by the plural components at the periphery. The monism is enabled through the pluralism and the pluralism is a dimension of the monism. The problem is to spot the interface. We return to the same conclusion. We may conceivably have absolutism without pluralism, but cannot enjoy pluralism without universalism. Federations are plural entities whose defence is secured monistically.

V

We have explored some of the complexity of the notion that there is 'a single best way', hinting (a) that this does not necessarily exclude pluralist theses, and (b) that pluralist theses do necessarily convey a positive, integrated, universal thrust. Now it is in order to explore the contradictory of this notion, to the effect that 'there is *no* single best way'.

'No single best way' seems to equate with such a popular aphorism as 'live and let live'. To relax in this way, to admit variety and the legitimacy of otherness, must be seen in turn to constitute a putative 'single best way'. No matter that it is a directive principle marked by a high degree of prospectively varied application. For all its apparent 'liberality', the injunction, 'live and let live', is as much a rule as any other. If we read 'live and let live' as one take on 'no single best way', we readily detect its moral animus. Every negative moral argument has the peculiarity that it negates only a particular moral claim, never moral claims as such. And given the role of morality, the negation must betray some positive commitment of its own. The negation has positive directive implications, locating the type of action that is understood to be morally correct. If a moral negation has no such implications, then it negates nothing.

Just as negative descriptive claims (e.g., 'a Bush is not a Legume', 'Clinton was not born in Hope') are still truth-claims, whether correct or not, so are negative moral claims truth-claims. Moral assertions, negative or not, remain assertions about what is right, or at least about what is assumed to be right. 'Thou shall *not* steal' as much belongs to the category of moral command as does the injunction, 'honour thy father and thy mother'. No one will dispute that 'laissez faire' is a social or moral imperative. But it is no more so than 'do *not* bully that child!' The morality of the command, 'thou shall *not* kill', is not tainted by the negative form in which it comes. Because pluralism commonly takes the form of negation of absolutism, it may be tempting to read it off as endorsing moral 'chaos' or 'relativism'. But the negation of an absolutist moral claim, indeed even of a universal absolutist moral claim, does no more than negate that particular moral claim; it replaces one moral claim with another; it is a move made within the game of morality.

To claim that there is a *best* way is obviously a piece of moral argument. Where we negate this, we introduce a matching piece of moral argument, to the effect that there is *no best* way, this being no less moral, for all that it is opposed. The universal, monistic affirmation that there is a single best way, implies that there is some one rule or set of rules under which we all ought commonly to fall. The universal, pluralist negation, to the effect that there is *no* one best way, implies that it is morally and socially *right* that different persons or communities should fall under divergent classes of rules. Both are moral claims. There is no 'relativism' either way.

To make a case in a moral context is never to escape morality. To make a case in a nay-saying manner is to do no more than advance moral-hand in negative-glove. If the morality and the negation are, so to say, hand-in-glove, then the negation, in the moral sphere, cannot just be negative, in the sense that it has a grip on nothing, conveys nothing, intends nothing. If the negative claim confutes a positive moral claim, the algebra of this is such that the negation is an affirmation, carrying some directive burden. To claim that 'there is no single best way' is therefore not to be non-political or non-moral or broadly relativistic. Rather, it is to express a variant form of morality – a commitment of a more pluralistic (but not relativistic) type.

Take such a case as 'liberty', where liberty is defined as 'non-oppression', the simultaneous burden of this being (a) to 'let a hundred flowers bloom', and contrariwise (b) to check those forces minded to clip that efflorescence. The right of every agent passively not to be oppressed translates out equally as an imperative actively to restrain oppressors. The way we gain 'non-oppression' is typically by obstructing or bearing down on those who violate our freedoms. The morality of liberty, accordingly, is not just positive; it is also negative. But the negative call to cancel oppression leaves no void, no relativism. The moral negative then, including pluralism, is still moral, still directive, and is in that sense positive.

In consequence of all this it does not seem to matter, on any general moral level, whether we say, 'there is a single best way', or 'there is not a single best way'. It seems not to matter in the sense that each position contains a distinct moral affirmation. Each, in the concrete setting given, will be read off to signal some specific policy that counters an opposed policy. No matter which of the two principles we embrace, at the point of application, there will be no moral difference between them – in the sense that both, appearances to the contrary, equally constitute, abstractly and in general, categorially moral principles. This is not to say that they are equally good or bad. It only says that each rightly seeks moral success. It is no different to the situation where a bowler lets fly a full-toss, only to be swatted away by the batsman for six; the one made a mistake, the other got it right; yet both were playing cricket. So where we are to do with two opposing moral principles, and even where one is better than the other, they both remain, in the general, categorial sense, *moral*. When inspecting antinomous claims, and in recognition of the fact that each polarity is technically moral, it becomes appropriate to try always to decoct the *positive* moral thrust of the negative term of the antinomy.

If pluralism has a genuinely independent moral status, the immediate consideration arising is whether it is logically self-contradictory in a way that universalism is not. It is plausible that it might contradict itself, as in the following argument: 'if there is no single best way, then a variety of options are plausible, some of which must contradict others, such that we are entitled to do both p and not-p at the same time, which is self-contradictory, a logical failure, in the moral sphere, known at the limit as relativism.' If pluralism can indeed be convicted of relativism, then the law of non-contradiction ('the excluded middle') condemns it as irrational.

We have already seen however that a pluralist approach – as with liberty or federation or indeed a 'pluralist' rule of the road – can be perfectly coherent in its admission of varied applications. And we can show the same again vis-à-vis the theory of toleration, which effectively contains a pluralist notion of morality. The logic of tolerance makes it clear that there are ways we can consistently – without self-contradiction – tolerate practices and beliefs of which we disapprove. Tolerance (as I have argued elsewhere) has its own moral logic, which need have nothing to do with relativism or indifference or overwhelming uncertainty. Religious tolerance is the classic case in point. Here the agent, B, approve's B's own religion, T1, but puts up with C's religion, T2, even though T1 and T2 contain mutually contradictory items of doctrine. Let us say that B does this, not because B is powerless vis-à-vis either C or T2, but because B prioritises respect for (or friendship with etc.) C over disapproval of the doctrinal content of C's religion, T2. Pluralism then need not be self-contradictory, and thus need not slide into any form of relativism. We have constantly to juggle rival (even if usually complementary) moral goods. Pluralism, qua tolerance, is one such *coup de théatre*.

The call for plurality is a claim that is (a) categorially moral and, if valid, (b) universally applicable. In this sense, moral pluralism, appearances possibly to the contrary, is no more than a certain type of universal. The real question raised by pluralism is not so much whether its tenets (in this, that or the other form) are valid – and in this stringent sense universal – but merely whether the degree of variation pluralism enjoins (however much that happens to be) is morally allowable. There is nothing logically contradictory or incoherent about allowing two or more forms of religion to be embraced in some one country. The real question is whether some given religious cluster – perhaps Baptists in the sixteenth century, or Methodists in the eighteenth century, or Scientologists in the twentieth century – ought or ought not to be tolerated. Pluralism in no way undermines morality as such, nor can or does it permit 'everything'. Pluralism, viewed thus, has nothing necessarily to do with relativism, and is characteristically designed to argue only that some given command or arrangement is too rigid or too narrow.

Pluralism might constitute an attack upon such a command as that: '*all* students in this school must wear headgear and it must be of type x'. A narrower and negative rule, but one that is similarly absolutist – meaning it allows no flexibility of application – might run to the effect that: '*no* scarves (*chador*) can be worn by students in this school'. (Absolutisms too can be entirely negative.) We shall often wish to claim that some such command or rule or law or norm is too narrowly or too rigidly drawn. In that case, we proclaim an oppositional pluralism. To seek to negate narrowness and rigidity of construction is only, in such cases, to seek to loosen or broaden the specific rule regarding headgear. It is not to have no rule whatever regarding headgear. For even where we have 'no rule' explicitly about headgear, we still implicitly have a rule, namely that 'pupils can robe their heads more or less as they like'. To broaden the rule, to allow variation in its application, is not to eliminate it. More stringently, even to drop the rule is always to leave some other rule(s) in place. Reconstruction or even replacement of a particular rule is nothing to do with terminating rule in general. Pluralism thus conceived only ever constitutes a modification of order or unity or morality or law; it can involve no grand pursuit of the final overthrow of any of these.

In the case of legal or moral antinomies, such as 'keep to the left; keep to the right', the problem may be to recognise that it will be proper to do x (keep to the right) in some given place, but then to do non-x (keep to the left) in some different setting. Similarly, on some occasions (listening to the Goons) it may be fitting to laugh aloud, whereas on other occasions (at one's aunt's funeral) to do quite the same thing would display a less than brilliant grasp of etiquette. In this sort of circumstance, the major question raised by pluralism is not to do with whether there is a narrowly constructed duty (such as that helpfully imposed by the 'rule of the road'), but with the unremitting applicability of that duty, no matter the time or place or circumstance. Here the argument between legal or moral absolutism, on the one hand, and pluralism, on the other, fixes upon the conflict between imposing some injunction along (a) more approximately 'universal' lines (as with the apparent duty to try to put one's self 'in the shoes' of prospective adversaries) and applying it (b) along more severely 'situational' lines (as with the entirely local obligation for traffic to keep to the left in one country and to the right in another. There is a sort of pluralism here (arguably along the lines of 'cannibalism for the cannibals and liberalism for the liberals') – but it is not a relativism.

Differences between rival views of the good or between rival religions may possibly be irresolvable. While this may well be so, it remains that we must distinguish between (a) 'mere differences' and (b) 'irresolvable differences'. It is difficult to say what makes a difference 'irresolvable'. Those differences that are *longstanding*, as between distinct religions, or as between distinct sects within a religion, may be so viewed. Yet it remains that a difference that has stood for a long time is not *per se* one that must last forever. Though 'the sun also rises', we have good reason to suppose it will yet burn itself out. Though France and Britain were at war for centuries, with no surcease of sorrow, yet we may be right to suppose that such grief is little likely to recur.

A key point about the endurance of difference between groups of humans is that the members, ideologies and laws of these groups change. Animosities cannot stand where the justificatory mental structures shoring them up fall. And mental structures, sometimes quickly, sometimes slowly, are in steady mutation. If the endurance of an outlook depends upon the immutability of mental structures, and assuming mental structures to be notoriously mutable, then we cannot calmly count upon such endurance. It must appear just as likely that differences will dissolve as endure.

VI

Even if we cannot be sure that 'there is a single best way for humans to live', we still cannot avoid moral judgements. We are non-vegetative agents on the move in a world inhabited by others such as ourselves. In so far as we are bound to distinguish 'I want' from 'I ought', and in so far as 'I ought' implies objective as distinct from merely personal or biased claims of interest or desire, then we assume rationality, where rationality seeks to establish the substance of that objectivity. We cannot manipulate 'I ought' judgements without assuming there to be *right* conduct, nor therefore without assuming that there is some *criterion* of right conduct. But to make these assumptions does not require that one know what this criterion might be. No more than one needs to know the laws of physics to ascertain that felled trees fall down, not up. We can and must assume some criterion of right conduct, even when we cannot reliably establish what the express criterion for it may be.

We cannot escape from the prison of moral judgement. We commit moral and other felonies within that prison, not outside it. The fact that we err as we do is not evidence for, nor a means by which we secure release from, the prison of morality. However satisfactory or not we find our abstract and shifting moral principles, not to speak of the concrete enactment of these, it remains that we do not avoid moral judgement as such. It is not clear how we can avoid commitment to some implicit principle of moral rightness, as an objective *possibility*, even if we find it hard coherently to say what it is – and even indeed if we entirely fail to do so. However much we rescind, or fail to discover, or feverishly dispute what we take to be the correct criteria of morality and of justice, we still appear inextricably enmeshed in a world of ethical claim and counter-claim, of ethical assumption and counter-assumption. Measured dispute is presumably best read off as a search for, not as evidence for the impossibility of, a higher rationality.

In the end, the question must be, not whether reasoning in general is open to disagreement, and is fallible, but whether there is anything one may fall back upon as an alternative. The only alternative to 'reasoning', whether descriptive or prescriptive, is better reasoning. We require as much research in ethics as in science for the fairly obvious reason that we are not born knowing what to do, and because present arrangements and interactions can almost always be somehow improved. The fact that we attend so earnestly to science (as a descriptive mode) and so limitedly to ethics (as a prescriptive mode) may tell a great deal about the moral impoverishment of our society. We need clever and apt invention as much in one area as in the other, though ethics probably represents the more obvious area of need.

The only relevant criticism of reasoning is where it happens – in this instance or that or the other – to fall on its face. The point cannot be that reasoning as such is evitable and should be abandoned. Reasoning is a category of engagement inescapable save thru death or near death, as in vegetative or prolonged sleeping states. The moral of this story is conventional: reasoning is not to be escaped.

One does not surrender to God. One deploys the impressive rationale of teleological subjection as a conduit for one's own, too-often emaciated, reasoning. One does not surrender to Nature. One deploys the rationale of abandonment as an expression of one's own perforce limited understanding and commitment. One does not surrender to Science. Science is the best (or worst: the science could be phrenology) that contemporaries can muster when asked. Thus it is never to be assumed that one can criticise rationality as such, for the reason that reason is all we have. To think to pontificate from a vantage point outside reason seems at the least un-reasonable. Wherever it leads us – to God, to gods, to Nature, to Science, to withdrawal or to affirmation or to negation – reason is hard-wired within us.

Whenever we are apparently led to the repudiation of reason, as to relativism, it is still by reason, however inadequate, that we are led there, and hence paradoxically have been led nowhere – at least nowhere outside the skin of the reasoning machine in which we set out. The mind has vastly many wheels and cogs, and takes off in surprisingly many directions. Whatever the reasoning machine does – bang or gurgle – it seems fair to say it is the machine that's doing it – not 'voices off'. It seems pointless generically urging others to embrace reason or to abandon it. After all, what choice has one? Where actors are advised 'to be rational', one may infer that the real intention is only to seek to have them play the game of reason in a more impressive way. In this game, the hope is less that one should stick to reason, than that the reason one is stuck with may bring a fair and improving measure of success.

2

Liberalism for the Liberals, Cannibalism for the Cannibals

STEVEN LUKES

My title is an aphorism coined by the late Martin Hollis. Well, almost. The relevant passage from which it derives occurs in one of his last papers, delivered at a conference in Florence in answer to a question I posed him, namely: 'Is Universalism Ethnocentric?' The passage reads:

> ...I see no way to secure liberalism by trying to put its core values beyond any but internal or consensual reasoning. The resulting slide into relativism leaves a disastrous parallel between 'liberalism for the liberals!' and 'cannibalism for the cannibals!' (Hollis 1999: 36)

Citing an aphorism is an appropriate way to begin. For the aphorism, as John Gross has reminded us, is 'a form of literature', which 'bears the stamp and style of the mind which created it; its message is universal, but scarcely impersonal', it embodies a 'twist of thought', and it 'depends for its full effect on verbal artistry, on a subtle or concentrated perfection of phrasing which can sometimes approach poetry in its intensity'. Aphorisms, he goes on, are 'shafts aimed at the champions of an established viewpoint or a shallower morality. They tease and prod the lazy assumptions lodged in the reader's mind' (Gross 1983: viii). Malesherbes observed that 'a new maxim is often a brilliant error' (Gross 1983: 1) and Karl Kraus that 'an aphorism never coincides with the truth: it is either a half-truth or one-and-a-half truths' (Kraus 1986: 67). According to Vauvenargues, 'men's maxims reveal their characters' (Gross 1983: 1).

Martin Hollis's aphorism certainly reveals his. His shafts were perfectly aimed and he loved to tease and prod, employing delicate witticisms and ingenious wordplay in the service of what was, I believe,

a rather unrestrained passion for reason and its claims. I have never
known a more passionate rationalist. His aphorisms, scattered
throughout his writings, distil his philosophical outlook, much as those
of Montaigne, Voltaire, Schopenhauer and Nietzsche distilled theirs. It
would be worthwhile, and undoubtedly huge fun, to collect them
together.

So let us turn to the aphorism in question. 'Liberalism for the liberals;
cannibalism for the cannibals.' Does it state a deep truth, or a brilliant
error, or a half-truth or, perhaps, one-and-a-half truths? The
juxtaposition is offered us as a warning: a way of characterising the
relativism into which we must not slide. Let us, then, analyse this
'disastrous parallel' in order to see what point this twist of thought is
meant to make. Why compare liberalism and liberals with cannibalism
and cannibals?

Let us begin with cannibalism and the cannibals. The word dates
from the sixteenth century and was coined by Columbus and comes from
the Spanish form of *Carib* or *Caribes*, meaning 'bold' or 'fierce' in the
language of an Amerindian people, thus called, in the Lesser Antilles,
held by neighbouring tribes to be *anthropophagi*, or man-eaters. I stress
'held to be' and will return to this shortly. Cannibalism is, we might say,
a culinary practice or, better, a way of dealing with one's enemies after
victory, held to be characteristic of totally alien cultures. In the context
of the aphorism its role is clearly to represent a practice that is at once
culturally embedded, exotic and utterly repellent.

But there is, of course, much more to say about cannibalism – and I
will only be able to say a very small part of it here (see Lestringant 1997
and Rawson 1997). It has played a significant role in the history of
Westerners' or Europeans' conceptions of 'the other' and thus in their
self-reflection since the sixteenth century. It has been a classic instance,
we might say, of adversary anthropology ('despotism' is another) to be
found in fiction, philosophical reflection, satire and caricature and even,
as we shall see, in anthropology.

Montaigne's essay 'On the Cannibals' (Montaigne 1991) reveals this
with great clarity. He begins, in a way of which Martin Hollis would
thoroughly have approved, by observing that we 'should be ... wary of
accepting common opinions; we should judge them by the ways of
reason not by popular vote'. So how does Montaigne judge the
cannibals' society? The answer is: highly favourably, in comparison with
his own. From what he has heard, he gathers that 'there is nothing savage

or barbarous about those peoples'. For, he goes on, 'every man calls barbarous anything he is not accustomed to; it is indeed the case that we have no other criterion of truth or right reason than the example or form of the opinions and customs of our own society'. Their ethical system respects only two things: 'resoluteness in battle and love for their wives' and indeed 'their steadfastness in battle is astonishing'. As for their cannibalism, he exonerates it, noting that 'Chrysippus and Zeno, the leaders of the Stoic school, certainly thought there was nothing wrong in using our carcasses for whatever purpose we needed, even for food'. Montaigne's purpose is to ask the question: 'who are the real barbarians?' and his answer is clear. We can, he says, indeed 'call these folk barbarians by the rules of reason but not in comparison with ourselves who surpass them in every kind of barbarism'. For

> I think there is more barbarity in eating a man alive than eating him dead, more barbarity in lacerating by rack and torture a body still fully able to feel things, in roasting him little by little and having him bruised and bitten by pigs and dogs (as we have not only read about but seen in recent memory, not among enemies in antiquity but among our fellow-citizens and neighbours – and, what is worse, in the name of duty and religion) than in roasting and eating him after his death.

Even their poetry Montaigne judges to be not barbarous because it resembles Greek poetry ('their language is a pleasant one with an agreeable sound ... rather like Greek') (Montaigne 1991: 228, 231, 234, 235, 236, 236, 235–6, 240). Obviously Tsvetan Todorov is right in seeing Montaigne's view of the cannibals as a 'projection onto the Other of an image of the self – or, more precisely, of an ideal of the self, embodied for Montaigne by classical civilisation'. Todorov characterises Montaigne as an 'unconscious universalist' disposed 'simply to declare that his own values are universal' (Todorov 1993: 41, 42).[1]

Defoe's Friday was a cannibal whom Crusoe rescues from the danger of being eaten and converts, as a penitent, to Christianity. The authors of the *Encyclopédie* were concerned to make a different point about the relationship between cannibalism and Christianity. If you look up *Anthropophages* you will find a summary of standard classical views and then a cross reference: 'see *Eucharistie, Communion, Autel*'. (In this they were taking up the longstanding Protestant view of the Catholic Mass as a sanguinary sacrifice), A different, political point is made by Gillray's cartoon *Petit Souper à la Parisienne* which depicts a party of Sanscoulottes feasting on the carcases of dead aristocrats in an extraordinary carnivalesque scene just after the 1792 massacres.

Nearer our own time, I cannot resist quoting the anthropologist Ruth Benedict, widely regarded as an archetypal cultural relativist, who in 1925 wrote in satirical (and thus non-relativistic) vein an extraordinary anti-war piece entitled 'The Uses of Cannibalism', that is highly reminiscent of Swift's *Modest Proposal*:

> We have done scant justice to the reasonableness of cannibalism.... We have already had recourse to many quaint primitive customs our fathers believed outmoded by the progress of mankind. We have watched the dependence of great nations upon the old device of the pogrom. We have seen the rise of demagogues, and even in those countries we consider lost in a morally dangerous idealism we have watched death dealt out to those who harbour the mildest private opinions. Even in our own country we have come to the point of shooting in the back that familiar harmless annoyance, the strike picketer. It is strange that we have overlooked cannibalism.... Without the infantile ostentations and unfortunate appeals to the hatred of one's fellow being which characterise our Black Shirts and our Red Shirts, the Indians of Vancouver Island found a heightened excitation, disciplined in endless ritual and taboo, in a ceremonial show of cannibalism ... nothing could be more harmless to the community: one useless body per year satisfactorily satisfied the craving for violence which we have clumsily supplied in modern times in the form of oaths, blood-and-thunder, and vows to undertake the death of industrious households.... The Maoris of New Zealand ... before the feast took from their enemies the exquisitely tattooed heads which were their incomparable pride.... No-one who is familiar with the breakdown of emotional satisfaction in warfare as it is recorded in postwar literature of our time can fail to see in all this a hopeful device for the re-establishment of an emotional complex which shows every sign of disintegration among us. It is obvious that something must be done, and no suggestion seems more hopeful than this drawn from the Maoris of New Zealand. (Benedict 1959: 44–8)

Cannibalism, in short, has played a continuing role in Westerners' constructions of what it is to be civilised, and it has served the ends of both conservatives and critics. Its imputation to 'savages' has mirrored the historical geography of successive empires, being variously attributed to early Christians, Amerindians, Irish, Africans and Polynesians. (It has even, it appears, played this role among the 'natives' themselves. In James Marre's film *Spirits of Defiance*, I am told, the members of the Mangabeta tribe sit around the camp fire discussing their suspicions about cannibalism among whites).

Which raises, of course, the interesting possibility that not only is the meaning of cannibalism a 'social construction' for purposes of self-understanding and critique, but that the cannibals are themselves largely or even entirely fictitious. This is, it appears, becoming an accepted idea among archaeologists. According to Professors Colin Renfrew and Paul Bahn, there has been a reappraisal of the archaeological and ethnographic evidence previously interpreted as proof of cannibalism, and all of it has been found open to other explanations, such as 'violence and mutilation done to enemy corpses in warfare, or the varied and complex range of mortuary rituals documented around the world.' Even if cannibalism existed occasionally, they write, 'the contribution of human flesh to human diet must have been minimal and sporadic' (Renfrew and Bahn 1996: 270). Anthropologists and others have recently been expressing a similar scepticism (see Arens 1979) – a scepticism which, however, Professor Rawson sees as 'denial' of its existence both at home and abroad by '*bien-pensant* pedagogues' overcome by 'post-colonial guilt and imperial self-inculpation'. According to him, instances of its practice, both historical and present-day, are 'amply demonstrable, by the kind of evidence usually accepted for other historical events: reports and descriptions by witnesses and a variety of archival, anthropological and journalistic sources' (Rawson 1997: 3).

Whatever the truth about this, I propose that, returning to our topic, we take cannibalism as a representation of a practice that is culturally embedded, exotic and utterly repellent to us. So the suggestion is that liberalism is, in parallel fashion, to be seen as a practice that is no less culturally embedded, familiar and wholly attractive to us.

This is a helpful beginning but of course liberalism does not denote a practice, but rather, let us say, an outlook which underwrites and justifies a range of typically liberal practices and institutions–such as constitutions, separation of powers, citizenship, toleration, rights of free speech, free assembly and association, due process, private property and so on. It is, as Raymond Geuss has recently observed, an outlook that is practically engaged and historically located and this has three important consequences: '[a] it has no definition, [b] it tends to rewrite its own past sometimes anachronistically, [c] it is open to very significant modification in the future' (Geuss 2001: 69). Nevertheless it is possible to identify elements that distinguish the liberal tradition from non-liberal over time and space. So what is the scope of this outlook? I propose that we should for the purposes of the present discussion help ourselves to the useful Italian distinction between *liberalismo* and *liberismo*, the latter referring to the economic doctrine of *laisser-faire*, and that we take 'liberalism' to denote the former understood as the political morality that underpins and justifies liberal practices and institutions.

Is liberalism, thus understood, culturally embedded? And, if so, does it mean that our capacity to justify it – the reasons we can offer in its defence – are similarly embedded and thus, presumably, uncompelling to bearers of non-liberal cultures? It may help to survey a few current statements of the case for and against this claim. Is liberalism, as Michael Walzer suggests, to be understood and interpreted and criticised mainly from within and only sometimes from without, since 'morality is thick from the beginning, culturally integrated, fully resonant, and it reveals itself thinly only on special occasions, when moral language is turned to specific purposes' – as in appeals for international solidarity, across cultural frontiers (Walzer 1994: 4). Early Walzer, in his *Spheres of Justice*, claimed that 'a given society is just if its substantive life is lived in a certain way, that is, in a way faithful to the shared understandings of the members'; there are 'no external or universal principles' and every 'substantive account of distributive justice is a local account' (Walzer 1983: 313, 314). This certainly looks like cultural relativism – a suspicion reinforced by what Walzer wrote there about the caste system and the injustice of overriding the understandings of the villagers who 'really do accept the doctrines' that support it (Walzer 1983: 314). In his later writings, Walzer extracts from this account a further notion of thin, 'minimalist' morality, accessible only from the outside, and expressed in terms such as 'truth', 'justice', 'life' and 'liberty', put together 'by abstracting from social practices reiterated in many countries and cultures'. So murder, torture and enslavement are wrongful features of any social order, but for reasons unconnected with the variable cultural meanings or 'shared understandings' of 'social goods'. But it remains unclear how the thin, minimalist component qualifies the relativism of the thick, maximalist morality, especially since, according to Walzer, 'minimalism is not foundational' (Walzer 1994: 15, 18).

Another, more colourful and less qualified version of the case for the cultural embeddedness of liberalism comes from James Tully in the form of a fable (like all the best fables an animal fable) to illustrate the mistakes of contemporary liberal constitutionalism. There is a sculpture of a black canoe occupied by various animals from the mythology of the Haida nation of *Haida Gwaii* (The Queen Charlotte Islands) off the north-west coast of Great Turtle Island (North America). Tully writes:

> Imagine the large father grisly bear at the bow of the canoe addressing the other passengers.... He claims that the ways of the bear clan are superior to all the others in their civility or efficiency. Alternatively, he may claim that they are not bear ways at all, but universal ways that the bears, being at a higher stage, are able to discern. Or he confidently asserts that his articulation of the association comprehends and sublimates the constitutional ways of the others in a higher synthesis. The other passengers would accept these ways if they were reasonable, if they would think through the following thought experiment, or if they would only speak the language of constitutionalism he uses.

And Tully asks: 'if we now view ourselves as members of the black canoe, what carries over?' (Tully 1995, 203, 204). I agree with Brian Barry's answer to this, namely: 'precisely nothing'. For, as Barry argues, 'there is nothing intrinsically absurd in any of the argumentative strategies that Tully attributes to the mythological bear, once we have substituted a human being for the bear'. Barry asserts that it is 'quite legitimate to hope that eventually a common standard of reasonableness will prevail over a certain range of ethical questions, in a way similar to that in which acknowledgement of the soundness of the physical sciences has diffused throughout the world'(Barry 2001: 262). It may be legitimate so to hope, but is such a hope well-founded? Here I am much less convinced and will return to this crucial point shortly.

A third, more equivocal version of the case we are considering is advanced by Bhikhu Parekh, who, in his article 'Superior People: the narrowness of liberalism from Mill to Rawls', maintained that we have not shaken off the legacy of Millian liberalism which

linked diversity to individuality and choice, and valued the former
only in so far as it was grounded in the individualist conception of
man. This ruled out several forms of diversity. It ruled out
traditional and customary ways of life, as well as those centred on
the community. It also ruled out ethnically grounded ways of life,
as well as those limited to a 'narrow mental orbit' or 'not in tune'
with the dominant trend of the age. Although it may not entirely
rule them out, Millian liberalism also takes a low view of ways of
life that stress contentment and weak ambition rather than a go-
getting character, or are centred on religion, or place little value on
worldly success and material abundance. As one would expect,
Millian liberalism cherishes not diversity *per se* but *liberal* diversity,
that is, diversity confined within the narrow limits of the
individualist model of human excellence.

Parekh is thus a critic of what he sees as the narrowness of this liberalism
which he portrays as representing 'the British and European self-
consciousness during the heyday of imperialism, and bears the deep
imprint of an age in which the liberal way of life and thought exercised
unchallenged intellectual and political hegemony over its defeated
rivals'. Yet Parekh's critique of narrow liberalism also purports to be a
defence of liberalism properly understood, since he argues for 'a more
broad-based liberalism in which it must 'reassess its Millian commitment
to a single mode of human excellence and evolve a view of the world in
which different ways of life, including the non-liberal can converse as
equals and enrich both individual and collective existence'. So a 'truly
liberal *state* cherishes and gives public recognition' to 'diverse ways of
life, both liberal and non-liberal', providing them, among other things,
with 'such resources and conditions of growth as they need and cannot
raise themselves' (Parekh 1994: 11–13). This last suggestion is clearly the
most contentious, since it asks liberals not merely to finance but to
promote the growth of non-liberal practices. If they are anti-liberal
practices involving injustices or the violation of individual rights, can a
liberal coherently justify them let alone advocate that a liberal state
finance and encourage them? But my main point is that Parekh is here
equivocating: criticising liberalism as culturally embedded and thus
confined and advocating a 'true' liberalism that would be, one supposes,
un-embedded and culture-free – or, at least, less embedded and less
confined (he doesn't tell us which).

One comment about these culturalist accounts of liberalism, that applies more particularly to Walzer and Tully (and also to Kymlicka, who focuses on the cultures of sub-state nationalities). They, and other writers in this vein, employ what Seyla Benhabib has called a 'poor man's sociology' (Benhabib 1995: 241–4 and Benhabib 1999) – a misconceived because far too holistic notion of culture. For cultures are always open systems, sites of contestation and heterogeneity, of hybridisation and cross-fertilisation, whose boundaries are inevitably indeterminate. Walzer's talk of cultural integration and shared meanings and Tully's analogy between animal species and cultural groups are deeply misleading. One should never forget that the simplifying perception of the internal coherence and distinctness from one another of cultures is invariably perpetrated by interested parties – by cultural entrepreneurs, by priests and elders, by populist and nationalist intellectuals and propagandists, and even by social anthropologists in search of unified and uncontaminated objects of study. As Mary Midgley has well put it, of course cultures differ but 'they differ in a way which is much more like that of climactic regions or ecosystems than it is like the frontiers drawn...between nation states' (Midgley 1991: 84). The important thing to see is that they are never coherent, never closed to the outside, never merely local, and never uncontested from within and from without – though, of course, the degree to which these things are true will vary from case to case.

The contrary case is that liberalism is culture-free – a set of principles formulable, intelligible and applicable anywhere and everywhere, though, of course, being responsive to local variations in circumstances. The classic formulation of such a case is, of course, that of the early Rawls. His *A Theory of Justice* concludes with an extraordinary irenic (that is, non-polemic) vision. He claims that to see our place in society from the perspective of the original position, from which liberal principles are to be derived, is

> to see it *sub specie aeternitatis*: it is to regard the human situation not only from all social but also from all temporal points of view. The perspective of eternity is not a perspective from a certain place beyond the world, nor the point of view of a transcendent being; rather it is a certain form of thought and feeling that rational persons can adopt within the world. And having done so, they can, whatever their generation, bring together in one scheme, all

individual perspectives and arrive together at regulative principles that can be affirmed by everyone as he lives by them, each from his own standpoint. (Rawls 1971: 587)

This of course contrasts with the answer of the later Rawls, in *Political Liberalism*, according to which the principles in question constitute a 'reasonable political conception of justice', without metaphysical foundations, constructed from an overlapping consensus among the 'reasonable, comprehensive religious, philosophical, and moral doctrines found in modern democratic societies' (Rawls 1993: 46. 36). 'Reasonableness' is, indeed, a tricky notion and one that seems to me, at least at first sight, to be vulnerable to Parekh's critique that the range of permitted doctrines is confined to those that are already liberal, or at least liberalism friendly. This becomes clear in a well-known passage in which Rawls expounds on reasonableness:

> Thus, it is not in general unreasonable to affirm any one of a number of reasonable comprehensive doctrines... .Others who affirm doctrines different from ours are, we grant, reasonable also, and certainly not unreasonable. Since there are many reasonable doctrines, the idea of the reasonable does not require us, or others, to believe any specific reasonable doctrine, though we may do so. When we take a step beyond recognising the reasonableness of a doctrine and affirm our belief in it, we are not being unreasonable. (Rawls 1993: 60)

But this is to juggle with different senses of 'reasonable': that in which a *doctrine* can be said to be reasonable, that is justifiable by convincing or adequate reasons, even if not acceptable to all (in view of the lack of 'a public and shared basis of justification ... in the public culture of a democratic society'[Rawls 1993: 61]) and that in which *people* can be reasonable that is disposed to behave co-operatively within certain justifiable constraints (by requiring only 'what free and equal citizens ... can require of each other with respect to their reasonable comprehensive views' [Rawls 1993: 62]). Nor does it help to elide these senses by defining a 'reasonable doctrine' as 'one that can be affirmed in a reasonable way' (Rawls 1993: 60). It is hard to evade the impression that liberal principles are here being justified as constructed from an overlapping consensus of doctrines that reasonable liberal, or liberalism-friendly, people are prepared to affirm or accept.

Brian Barry firmly rejects this development in Rawls's thought, seeing it as a 'rather muddled version of Michael Walzer's anti-Enlightenment particularism'. Indeed, he caustically observes that the same should be said about Walzer's later thoughts about combining thick maximalism and thin universalist minimalism. Rawls and Walzer, he suggests (inaccurately), have now converged: 'if anything, they have gone past one another, calling to mind Mark Twain's story about the two drunks who fought so hard that they finished up by struggling into one another's overcoats' (Barry 2001: 331, 346). In *Culture and Equality* Barry advances a defence of culture-free egalitarian liberalism of which I suspect Hollis would, in part, have approved. This defence consists in a detailed case for difference-blind liberal policies, negative and positive; an extended argument for a theory of group rights that seeks to specify what limits liberalism requires be set to the freedom of groups, such as illiberal religions, from external intervention in handling their own affairs (an argument aimed at refuting Parekh's claim that liberalism restricts their diversity); and a robust defence of 'moral universalism' and attack on the currently widespread idea that, in Hollis's words, liberal values cannot lie 'beyond internal or consensual reasoning'. This last involves showing how an appeal to culture has no justificatory force in defending liberal principles, and nor does contribution to cultural survival or cultural diversity. Nor does Taylor's idea of presuming the equal value of cultures convince, nor can it coherently be practised. Nor, finally, to be specific for once, is the right defence of the British government's not punishing Rushdie or handing him over to others for punishment (whether within some legal process or outside it) that 'this is the way we do things here' (the phrase is Richard Rorty's); it is, in Barry's words 'this is the way things ought to be done everywhere: we do things that way here not because it is a part of our culture but because it is the right thing to do' (Barry 2001: 284). But are things quite so straighforward?

Let us turn to this question of moral universalism. Hollis's approach to this issue suggests, as I have indicated, that he would have been sympathetic to Barry's, yet he would also, I believe, have been troubled by it – as indeed am I, though I am more troubled than he would have been. Liberals, he writes, 'are indeed universalists, committed to universal reason in pressing their ideas of a free, just and equal society on persons or cultures not of liberal persuasion'. 'Enlightenment liberalism', he spiritedly writes, echoing a phrase of Charles Taylor's, 'was a fighting creed, armed with a universal account of human nature and of how societies arise and function, universal notions of human interests and human freedom, and universal prescriptions for education and moral progress, all of which could be established from a scientifically objective and universally attainable point of view' (Hollis 1999: 36). The question is: how much of this picture can we retain?

Liberalism, Hollis wrote, 'has to remain a fighting creed with universalist pretensions':

> Liberal declarations of human rights, for instance, are robust and sharp-edged declarations, intended to lay anyone who breaches them open to moral condemnation. Their neutrality, if they have it, is to do with their being so undeniably well-founded that they can be assumed in all further discussion of how a just society should be organised. This has to remain a claim to universal standing, even if one becomes coy about quite what lies behind it. Otherwise Amnesty International could not speak out globally. (Hollis 1999: 36)

Compare what Walzer says about Amnesty International – that its success depends on self-restraint, on restricting itself to 'moral minimalism, since there is no single, correct maximalist ideology' (Walzer 1994: 49). Hollis also views liberalism's procedural values as 'a minimal universal morality, yet one with a cutting edge' (which 'weigh in somewhere between telling cannibals to use a knife and fork and forcing them to turn vegetarian'). But Hollis's strategy, to which I now draw attention, is to exert pressure on Walzer's suspect thick/thin distinction. Liberals, says Hollis, should stick to reason 'through thick and thin', and, by 'arguing that thinner concepts are still action guiding', 'open the way to a thinly developed local politics'. But this, he says, requires that there is 'a notion of "reasonable persons" able to hover between heaven and earth' (Hollis 1999: 36, 37, 40).

He suggests that there are two defences against the charge, expressed by the aphorism with which we began, that liberalism is ethno- (that is culture-) centric. One is empirical: that liberal values are in fact values which everyone does recognise, and I shall return to this at the end of this article. The other, which is of more interest to him, is metaphysical: 'a contentious, objectivist universal story about, for example, human nature, human interests, the fundamentals of law, the conditions of flourishing for civil society, or the character of citizenship'. So which values should liberals defend as universal? Hollis's answer is that the standard answer is 'procedural values backed by a separation of the right from the good' – an answer which needs 'substantive support', for

> procedural values which extend to a distributive principle of social justice and a robust view of what counts, for purposes of drawing a circle round every human being, as harm to others, call for reasoning which strains any separation of the right from the good. In short, even if muted for reasons of tactics or tact, a liberalism which believes in freedom, justice, inalienable rights, and equality is still a fighting creed. (Hollis 1999: 41)

Here you see Hollis expressing worries which Barry plainly does not share. For Hollis 'there is trouble over both "procedural" and "neutrality"': 'what counts as procedural is itself a substantive question'. Indeed, whether 'an appeal to neutrality has special force depends on the robustness of liberal distinctions between procedural and substantive values and between the right and the good'. 'Neither distinction', he remarks, 'seems very robust to me' (Hollis 1999: 36).

Brian Barry's approach is altogether less squeamish. Unlike the animals on Tully's canoe, he writes,

> precisely because human beings are virtually identical as they come from the hand of nature – at any rate at the level of groups – there is nothing straightforwardly absurd about the idea that there is a single best way for human beings to live, allowing whatever adjustments are necessary for different physical environments. Disagreements will in fact arise because there are bound to be differences of opinion about what is the best way to live – what, for example, is the true religion, if any – and there is no known method of resolving such disagreements. But it is consistent with that to hold that the human situation is sufficiently uniform to make it possible to say that there are quite a number of things that every society ought to achieve if it is to provide a tolerably good life for all its members. Moreover, the very fact of irresolvable disagreement over the nature of the good life, once we get beyond the basics, is itself a premise in the argument for liberal institutions. For, in the face of these disagreements, what we need is a fair way of adjudicating between the conflicting demands that they give rise to. This is what liberalism offers. But saying that is to make a universalistic claim. (Barry 2001: 262–3)

But, to state that the idea that there is a single best way for human beings to live is not straightforwardly absurd is far from showing that it is plausible; and certainly the idea as thus stated does look (how can I put it?) somewhat incautious, and it is in no way supported by the premise that human beings come virtually identical from the hand of nature. Why should where they come from, and how they come, have any bearing on where they go? The human situation may be viewed as 'uniform' but there is no reason to think all will ever agree on what that uniformity consists in, or on what a 'tolerably good life' is or, indeed, that it should be 'provided' or that it should be available to all a society's members. Nor is it convincing to suggest that the admittedly irresolvable differences about what constitutes the good, arising from different religions for example, have no bearing upon the warrant of any claim to have given it an objective and universal answer. It is just this crux that leads Rawls and Walzer to their respective, but quite different, bolt-holes – Rawls to reasonable pluralism, based on the 'burdens of judgment', and Walzer to his idea of moral maximalism incorporating variable cultural meanings. Nor does the point that the fact of irresolvable disagreement over the nature of the good life is itself a premise in the argument for liberal institutions show that that argument can be conducted from a standpoint external to one of the contending sides in the argument. But nor is it clear that Barry thinks it can, since he has argued that we can no longer maintain the hope of the Enlightenment that liberal attitudes will, in the absence of persecution and censorship, prevail over time and thus that, faced with the choice between trying to persuade non-liberals to accept the principle of neutrality and trying to discredit their beliefs, 'I think that the second is clearly the better strategy'. (Barry 1990: 14). Nor, finally, is it clear how to arrive at a univocal answer to the question of what is a fair way of adjudicating conflicting demands that arise from conflicting moral viewpoints, where the very answer to what counts as such a fair way and indeed what counts as a reasonable answer may well be in dispute among such viewpoints. Martin Hollis saw these difficulties, or some of them, and was (perhaps insufficiently) troubled by them and Brian Barry is not.

So can we 'secure liberalism' by putting its core values 'beyond internal or consensual reasoning'? To approach an answer to this, we must ask: internal to and consensual within what? One answer, suggested by several of the writers we have been considering is: *culture*. So the question becomes: can we secure liberalism by trying to put its core values beyond the reasoning internal to and shared within liberal cultures, or to cultures hospitable to liberalism? But, in the light of what was said above about the erroneous 'poor man's sociology' that views cultures as undifferentiated and integrated wholes, this cannot be the right answer. For cultures, and in particular liberal cultures, are sites of contestation. Those who proclaim the latter's virtues count as prime among these their very openness to such contestation, their commitment to debate and pluralism – though, of course, in reality, such cultures all fail to live up to this ideal; some do so poorly, some less poorly and all patchily and inadequately. From Mill to Rawls (as Parekh might say), *dissensus*, in the form of open public debate and the clash of value positions, is what liberal cultures are supposed to promote and sustain. Mill, of course, thought that out of such conflict conclusions would be reached that would come to be widely accepted: that both individuals and societies would progress, through 'experiments in living' towards higher rather than lower ways of living, while Rawls makes no such assumption. But whatever its predicted outcome, most liberals defend liberal cultures in the hope that they will be maximally open to the challenge of non-liberal and illiberal reasoning.

So perhaps the answer to our question should be to return to our original characterisation of liberalism as an *outlook*, or, to use Rawls's terms, *perspective* or *standpoint*. Can we secure liberalism by putting its core values beyond the reasoning that is internal to and consensual within a liberal outlook? I suggest that two distinctions need to be made here. One concerns the *content* of such an outlook – which, as Geuss has been quoted as observing, is undefinable and continuously self-reinterpreting. Assuming that it nevertheless exhibits core beliefs, some of these will be seen (from such a perspective) as first-order beliefs about substantive issues. At this level we are discussing norms of conduct, and in particular norms of conduct enforceable by the State. Which freedoms should be guaranteed and protected – of speech, of association, of religion, of property ownership, and so on? How should benefits and burdens, freedoms, resources and obligations be distributed? Even more specifically, how should the abortion question be decided? What should the policy on immigration be? Typically, within liberalism, such questions are answered in the language of rights – whether human or civil or social or economic or cultural and whether attributed to individuals or collectivities (liberalism displaying generally some reluctance here). Such rights are enshrined in Bills of Rights and constitutions, but the language of liberal politics is increasingly pervaded by rights talk. And these answers, framed in this way, are typically justified by distinctively liberal background assumptions: chief among them humanism, individualism ('giving pride of place to autonomous individuals, determined to demand their rights, even (indeed especially), in the face of widespread social consensus' [Taylor 1999: 128]) and equality as non-discrimination, arising with the idea of Natural Right and challenging the alleged naturalness of successive forms of human differentiation, held by pre- and non-liberal world views to be rooted in the cosmic order of things.[2]

But such first-order beliefs and their justifying assumptions contrast with second-order or meta-beliefs characteristic of (internal to and consensual within) the liberal outlook. These are beliefs about how to argue and how to justify your political morality. So liberals typically say that alternative principles, dictating norms of conduct and policies have to be stated in universalistic form, they have to be accessible to 'public reason', they have to be acceptable to all those affected by the consequences of their implementation, or to all those engaged in a free and unforced discussion on equal terms, and so on. So liberalism, seen as an outlook or political morality, contains meta-principles that specify what is going to count as adequate reasoning, whether directed to liberal conclusions or not.

The second distinction we need to make concerns the very standpoint from which we ask the question at issue here: can liberalism be secured by putting its values beyond internal or consensual reasoning? We can ask this as enquiring anthropologists who view political moralities as specimens, each with its own organising principles of reasoning. From this viewpoint what counts as a compelling reason is whatever convinces the relevant community. A good reason, from an anthropological standpoint, is *a reason apt to convince*. Alternatively, we can ask it as engaged participants in political discourse, seeking answers to practical, first-order substantive questions of the kind indicated above: what freedoms should be protected? What would be the just solution? What should we tolerate? and so on. Here liberal and other answers are in competition, and the question is: which answer is the more convincing? A good reason, from a participant's standpoint, is *a reason fit to convince*.

It is evident that, from the anthropological standpoint, the answer to our question is obviously no, since what counts as reasoning is taken to be both internal and consensual. How about the participant's standpoint? Liberalism offers the questioning participant not only first order answers (or rather principles from which to generate answers) but also principles specifying what good reasoning – reasons fit to convince – consist in. Moreover, these meta-principles are tightly linked to the rest and in particular to what I have called the background assumptions. Thus, for instance, the idea that political principles, of justice for example, must be acceptable to all those affected by their implementation is, obviously, itself an expression of humanism, individualism and equality. So, it would appear that, although there are obviously canons of reasoning that are, and must be, common to all those who reason, in crucial respects, liberalism, as an outlook, is, at once, both fighting creed and referee.

But suppose we now modify the question and treat 'liberalism', not as an outlook, but as a set of practices and institutions, as specified at the beginning of this paper – such as constitutions, separation of powers, citizenship, toleration, rights of free speech, assembly and association, due process, private property, and so on. Can these be secured only by reasoning internal to a liberal outlook? And, even if they can be so secured from within alternative outlooks, are those practices themselves equally secure when motivated by non-liberal beliefs? (How secure are they when motivated by liberal beliefs?) I believe these to be genuinely open and important questions. The process of answering them will involve debate and mutual efforts at understanding that may well change both liberal and non-liberal outlooks, perhaps in convergent ways (along the lines of what Gadamer calls a 'fusion of horizons') but perhaps not. Charles Taylor has suggested, for example that reformed or 'protestant' interpretations of Theravada Buddhism can exemplify the possibility of alternative variations in 'philosophical justifications or in legal forms that would still be compatible with a meaningful universal consensus on what really matters to us, the enforceable norms'. Others have made similar claims for contemporary interpretations of Confucian ethics (Taylor 1999: 129; see Gombrich and Obeyesekere 1988).[3]

Let me, finally, turn to what Hollis refers to as the empirical defence against the charge that liberalism is culture-centric. Here we return to the cannibals. For recall that, whatever the actual prevalence of man-eating may have been, both abroad and indeed at home, 'cannibalism' was a social construction of the self-reflective Western mind. As Rawson well puts it, the common factor in the long history of cannibal imputation is the combination of denial of it in ourselves and attribution of it to 'others', whom 'we' wish to defame, conquer, appropriate or 'civilize'. (Rawson 1997: 3)

Recall that in Hollis's evocative aphorism, the cannibals stood for culturally embedded, exotic and utterly repellent practices. I have in what I have said put in question the idea of cultural embeddedness. I want to conclude by putting the idea of the exotic into similar doubt. To what extent, I wonder, are the very ideas of culturally-based 'difference', 'otherness' and diversity themselves (as the current jargon goes) 'socially constructed'? To what extent have these notions been promoted and exaggerated for a variety of reasons and in pursuit of a variety of interests, including group interests but also liberally minded generosity and compassion, perhaps inspired by post-colonial guilt and imperial self-exculpation? I believe that these questions merit close attention from philosophers, but especially from sociologists and anthropologists. We need, I think, to return to a lost discipline, or sub-discipline, the sociology of morality and to a question that used to be central to studies and debates among sociologists and anthropologists, a question captured by the title of a book by Morris Ginsberg: *The Diversity of Morals*. I think we have no real idea either how to answer or even properly to investigate the question; how much moral diversity is there? I was struck when conducting an interview with the late Sir Isaiah Berlin, often thought of as an arch-advocate of value pluralism, by his statement that 'more people in more countries at more times accept more common values than is often believed' (Berlin 1998: 119). Political philosophers and others talk and write as though we have a handle on this question, but we do not. Perhaps, after all, the cannibals have more to teach us liberals than we realise.

NOTES

1. Todorov continues:

    Bravery in warfare and polygamy, cannibalism, or poetry will be excused or offered as examples, not in terms of the ethics of the other but simply because these features are found among the Greeks, who embody Montaigne's personal ideal.
    The relativist does not pass judgment on others. The conscious universalist

may condemn others, but he does so in the name of an openly assumed morality, which may therefore be called into question. The unconscious universalist is unassailable, since he claims to be a relativist; however, this does not prevent him from passing judgments on others and imposing his own ideal on them. He has the aggressiveness of the latter and the clear conscience of the former: he is an assimilator in all innocence, because he has not noticed that the others are different. (Ibid.)

One difficulty with Todorov's view of Montaigne is that it attributes unconsciousness to this supremely self-reflective thinker.

2. As Taylor writes: 'once right inheres in nature, then it is hard in the long run to deny it to anyone. The connection to equality is the stronger because of the thrust of modern humanism..., which defines itself against the view that we are embedded in a meaningful cosmic order.... This has been a very common form of thinking in almost all human societies' (Taylor 1999: 139).

3. For a somewhat similar argument, see Chan 1999. Several Chinese scholars, some less skeptical than Chan, are currently working along these lines.

REFERENCES

Arens, W. 1979. *The Man-eating Myth. Anthropology and Anthropophagy.* New York: Oxford University Press.

Barry, B.M. 1990. 'How not to defend liberal institutions'. *British Journal of Political Science,* 20/1, 1–14

2001. *Culture and Equality. An Egalitarian Critique of Multiculturalism.* Cambridge, Mass.: Harvard University Press.

Bauer J.R. & D.A. Bell, eds. 1999. *The East Asian Challenge for Human Rights.* Cambridge: CUP.

Benedict, R. 1959. 'The uses of cannibalism'. Mead 1959: 44–8.

Benhabib, S. 1995. 'Cultural complexity, moral interdependence and the global dialogical community'. Nussbaum & Glover: 235–59.

1999. '"Nous" et "les autres": the politics of complex cultural dialogue in a global civilization'. Joppke & Lukes 1999: 44–62.

Berlin, I. 1998. 'Isaiah Berlin in conversation with Steven Lukes'. *Salmagundi,* 120, Fall, 52–134.

Chan, J. 1999. 'A Confucian perspective on human rights for contemporary China'. Bauer & Bell 1999: 44–62.

Geuss, R. 2001. *History and Illusion in Politics.* New York: CUP.

Gombrich, R. & Obeyesekere, G. 1988. *Buddhism Transformed: Religious Change in Sri Lanka.* Princeton: Princeton University Press.

Gross, J., ed. 1983. *The Oxford Book of Aphorisms.* Oxford: OUP.

Hollis, M.. 1999. 'Is Universalism Ethnocentric?' Joppke & Lukes 1999: 27–43.

Joppke, C. and S. Lukes, eds. 1999. *Multicultural Questions.* Oxford: OUP.

Kraus, K. 1986. *Half-truths and One-and-a-half Truths.* Selected Aphorisms translated by Harry Zohn. Manchester: Carcanet.

Lestringant, F. 1997. *Cannibals: The Discovery and Representation of the Cannibal from Columbus to Jules Verne.* Oxford: Polity.

Mead, M., ed. 1959. *An Anthropologist at Work. Writings of Ruth Benedict.* Boston: Houghton Mifflin.

Midgley, M. 1991. *Can't We Make Moral Judgments?* Bristol: Bristol Press.

Montaigne, M. de. 1991. 'On the cannibals'. Screech 1991: 228–41.

Nussbaum, M. & J. Glover, eds. 1995. *Women, Culture and Development. A Study of Human Capabilities.* Oxford: Clarendon Press.

Parekh, B. 1994. 'Superior People: the narrowness of liberalism from Mill to Rawls'. *Times Literary Supplement,* 25 February, 11–13.

Rawls, J. 1971. *A Theory of Justice* Cambridge, Mass.: Harvard University Press.

1993. *Political Liberalism.* New York: Columbia University Press.

Rawson, C. 1997. 'The horror, the holy horror. revulsion, accusation and the eucharist in the history of cannibalism'. *Times Literary Supplement,* 31 October, 3–5.

Refrew, C. & C. Bahn. 1996. *Archaeology: Theory, Methods and Practice.* 2nd ed. London: Thames & Hudson.

Screech, M.A., ed. & trans. *The Essays of Michel de Montaigne.* London: Allen Lane.

Taylor, C. 1999. 'Conditions of an unforced consensus on human rights'. Bauer & Bell 1999: 124–44.

Todorov, T. 1993. *On Human Diversity. Racism and Exoticism in French Thought.* Cambridge, Mass.: Harvard University Press.

Tully, J. 1995. *Strange Multiplicity. Constitutionalism in an Age of Diversity.* Cambridge: CUP.

Walzer, M. 1983. *Spheres of Justice. A Defence of Pluralism and Equality.* New York: Basic Books.

1994. *Thick and Thin. Moral Argument at Home and Abroad.* Notre Dame & London: University of Notre Dame Press.

3

Hollis, Rousseau and Gyges' Ring

TIMOTHY O'HAGAN

Prologue: Gyges' Ring

They say that there was a shepherd, and that he was the serf of the ruler of Lydia. One day there was a great rainstorm and earthquake ... Part of the ground opened up, and a great hole appeared in it. He was astonished when he saw it, but went down into it ... Among many marvels he saw a hollow bronze horse with windows in it. Peeping through them, he saw inside what appeared to be a corpse, larger than human, wearing only a golden ring on its hand. They say he removed the ring and came out. [Later] the shepherds were having one of their regular meetings, so that they could give the king their monthly report on the flocks, which he attended, wearing the ring. As he sat with the rest of them, he happened to twist the setting of the ring towards him ... When he did this, he became invisible to those who were with him, and they started talking about him as if he had gone. He was amazed, and twisted the ring again, turning the setting to the outside. As soon as he did so, he became visible. When he realized this, he experimented with the ring, to see if it did have this power. And he found that that was how it was ... Once he had established this, he lost no time arranging to be one of those making the report to the king. When he got there he seduced the king's wife, plotted with her against the king, killed him and seized power.

The legend of Gyges' ring is one of the great thought experiments in moral philosophy. In book two of his *Republic* Plato puts it into the mouth of Glaucon, Socrates' chief interlocutor in the dialogue, in order to challenge the view that people are naturally inclined to act in a moral and trustworthy fashion. Gyges' ring, says Glaucon, provides 'a strong argument ... for the claim that no one is just voluntarily, but only under compulsion'.[1] In response to this challenge Socrates will go on to construct a gigantic edifice of political and moral theory, depicting a perfect correspondence between the well-formed individual and the well-formed state. In the new order of things, the just citizen will flourish in the just polity. As Socrates concludes in the last book of the *Republic*, 'justice is best for the soul itself, and the soul should do what is just, whether or not it possesses Gyges' ring'. (Plato 2000: 334 [612b])

Throughout his writing, Hollis sought a way of mediating between two apparently irreconcilable approaches to morality: one based on some version of self-interest, revealed by instrumental reason, the other based on duty, revealed by disinterested reason. In his last, and greatest, work, *Trust Within Reason*, Hollis (1998) focused on the all-important social virtue of trust, as it is understood according to these two approaches, taking the philosophers and political economists of the eighteenth-century Enlightenment as his starting point, and engaging with twentieth-century game theory in the heart of the book, before returning to Jean-Jacques Rousseau by the end. Each position was subjected to the challenge of Gyges' ring, and each (with the possible exception of Rousseau's) was found to be wanting.[2]

It is, in fact, the first approach, that of self-interest, which occupied most of Hollis's attention. Writers in the tradition of Hume and Adam Smith expanded and enriched the idea of self interest until it included a concern for one's reputation, a sympathy for those to whom one is more or less closely attached, a hierarchy of preferences in which one prefers to be the sort of person who prefers to 'keep covenants made'. In this process of socialisation, the self becomes increasingly conscious of the price to be paid for unbridled, short-term egotism. But the agents conceived by thinkers from Hobbes to the most sophisticated modern game theorists still reason instrumentally. Such agents keep promises because failure to keep them will, in any games other than the simplest one-shot game, damage their own interests (and those interests may include their own self-esteem). Until people have changed their way of reasoning, so Hollis argued, they can never be relied on, since they will always be subjected to the temptations of Gyges' ring. A society made up of instrumental reasoners will lack the crucial element of trust.

The second approach, in which trust is based on disinterested reason, was espoused most famously by Kant. He held that the moral worth of an action is derived from the fact that it is performed 'from duty', not from inclination. Truly moral behaviour, according to Kant, is motivated by respect for the law of duty itself. Reverence for the moral law is inspired not only by its majestic universality, but also by the realisation that its source of legitimation lies within oneself, as a moral agent. In the principle of moral autonomy, 'there is nothing left to determine the will except objectively the *law* and subjectively *pure reverence* for this practical law and therefore the maxim of obeying this law even to the detriment of all my inclinations' (Kant 1963: 68–9). Hollis was impressed by the austerity of Kant's principles, in particular by his insistence that you 'always treat humanity, whether in your own person, or in the person of any other, never simply as a means, but always at the same time as an end' (Kant 1963: 96). In a world of consistent Kantian agents, there would be no problem about trust, since all parties could be trusted to keep their word, whatever the outcome. But Kant, is, finally, just *too* austere for Hollis (1998: 90): 'critics still deem it artificial to detach us morally from our inclinations and from all concern for consequences'. It is evident that Hollis counted himself among those critics.

So the eighteenth century provided Hollis with a stark choice, between the legacy of instrumental reasoners of enlightened self-interest on the one hand, and the legacy of disinterested reasoners of Kantian duty on the other. But both these legacies are flawed, the former because no instrumental reasoners can ultimately resist the temptations provided by Gyges' ring, the latter because, although disinterested reasoners would successfully resist, they would do so only by being subject to an unrealisable moral code, one which is 'too high-minded to serve as the bond of society' (Hollis 1998: 102).

In seeking a way out of that dilemma, Hollis aimed to reconcile the claims of reason with the equally pressing demands of human motivation. The motto of the book, repeated several times, comes from another Enlightenment writer, the Marquis de Condorcet (1988: 286): 'Do not all these observations .... prove that the moral goodness of man, the necessary result of his organization, is, like all his other faculties, susceptible to indefinite improvement, and that nature unites truth, happiness and virtue with an indissoluble chain?' Like Condorcet, Hollis implicitly rejected any absolute opposition between empirical questions concerning motivation and normative questions concerning the rightness or wrongness of actions. In that sense his procedure was more *naturalistic* than Kant's. That is why he reached Rousseau *after* Kant, holding that Rousseau had anticipated a way of naturalising Kant's abstraction in *Social Contract* I.8: 'this passage from the state of nature to the civil state produces a remarkable change in man, by substituting justice for instinct in his behaviour and giving his actions the morality they previously lacked. Only then, when the voice of duty replaces physical impulse and right replaces appetite, does man, who until that time considered only himself, find himself forced to act upon other principles and to consult his reason before heeding his inclinations' (Rousseau 1994b: 141). The two axes of Hollis's extraordinary book are thus both rooted in the eighteenth century, Condorcet's 'indissoluble chain' and Rousseau's 'remarkable change in man'.

Rousseau's Naturalism and the 'Remarkable Change in Man'

Why was Rousseau's insight so important to Hollis? *Trust Within Reason* marked his final attempt to come to terms with Rousseau's 'remarkable change in man', a theme to which he had returned on several previous occasions.[3] In 'Honour among thieves', Hollis (1990b: 177–8) found in it the contrast between two forms of rationality:

> [Rousseau's] contrast between individuals and citizens goes irresistibly with that between instrumental and expressive reasons. Like the honourable or principled thing to do, the public interest may be hard to discern. The search for it motivates the citizen, however, because that is the condition of being a citizen. In this way of taking the social contract, it sets up the widest game, the one in which the player is himself and acts from expressive reasons, which are not instrumental in some yet wider game.

Seven years later, addressing the text rather more closely in his lecture 'A remarkable change in man', the liberal Hollis was still attracted, but at the same time alarmed, by Rousseau's ambivalent idea:

> As citizens, we bring to collective decision-making the intimate aims, emotions and relations which make us particular human beings, and yet stand ready to revise these identities. This can make sense only if rational choice in public matters is not construed wholly, or even basically, as instrumental choice of means to satisfy our individual self-regarding preferences. We are who we are, not what we want; our moral freedom lies in self-direction, not

consumer-slavery. That much strikes me as clear. But the ambiguity is pervasive and goes deep. The self in Rousseau is neither fully encumbered nor Kantianly detachable, neither prior to its ends nor posterior to them. It slips from view in the interplay of 'I' and 'we', but maintains the individuality of its particular interests, even though it has a civic identity and duties. That makes Rousseau's solution to his own problem of finding the right form of association teasingly incomplete. (Hollis 1997: 64)

Following Rousseau, Hollis held that the 'remarkable change in man' comes about as we learn what it is to be members of what Edmund Burke called the 'little platoon'. The word 'loyalty' is notably absent from *Trust Within Reason*, yet it is the phenomenon of group loyalty that allowed Hollis to bring the excessively 'high-minded' Kant down to earth (Hollis 1998: 101), and discover a self which is 'embedded in the games of social life but not lost in them'. (Hollis 1998: 161–2). For all the dangers inherent in his work, Rousseau appealed to Hollis just because he seemed to combine (at least in the *Social Contract*) an Enlightenment faith in universal principles of reason and morality with a naturalistic commitment to seeking the real, material conditions in which those principles could be realised. As we saw above, Hollis translated Rousseau's 'remarkable change in man' into a modern idiom, interpreting that change as one from instrumental to expressive rationality. According to Hollis's understanding of *Social Contract* I.8, once you become an agent in Rousseau's new, transformed world, you come to express your identity by acting according to the norms of the society which you yourself, along with your fellow citizens, create and sustain. You make yourself what you are by engaging in a common project with them. This is the up-side of the 'remarkable change in man'. It is better to engage with others expressively rather than instrumentally. The down-side is that, by absorbing yourself in the common project, you risk losing the critical distance provided by universal Enlightenment reason. For a group can have an internal structure that is inegalitarian and oppressive of some of its members, yet still enjoy their loyalty. It can also act wickedly towards those outside the group. If the highest we can aspire to is self-realisation by identifying ourselves with a greater whole, then there seems to be no difference between belonging to Friends of the Earth and belonging to the Mafia.

In *Trust Within Reason* Hollis dealt with this problem, as he did with many others, by appeal to striking anecdotes. He told the story of the motorist who picks up the hitchhiker because he feels solidarity with the needy traveller, a feeling generated perhaps by memories of his own student past or by sympathy with his own present-day student children. In another story, the blood-donor is motivated by a feeling of interdependence between fellow human beings. People who engage in such behaviour, he suggested, feel themselves subject to obligations which are 'neither straightforwardly moral nor morally neutral' (Hollis 1998: 148). They find themselves part of a network of 'generalized reciprocity', which is like a system of gifts with 'no implicit or explicit right to return gift or action' (Hollis: 1998: 146). Despite the anecdotal presentation, it is clear that the transformation process is teleologically driven. Characters like the kind-hearted motorist and the blood-donor are playing their roles in a drama whose final act could be entitled 'the Generalised Other'. When Reason finally triumphs, a 'remarkable change' will have been wrought, but it will be a naturalistic change, following Rousseau's requirement that we should 'take men as they are and laws as they can be'.

Optimistic to the last, Hollis thought that his new naturalism would split the difference between the loyal, unquestioning member of the group, on the one hand, and the impartial spectator, on the other. His new order would be populated by people who would be both team players and citizens of the world (Hollis 1998: 143). Hollis's story was naturalistic since it told of a real transformation in the way in which people respond to each other. Where Kant asserted the universality of the categorical imperative as a matter of normative logic, Hollis, like Rousseau before him, was interested in the feelings which might motivate people into action, and which would fuel the drive towards universality. That drive, he seemed to think, was somehow secreted within expressive rationality itself, but he did not have a chance to investigate its psychological mechanisms in his last great book before his death.

The Drive towards Universality: Rousseau's Rich and Cautious Story

Jean-Jacques Rousseau took at least some steps in investigating those mechanisms, and Hollis's reference to 'citizens of the world' suggests that he would have been sympathetic to Rousseau's approach to this topic. From Rousseau's vast corpus of writing, we have so far mentioned only *Social Contract* I.8, the 'remarkable change in man'. Taken in isolation, that chapter is somewhat mysterious, and its mystery is strengthened by its high rhetorical tone. It seems to suggest that the 'remarkable change' comes about through a miraculous transfiguration in which each natural human characteristic is negated and converted into its opposite. In that chapter, Rousseau offers no causal explanation of the change and no account of what, if anything, remains constant in the identity of human beings across the process of change. Justice, morality, duty, right and reason simply replace instinct, physical impulse, appetite, egotism and inclinations. Absent from either side of the ledger is compassion or pity. That characteristic, according to the model of human psychology which Rousseau elaborated in the *Discourse on the Origin of Inequality among Men* (1755), is part of our natural endowment, expressed in our 'innate repugnance at seeing a fellow creature suffer'. But compassion can be corrupted, even annihilated, by a bad social environment, where we learn to turn away from our neighbour's distress and channel our sympathy into sentimentality or self-pity. Where the social system is particularly hard, then the other innate drive, that of self-preservation, will entirely displace compassion when our own survival may be threatened if we give way to it. In the *Social Contract* Rousseau seeks to generate an entirely new order. It will be different from the pure state of nature of the *Discourse on the Origin of Inequality*, in which isolated human beings roam the forest, self-preserving, compassionate, idle animals, untouched by either the vices or the virtues of any social order. It will be different too from the highly socialised but disordered world which we now inhabit, marked by mutual aggression and zero-sum competition. Implicit in Rousseau's solution is the idea that our innate compassion can be rescued from its corrupting environment and harnessed to produce a new order. Compassion, for Rousseau, generates fellow-feeling, a sense of identification with those who are close to us, and from that root all the social virtues grow.

The sense of identification can be educated and focused. The narrowest, most natural degree of identification is found within the family. It is there that we experience the feelings idealised by Rousseau in the description of the 'Youth of the World' in the *Discourse on the Origin of Inequality*: 'the habit of living together gave rise to the sweetest feelings known to men, conjugal love and Paternal love. Each family became a little society all the better united because mutual affection and freedom were its only bonds' (Rousseau 1992b: 46). In the family we encounter the world, both as parents and as children, through identification. We must take with us from nature to society the feeling of identification with others which we have learnt within the family, yet once we have made the transition, we must learn to distance ourselves, particularly when we hold office, from those very feelings of family loyalty. Here we are at the middle point between the family, at one extreme, and humanity, at the other, as citizens of a fatherland. What then is the fatherland? The word is linked, etymologically, to father, the natural parent. But at the same time it is constituted by non-natural ties. As Rousseau expressed it in a letter (1964: 1397): 'it is neither the walls nor the men which make the fatherland: it is the laws, the norms, the customs, the Government, the constitution, the way of being that results from all that. The fatherland is [exists] in the relations of the State to its members; when those relations change or are annihilated, the fatherland vanishes'.

Rousseau's model of the legitimate fatherland is thus complex. Its citizens are tied to it by a love learnt in the family. Indeed it embodies both parents in one, in that the fatherland also 'shows itself as the common mother of the citizens' (Rousseau 1992c: 153). Identification will take place when citizens come to recognise that their particular interests coincide with those of the fatherland. And that will happen when the fatherland is governed justly by laws emanating from the citizens themselves.

Adult citizens will come to identify themselves with the fatherland to the point where they will sacrifice themselves for its defence. In the words of Rousseau's 'Political Fragments': 'they will know no other true life than that which it provides, no true happiness except to use their life to serve it. And they will include among its benefits the honour of shedding their blood to defend it if necessary' (Rousseau 1994c: 58). Political virtue in turn is defined as a pure identification between the aspirations of citizen and fatherland: '... according to the definition I have given of virtue, love of the fatherland necessarily leads to it, since we willingly want what is wanted by those we love' (Rousseau 1994c: 59). According to his epigrammatic definition in the *Discourse on Political Economy*: 'virtue is only this conformity between the particular will and the general will' (Rousseau 1992c: 149).

From this perspective, the legitimate fatherland is the environment within which one can best live an integrated life at the political level. The fatherland is immediate in that it focuses the love and loyalty of individuals who identify their private with their public interests. But it is universal in that it is the bearer of the universal values of freedom and equality. Within a well-ordered fatherland, families flourish, providing the primary lessons in love and identification. At the same time it embodies the public space within which citizens live a republican life, identifying themselves with the whole through political participation. The particular fatherland constitutes a particular environment, a geography, climate, history and culture, encountered and transformed by its citizens. Rousseau recognised that political virtue is both created and reinforced by this immediate environment. His hostility to cosmopolitanism was based on the naturalistic assumption that 'the feeling of humanity seems to evaporate and become feeble as it extends over the whole earth' (Rousseau 1992c: 151). But it was reinforced by his characteristic bitterness about the hypocrisy of the *bien-pensants*, '...those supposed Cosmopolitans who, justifying their love of the fatherland by means of their love of the human race, boast of loving everyone in order to have the right to love no one' (Rousseau 1994d: 81).

But the closure is not absolute. The drive to extend compassion and to identify with people beyond one's immediate circle appears to be a natural one. Even 'cosmopolitan', so often a term of abuse, can take a positive charge, as it does, surprisingly, in the *Discourse on the Origin of Inequality*, at the point where Rousseau describes international law. At that level, he says, since the parties are too distantly related to feel any immediate identification with one another, the most we can hope for are 'some tacit conventions'. These would serve

> to make intercourse possible and to take the place of natural commiseration which, losing between one Society and another nearly all the force it had between one man and another, no longer dwells in any but a few great Cosmopolitan souls, who surmount the imaginary barriers that separate Peoples and who, following the example of the sovereign Being who created them, include the whole human race in their benevolence. (Rousseau 1992b: 54)

Rousseau thus recognised a dynamic within the feeling of identification, but was not confident in its power. As things are, he suggests, most individuals, apart from the 'great Cosmopolitan souls', are united by shared feelings of identification within families and in the few well-ordered fatherlands. But at the level of the fatherland those feelings are more than gut loyalty to blood and soil, since they are mediated by recognition of the normative demands of just, self-imposed laws. As in the well-ordered fatherland individuals can transcend, without betraying, loyalty to family, so too, in a better world, groups of individuals might come to experience ties of fraternity which would transcend those of the fatherland. In such a world cosmopolitanism could be more than a hypocritical excuse for failure to perform one's immediate duties. Rousseau was pessimistic about the possibility of extending ties of fraternity so far, and for that reason he gives cosmopolitanism its predominantly negative charge, even though he allowed for the possibility, however remote, that a transformed world order might eventually be realised.

Hollis beyond Rousseau: The Moral Significance of one's Philosophy of Science

But there is one further move in *Trust Within Reason*, the boldest, and the most characteristically Hollisian one, which goes beyond anything to be found in Rousseau. 'A fighting liberalism', Hollis suggested, 'need not be an imposition if the Enlightenment project can rethink the basis of the moral and political sciences. The starting point might be to regard the social world as an intersubjective fabric spun from shared meanings which persist or change as we negotiate their interpretation among ourselves' (Hollis, 1998: 156). The suggestion is that the practical behaviour of real people is modified to a greater or lesser degree by the principles embodied in the human sciences used to study them, principles which they have themselves implicitly absorbed. The approach to the social sciences which Hollis advocated was based on Max Weber's insight that there is a radical difference between the objects and the methods of the human sciences on the one hand and those of the natural sciences on the other. The human sciences, unlike the natural ones, are addressed to *meaningful* relations and interactions between human beings. For writers in this Weberian tradition, rule-governed systems are categorically different from mere regularities of behaviour, and the former are not reducible to the latter. H.L.A. Hart was an influential proponent of this approach, arguing that there is a categorial distinction between the 'external' and the 'internal points of view' concerning a rule-governed system. Only those who adopt the 'internal point of view' are fully members of a normative community.

For them, a red traffic light 'is not merely a sign that others will stop: they look upon it as a *signal for* them to stop, and so a reason for stopping when the light is red, a standard of behaviour and an obligation' (Hart 1961: 87–8). In advocating that approach to the human sciences, Hollis was implicitly rejecting the rival approach, propounded by stimulus-response behaviourists like B.F. Skinner, who held that meaningful, rule-governed interaction is secondary, a mere epiphenomenon on some more basic drives. Hollis proposed that we should adopt the approach of Max Weber rather than that of B.F. Skinner for two reasons: first because it is superior to its rival at the bar of theory, and second because, in practice, by adopting it we will come to engage with our fellow men and women in a different and better fashion. If we adopt a Skinnerian stimulus-response approach to the human sciences, we will treat other human beings as external items, subject to instrumental, at best humane, manipulation. If we are influenced by Weberian principles, on the other hand, we shall have the intellectual resources to relate to others in a rule-governed game, interpreters of a shared language and culture.

So far, so good. So far there is nothing to perturb the liberal. Indeed the theoretical principles advocated by the Weberians seem more congenial to liberal sensibilities than the brutish externalism of the behaviourists. But in these last few pages of the book, Hollis was toying with other, riskier ideas, particularly with (i) 'a communitarian idea about persons', and (ii) 'a constructivist understanding of free action and the common good'. With (i) we can understand how a self emerges through a play of meaningful interactions with others, since there are no 'naked selves' pre-existing our encounters with them. With (ii) we can understand that to act freely is to act as a member of a team in co-operation with others, engaged in the formulation and realisation of a 'common good'.[4]

Principles (i) and (ii) together provide the resources for understanding expressive rationality and group action. They yield the grand rhetorical manifesto which brings the book to a close:

> liberals are citizens of the world which they construct on liberal principles. They subscribe to a communitarian idea about persons *but trump it by insisting that communities must accept liberal ideas about universal demands of the right and the good* ... Practical wisdom ... relies on a constructivist understanding of free action

and the common good, *while also submitting its constructions to a universal and a priori test of truth.* (Hollis 1998: 162–3) [italics added]

But – and this is what worried Hollis to the last page of his book – in adopting the two principles we may have lost the critical ground from which we could judge the different communities which provide different materials for constructing any particular 'understanding of free action and the common good'. As he observed, 'no doubt it helps to regard the good as in part a construct, rather than a discovery. But, if it were solely a construct, all sorts of further trouble would arise. Nor, if all reduces to struggle for who determines the kind of construct, can liberalism always win' (Hollis 1998: 162). How, in other words, can the recommended approach be prevented from sliding into relativism? Liberals, we were told, are (or become) 'citizens of the world they construct on liberal principles'. A relativist could interpret that phrase as meaning that liberals construct their liberal world and non-liberals construct their non-liberal world, and the two worlds must just coexist.[5] Hollis, of course, did not intend it to have that relativist meaning, as is made clear by the two italicised phrases, which invoke 'universal demands of the right and the good' and 'a universal and a priori test of truth'. But just what could be the source of those 'universal demands' and that 'a priori test'?

In earlier times, writers were more confident than they are now that there is such a thing as human nature, even if it is infinitely plastic, capable of being transformed almost beyond recognition by the environment. They were equally sure that they were equipped to prescribe the treatment necessary for that human nature to flourish. Rousseau, as we have seen, had at his disposal a model of human nature which allowed him both to test the relative success of different societies in realising fundamental human goods, and also to sketch the mechanisms available to reach a successful outcome.

In previous books, including *Models of Man*, Hollis (1977) had engaged in that endeavour. But here, at the end of his last work, we are left with only hints concerning the nature of *homo sapiens* that would provide the template against which we could subject particular constructions of the good to universal critical demands and universal a priori tests.

At all the earlier stages on the Enlightenment Trail we had been guided by waymarks, allowing us to escape from alluring, but dangerous, deviations. But here, as we approach our destination, the signposts run out. We are told that 'a well-ordered society can indeed be founded on a truth of reason, which stands outside any construct and serves as a criterion', but we are given no indication as to where that criterion might be found.

The signs might have pointed in the direction of writers who have returned to the high ground of liberalism. Those 'fighting liberals' (as Hollis called them) have argued, against the later Rawls, that liberalism can and must be defended in terms of universal values. Their outstanding representative is Joseph Raz, who has for many years been arguing that 'personal autonomy' is 'an essential element of the good life' and that 'the state has the duty not merely to prevent denial of freedom, but also to promote it by creating the conditions of autonomy' (Raz 1986: 424–5). Against the later Rawls, Raz has maintained that liberalism requires foundations in a deep underlying moral philosophy (Raz 1990). He has also assimilated the challenge of the communitarians, holding that individuals relate to their cultures in an expressive, not a purely instrumental, fashion, since membership of a 'pervasive culture' is 'important to one's self-identity' (Margalit & Raz 1990: 448–9). And he has argued that the fundamental value of human autonomy requires that society should contain a plurality of cultural forms ('moral pluralism') and a legal-political system to guarantee it. Although we shall never know what the final destination Hollis's Enlightenment Trail would have been, we can be sure that it would have passed through some of the country described by Raz. Beyond that, we shall have to make our own maps.

ACKNOWLEDGEMENTS

I am indebted to the Editor, Preston King, whose meticulous comments on an earlier version of this piece allowed me to revise it in structure and in detail. My thanks also to Angus Ross, friend and critic, who pointed out further mistakes which I have done my best to correct.

NOTES

1. Plato 2000: 39–40 [359d–360b. Confusingly, Plato attributed the ring to an 'ancestor of Gyges' in the passage quoted here from Book I. When he returned to the story at Book X, he referred simply to Gyges. Ferrari discusses this discrepancy at pp.353–4 of his edition of the translation. In any event, the legend has come down to posterity as 'Gyges' ring'.

2. He had already addressed Gyges' ring in detail in Hollis 1985: 122–37. Its challenge was never far from his reflexions on morality and social choice throughout his later work.
3. In addition to the three passages considered in this paper, he also discussed *Social Contract* I.8 in Hollis 1987: 212, and in Hollis 1990a: 162.
4. It might have been better if Hollis had used the term 'constructivist' in formulating (i) as well as (ii). In using 'communitarian' in (i), he might seem to be siding with those 'communitarian' theorists who hold that our identity is determined for us by the particular community to which we belong, a relativist position which is the very opposite of his own.
5. 'Liberalism for liberalism and cannibalism for cannibals' was Hollis's epigrammatic and ironic conclusion of that kind of relativism (Hollis 1999: 36).

REFERENCES

Condorcet, Marquis de. 1988 [1795]. *Esquisse d'un tableau historique des progrès de l'esprit humain*. Dixième époque. Paris: Garnier-Flammarion.
Hart, H.L.A. 1961. *The Concept of Law*. London: OUP.
Hollis, M. 1977. *Models of Man*. Cambridge: CUP.
    1985. *Invitation to Philosophy*. Oxford: Blackwell.
    1987. *The Cunning of Reason*. Cambridge: CUP.
    1990a. 'Friends, Romans and Consumers'. Hollis 1996: 150–69.
    1990b. 'Honour among Thieves'. Hollis 1996: 109–30.
    1996. *Reason in Action*. Cambridge: CUP.
    1997. 'A remarkable change in man'. O'Hagan 1997: 56–65.
    1998. *Trust Within Reason*. Cambridge: CUP.
    1999. 'Is universalism ethnocentric?'. Joppke & Lukes 1999: 27–43.
Joppke, C. & S. Lukes, eds. 1999. *Multicultural Questions*. Oxford: Clarendon Press.
Kant, I. 1963 [1785]. *Groundwork of the Metaphysic of Morals*. Trans. H.J. Paton. London: Hutchinson.
Margalit, A. & J. Raz.1990. 'National self-determination'. *Journal of Philosophy* 87/9, 439–61.
O'Hagan, T., ed. 1997. *Jean-Jacques Rousseau and the Sources of the Self*. Aldershot: Avebury Press.
Plato. 2000 [c.380 BCE]. *Republic*. Trans. T. Griffith, ed. G.R.F. Ferrari. Cambridge: CUP.
Raz, J. 1986. *The Morality of Freedom*. Oxford: Clarendon Press.
    1990. 'Facing diversity: the case of epistemic abstinence'. *Philosophy and Public Affairs*, 19/1, 3–46.
Rousseau, J.-J. 1964. *Oeuvres complètes*. Vol.3. Ed B. Gagnebin & M. Raymond. Paris: Gallimard (Bibliothèque de la Pléiade).
    1992a. *Collected Writings*. Vol.3. Ed. R.D. Masters & C. Kelly. Hanover, NH: University Press of New England.
    1992b [1755]. *Discourse on the Origin of Inequality Among Men*. Rousseau 1992a.
    1992c [1755]. *Discourse on Political Economy*. Rousseau 1992a.
    1994a. *Collected Writings*. Vol.4. Ed. R.D. Masters and C. Kelly. Hanover, NH: University Press of New England.
    1994b [1762]. *Social Contract*. Rousseau 1994a.
    1994c. 'Political Fragments'. Rousseau 1994a.
    1994d. Geneva Manuscript of the *Social Contract*. Rousseau 1994a.

4

Trust and Political Constitutions

ALBERT WEALE

Trust Within Reason should be read as a work of political philosophy. It is, of course, many other things besides. It is an exercise in the philosophy of the social sciences concerned to explore the theory of choice and action and the relevance of that theory for our understanding of social organisation. It is a playful piece of problem posing for those who think that the instrumental conception of rationality is the only view worthy of the name of reason. It combines whimsical story telling with sharp observation of how institutions work. And it is an engaging rehearsal of some of the principal moves made in Enlightenment thought seeking to reconcile the tension that Sidgwick (1931: 165–70) identified as the chief problem of modern ethics, namely how to make morality reasonable once the classical assumption that it was ultimately to an agent's good to be virtuous had been undermined by Hobbes.

Despite all of these diverse elements, so characteristic of Martin Hollis's wide-ranging and elegant mind, I propose to treat *Trust Within Reason* as a work primarily concerned with advancing a political philosophy. The main tenets of that political philosophy are anti-individualist. Showing that pure instrumental rationality is self-defeating for those agents who employ it as the basis of decision is a way of undermining the intellectual assumptions of market individualism. Durkheim's (1933: 215) thought that a contract is not sufficient unto itself but requires a regulation that is originally social points to forms relationship that are not founded upon mutual back-scratching by otherwise autonomous and self-contained individuals. The observation that even economic organisations will not work when based purely on force or incentives should be taken as a serious part of the argument.

What is the notion that is supposed to move our understanding of social relationships from a politics of mutual advantage to more solidaristic forms of social union? The answer is the principle of generalised reciprocity. The politics of mutual advantage can be supported by a principle of specific reciprocity, which says that agents should do good only to those who have done good to them. The principle of generalised reciprocity tells agents to return to non-assignable others the good that someone else has done to them. Drivers give lifts to hitch-hikers because someone once gave a lift to them or to their children, and of course today's hitch-hikers will become tomorrow's drivers obligated in their turn by the same principle of generalised reciprocity. Acting on this principle is rational from the social point of view, though it may not be a rational *ex ante* decision for any particular individual driver. (The hitch-hiker might be scruffy or boring, thus lowering the expected utility of an otherwise solitary drive.)

The most famous piece of modern political philosophy based upon the principle of generalised reciprocity is Richard Titmuss's *The Gift Relationship* (Titmuss 1970). Titmuss's work is cited in *Trust Within Reason* as illustrating how the principle of generalised reciprocity is superior to a principle of mutual contractual advantage as the basis of social policy. Titmuss was able to show that the UK's system of voluntary blood donation was superior to systems in which blood donors were paid. The UK system produced a greater volume of blood at higher quality than commercial systems like that of the USA in which blood donors were paid. It could do this because it relied upon the altruistic motives of donors and this conferred upon it certain advantages. For example, voluntary unpaid donors had no incentive to lie about any illness they suffered which might lead to the contamination of blood supplies. Paid donors, by contrast, did have such a motive. Clearly, however, keeping blood free of contamination was an important component of quality, particularly at a time when screening for contamination was not technically advanced.

The system of voluntary blood donation is a clear example of what policies based upon the principle of generalised reciprocity might look like, but it is by no means the only instance. Support for redistributive taxation as well as contributions to public goods are others. Moreover, according to the argument of *Trust Within Reason*, public policies in which priority is given to public investment and infrastructure is nurtured in a civic culture that maintains high levels of social capital through practices like tipping for service or being honest in contractual dealings, as well as being helpful to strangers.

Underlying this political argument is the general argument about the self-defeating quality of instrumental rationality. If agents are rational they seek to maximise their own utility. Their utility may depend upon the well-being of others as well as their own well-being (in this sense utility-maximisers may not be pure egoists). However, unless the marginal gain from an action for an individual exceeds its marginal cost the instrumentally rational individual will not undertake that action. With such a conception of rationality, individuals may often miss taking decisions that would be to their benefit if they could co-ordinate successfully with others.

In terms of the goals of public policy, *Trust Within Reason* seeks to justify the politics of an extensive welfare state. However, there is another side to its political philosophy, namely its account of the relationships that suit the project of a welfare state. Here the argument turns Rousseauian. If we aspire to the welfare state as an outcome of our political choices, then citizens must learn to make political choices in a way that enables the general will to substitute for the will of all. It is this claim about the logic of political choice that I wish to concentrate on in the remainder of this paper. In particular, I shall argue that it is ambiguous between two claims:

1. Instrumental rationality is often not sufficient to make decisions in the public interest.
2. There are forms of political life that can dispense with instrumental rationality.

The first of these claims is true; the second false. But a Rousseauian ought to hold to the stronger, second claim. The 'remarkable change in man' that Rousseau required his citizens to undergo forms an implausible basis for a politics of constitution building.

Does the Enlightenment Trail Lead to Philadelphia?

The central argument of *Trust Within Reason* is that instrumental rationality is self-defeating because its exercise will produce Pareto-inferior outcomes for all parties. The argument is maintained and illustrated by one central example, Adam and Eve moving up (or failing to move up) the Enlightenment Trail. *Trust Within Reason* presents this game in 'extensive form', meaning that it is presented as a decision tree in which nodal points and associated outcomes are identified. However, I find it helpful to present the relevant information about the game in the form of a table, in which total and marginal gains and losses for each of the parties are explicitly identified. Table 1 therefore sets out the relevant information.

TABLE 1
THE ENLIGHTENMENT TRAIL GAME

Stage	Adam	Eve	Sum	Increase Adam	Increase Eve	Increase Joint	Power of Decision at Stage
The Rational Choice	1	0	1	+1	0	+1	Adam
The Social Contract	0	2	2	–1	+2	+1	Eve
The Foole	3	1	4	+3	–1	+2	Adam
The Sensible Knave	2	4	6	–1	+3	+2	Eve
The Extra Trick	5	3	8	+3	–1	+2	Adam
The Triumph of Reason	4	5	9	–1	+2	+1	Eve

Note in the table in particular the final column, which assigns to either Adam or Eve the decision-making power to move from one level to another. The assignment of decision-making power in this way can be regarded as a political constitution for the community composed of Adam and Eve. According to this constitution, one of the players has veto power, the exercise of which would prevent both players getting to the next stage of the game.

Table 1 exhibits the basic logical features of the Adam and Eve game. Although *Trust Within Reason* always presents those features in terms of the Adam and Eve story, there is no reason in principle to stick with this particular interpretation and it is helpful to think about an alternative model for the game that enables us to gain insight into its most important aspects. We can think about the game as a mini-political system, in which a political constitution assigns decision-making powers. For example, we can think about the game as being represented by a political constitution in which for any legislative measure to be passed, the agreement of two chambers representing different constituencies or different types of voters is required. Looking at the rows in Table 1, we could then say that for a measure providing maximum joint advantage to be passed, an original proposal needs to go through three readings in each our two chamber political system and assent is sequentially required from each of the chambers in turn.

We can see what is involved in such an interpretation if we think through the example a little more. For example, suppose a proposal for some public works that would benefit the constituents of the first chamber. The members of the chamber pass a measure which provides for one unit of benefit for their constituents. That measure then goes to the second chamber which is free to amend it, so that the rewritten measure now provides for two units of benefit to the constituents of the second chamber, and minus one unit of benefit for the constituents of the first chamber (perhaps by the way in which taxes are levied to finance the measure). If this rewritten proposal is then passed back to the first chamber, the representatives there will be able to rewrite the proposal on their second reading, so that their constituents gain three units of benefit, this time financed by a loss to the constituents of the second chamber. However, if the measure is passed back to the second chamber for its second reading, those representatives will in turn be able to rewrite and so on.

Let us call such a constitution a system of concurrent decision making. There are three points to make about the political constitution of this joint system. The first is that the veto power that is built into the decision-making process is extensive. This is partly because getting a measure through three pairs of readings in two houses requires a high degree of concurrence of judgement by the decision-making bodies. However, it is also because the veto power that each chamber has is tied to a particular rule about the situation in default of agreement to carry a measure through all three stages. The normal default in legislative decisions is that the *status quo ante* prevails in the absence of being able to carry a measure through its full legislative process. In our hypothetical concurrent legislative system, by contrast, the default, when a measure does not succeed in passing through all the relevant legislative stages, is whatever amended version of the proposal is in the hand of the chamber with the veto at the time. In terms of real-world legislative systems, this sort of default rule seems highly unusual, but it is not entirely without some exemplars. For example, under the co-operation procedure of the European Union, if the Parliament cannot summon up a majority against a Council of Ministers proposal, then the Council measure prevails.

The second point is that the disincentives to initial action – to even making a proposal – that Martin Hollis identified in the Adam and Eve game is also present in our concurrent legislative version of the game. Because each chamber at each stage knows that it is handing over power to another chamber to rewrite the proposal and then veto any further moves, the same incentives not to proceed are found in the legislative version of the game as are found in the Adam and Eve story.

The third point to make about the game, viewed as exemplifying a political constitution, is that it embodies the principles of a particular political theory, namely the tradition that springs from the work of James Madison. When Madison argued for a theory of checks and balances within a constitution based on the separation of powers, he was arguing for a political constitution within which there would be considerable veto power. One version of the Madisonian tradition was notoriously extended by Calhoun in his advocacy of the principle of the 'concurrent majority' to defend the southern states and protect the south's 'peculiar institution' of slavery against federal legislative intervention. Calhoun's (1853) defence of the principle of concurrent majorities was taken up in the twentieth century by the 'Virginia' school of public choice, and in particular by Buchanan and Tullock (1962).

The main reason usually advocated for adopting Madisonian principles of design in the forming of constitutions is to avoid tyranny, understood within the tradition as preventing a popular majority from exploiting or taking unfair advantage of a minority. However, there is another effect of Madisonian principles of design usually identified by analysts, namely a tendency towards log-jam or immobility in the passage of measures. In political systems that are based upon the principle of the separation of powers and the system of checks and balances, it can prove time-consuming or impossible to secure reforms that would be of general benefit. In the US, for example, civil rights legislation was held up for decades primarily through the opposition of southern Democrats who were able to exploit their veto position in the Senate, until 1965. Similarly, the US remains the only country in the OECD world not to have passed legislation providing for some form of universal health care coverage. The problems are not limited to the US however. The difficulties in the European Union of securing reform in the Common Agricultural Policy or passing some form of energy/carbon tax to ensure an equitable contribution by member states to the control of climate change reflect a decision system in which veto power is lodged at a number of nodal points of decision.

These 'joint decision traps' (Scharpf, 1988) are not accidental features of systems that depend upon the principle of concurrent majorities, but stem from the basic properties of such systems. As Brian Barry (1965: 327) pointed out many years ago the problem with a power-diffusion system is that a determined minority can block not only substantive decisions but also the constitutional changes necessary to change the allocation of power. This intuition about substantive decisions has subsequently been formalised by Tsebelis (1995) in his identification of the importance of the distribution of veto power in the analysis of constitutions.

These insights from the formal analysis of constitutions provide the underpinning for the deadlock of decision making that *Trust Within Reason* identifies. Working with the instrumental concept of rationality, Adam and Eve find it impossible to attain the goal that is to their joint advantage. However, the problem is not simply the instrumental concept of rationality, but the exercise of this form of reason with a constitution of decision making that allows collectively self-defeating veto power to be exercised.

To say that a system of decision making uses a complex system of veto power is not to say that the possibility of all action is blocked. Even in constitutions where there is a strong bias towards conservatism or stasis, ingenuity can be used to get round the barriers to reform. Iain McLean has shown for example how the House of Lords was moved to pass corn law reform, an proposal over which it has veto power and which if passed would be contrary to the interests of those represented in the Lords, by a clever framing of the issue in terms of public order and the business management of the Duke of Wellington (McLean, 2001). Lyndon Johnson was able to use the circumstances of his large majority in the 1964 presidential popular vote in the wake of the Kennedy assassination to secure passage of the 1965 civil rights legislation. Reformers can use ingenuity to bring about change. But ingenuity needs the right circumstances, and the right circumstances can be few and far between. Where joint gains are difficult to capture because decision moves have to be made sequentially, with possible short-term losses to be incurred by key actors, it will be difficult for those actors to work to their mutual advantage, even where the potential gains are large.

Why, given the obvious difficulties or blockage or immobility, do political constitutions exist with a large number of veto points built into them? The obvious answer is the lack of trust on the part of political actors in the good intentions of those with whom they will have to interact. This lack of trust potentially has a number of sources, but one obvious basis is that the political actors who have to operate within the political constitution represent heterogeneous interests or ideologies. For example, veto points may be built into federal political systems because when the constituent units come together their representatives fear that in pooling their sovereignty with others they may be handing over control over their vital interests to others who may not respect their wishes. Similarly, territorially based second chambers, in which units of very different sizes are assigned equal voting weights, can provide a means by which sparse rural populations feel they can protect their interests against numerically superior urban and industrial interests. Within the European Union, to take another example, the extremely elaborate decision rules – including weighted majority voting in the Council of Ministers and complex, sequential decision making between the Commission, the Council and the Parliament – reflect the desire of the member states to protect their national interests.

There are two competing interpretations that one can offer about veto power as a solution to the problem of political mistrust. The first draws upon the principle that strong fences make for good neighbours. This line of reasoning accepts that instrumental rationality and opportunistic behaviour are ineradicable features of political interaction and seeks to provide constitutional protection to political actors in the hope that, protection having been provided, actors will have more confidence in seeking out the potential for measures of common gain when it is there. The principle here is that protection for one's vital interests, in the form of constitutional guarantees, provides the security for actors within which they can act to upgrade the common interest. The problem with this line of reason, however, is that it may prove to be self-defeating. The conditions under which protection is granted are just the conditions that make it virtually impossible to act in the common interest. The EU, for example, found that moves towards integration were blocked for more than twenty years after de Gaulle insisted in 1965 on the 'Luxembourg compromise', which allowed individual member states to veto measures that were regarded as contrary to their national interests.

The second line of reasoning is precisely the reverse of the first. It is based upon the thought that institutionalising mistrust in the distribution of decision-making powers is just the wrong way to go. Mistrust breeds mistrust. What is needed is a change of culture from a competitive political system to a co-operative one. It is this line of reasoning which is, of course, explored by Martin Hollis in his appeal to the Rousseauian transformation.

From Philadelphia to Geneva?

In a short but important section of *Trust Within Reason* Martin Hollis sought to exhibit the logical basis for a theory of co-operative citizenship, via an appeal to Rousseau's account of the transformation in human nature that occurs in the move from the state of nature to civil society. The kernel of the argument is stated as follows: 'to make citizenship robust enough to underwrite trust, a society must be more than a club for self-interestedly rational individuals who want their backs scratched. Our sociality is less instrumental and more genuine than that'. (Hollis 1998:153) What is it about Rousseau's political theory that made Martin Hollis think that he provided some of the conceptual resources necessary for making good this claim?

According to *Trust Within Reason* Rousseau's account of the transition from the state of nature to civil society is based upon three conceptual contrasts. The first of these is that between animal instinct and human intelligence. For Rousseau, as for Hobbes, life in the state of nature was brutish, but Rousseau understood this in a more literal sense than Hobbes, as any reader of the *Discourse on the Origin of Inequality* (Rousseau, 1754) will know. For Martin Hollis the development of intelligence in the state of civil society is important because one of his central ambitions is to show how morality can be grounded in reason, and this means showing how morality is consistent with the motives derived from intelligent reflection, which in turn is thought to be the distinctive human form of freedom. Martin Hollis quotes from Rousseau as follows: 'the impulse of appetite alone is slavery, and obedience to the law one has prescribed for oneself is freedom'.

The second aspect of Rousseau's account of the transition that is important is his contrast between natural liberty and civil liberty. In the state of nature humans enjoy natural liberty, meaning that they can acquire whatever they want, subject only to the constraint of others being free to acquire whatever it is they want. It is this natural form of liberty that is, of course, so self-defeating, for it creates just the type of social order in which the stable enjoyment of the fruits of proprietorship is not possible. Only civil liberty in which there is a mutual recognition on the part of all citizens of mutual limits is consistent with the freedom that allows individuals legally to enjoy what is theirs.

The third conceptual contrast in Rousseau is between the will of all and the general will. Hollis interprets this distinction (rightly in my view) as a version of the collective action problem, in which the pursuit of what is best for each does not lead to the achievement of what is good for all. The will of all would be exemplified in such situations as individuals continuing to use water in a drought, because their contribution to the common good by rationing their use of water seemed insignificant in the attainment of the overall social goal, or fishing fleets continuing to over-fish depleting stocks because it was in their individual interest but not in the collective interest. The general will by contrast consists in individuals acting for the common good, in a situation in which only the good of all can contribute to the good of each in the long run. It is, of course, precisely on this contrast between what is rational for each and what is rational for all that the argument of *Trust Within Reason* is built. If the rational, instrumental pursuit of self-interest always led to the best outcome for all, there would be no reason to ponder the paradoxes of rationality.

The most important fact about the Rousseauian transformation, however, is not the significance and plausibility of these conceptual contrasts, but the fact that for Rousseau all three of these contrasts line up with one another. The move from the state of nature to the state of civil society is a movement from the natural liberty of animal instinct governed by the will of all to the civil liberty of reason governed by the general will. This conceptual alignment is, I think, the reason why Martin Hollis thought that the Rousseauian turn was so important. All political theory is grounded in an understanding of human nature, and the central part of that nature to study is the character and activity of the mind. If the operation of human intelligence were simply a form of local optimising according to the logic of the will of all, then there would be no hope for overcoming the problems that the collective action problem poses for citizens and society. However, Rousseau has shown us how the character of intelligent action is linked to the form of our social relations and this in turn has implications for our understanding of the place of freedom in human affairs. What Rousseau offers in other words is not simply an alternative way of reasoning but also a potentially liberating account of the character of human social relations: '...for the purpose of deciding what reason is to say about trust, he challenges individualism at just the right depth' (Hollis, 1998, p.153).

It is important for Martin Hollis that the resolution of the problem of self-defeating instrumental reason is seen to involve an appeal to the political relations involved in active citizenship. One of the reasons why Rousseau is not to be confused with Kant is that Kant prescribes universally, whereas Rousseau sees citizens as legislating for themselves in their own local communities. The general will is made not discovered, and it can vary with circumstance depending on the collective decision that is made. However, this does not mean that individuals are simply caught up in the ethics of their own local community. Rousseauian legislation is still legislation by individuals, albeit individuals who are prepared to accept the decisions that emerge from their collective deliberations. So our sociality is genuine, but not pre-emptive. We do not simply follow the customs or conventions of our own clan:

> Reciprocal relations like love, friendship honour and patriotism extend the self into a wider community, which does indeed offer to settle who we are and where we belong. But they do not define us immutably, nor are schemes of generalised reciprocity beyond criticism. (Hollis, 1998: 153–4)

The role of citizenship is one, therefore, in which we both accept the obligation to respect the collective decision of the community and take on the responsibility of critically evaluating the standards by which the community is governed. This is a sober, but penetrating, reading of Rousseau's exaltation of the value of citizenship.

There are, of course, many questions that can be raised about Rousseau's attempt to show how those born free can nonetheless be in legitimate chains, and by extension many questions can be posed to those who wish to appropriate the logic of Rousseau for contemporary purposes. One obvious problem is that Rousseau's morality is ultimately conventionalist, in the sense that what is right is made to depend upon the collective choices of the citizenry. This conventionalist aspect is well revealed in his discussion of the morality of capital punishment, in which the rightness or wrongness of capital punishment is made to depend on a probabilistic calculation by those seeking the general will which balances the likelihood of being convicted oneself as a murderer as against the reduction in the chance of being a victim given a presumed deterrent effect from capital punishment (Rousseau, 1762, book II,

chapter 5). (Rousseau is uncharacteristically conventional for his time in
thinking that the balance of advantage will come down on the side of
capital punishment.) Any form of conventionalism will pose problems
for those who hold to a deontological standard, and who wish to see the
prohibition of capital punishment on the grounds that it violates human
rights. For pure contractarians this will not be a problem, but it ought to
be a problem for those, like Martin Hollis himself, who do not want the
communitarian sentiments to drive out respect for universal standards of
human rights (Hollis, 1998: 154).

However, that is not a line of criticism that I shall pursue here. For
my money, one of the impressive features of Rousseau's philosophy is
how much by way of justifying political authority he seems to accomplish
with unprepossessing premises. The 'remarkable transformation' to
which Martin Hollis points is not ultimately a transformation in human
nature but a theoretical and conceptual transformation in the way we are
to think about human nature. Rousseau shows us how far the rational
animal has to have travelled to have gone from animal to rational. It is,
moreover, sheer perversity to see Rousseau's praise of the positive
freedom that comes with the arrival of the civil state as a forerunner of
totalitarianism.

The issue I wish to raise, therefore, is not with the tools that are
used to attack individualism but with the target of attack itself. One
way of putting this is to ask whether there is the direct line from
sociality to citizenship that Martin Hollis supposed in his
appropriation of Rousseau. Rousseau thought that there was this direct
line because he thought that any partial or sectional attachments were
incompatible with citizens determining the general will. If every form
of social relationship apart from that of citizenship threatens to cut
across the exercise of the responsibilities of citizenship then sociality
has no other outlet than in the political relation. However, there is
clearly a logical gap opening up here. Sociality is compatible with a
variety of non-individualistic attachments, including those to church,
class, language or ethnic group, region or status group. It is an
empirical matter how high up the list of attachments citizenship comes
for the members of a particular society.

In this respect the model of Adam and Eve is somewhat misleading.
The logic of their choice situation generalises to any corporate entity that
is involved in collective decision making with other corporate entities,
whether they be political representatives, social partners or nation states.

However, assuming that the political problem is how Adam and Eve are to co-operate to mutual advantage despite the temptation on each to defect at suitable veto points ignores the sociality that is involved in aggregating to a collective level short of the relationship of citizenship. Suppose Adam and Eve are not natural individuals but the names of corporate actors or social groups (say labour and capital or religious and secular). Sociality will occur within those corporate entities, but it will not be the sociality of citizenship.

What this means is that reciprocal relations may flourish in extensive, but nonetheless bounded, forms of association. The optimist will hold that this is the form that 'social capital' takes, and there is every reason to think that there is a positive association between a flourishing set of secondary associations and democratic performance. However, there are large and contested empirical and evaluative questions to be settled here, and we cannot assume a benign effect on democratic values from a dense network of civic associations.

From Rationality to Reasonableness?

We are, I think, back to the problem of the design of a political constitution for individuals and groups whose rationality may not be purely instrumental but who cannot be assumed to be able to internalise an intense association with the logic of the general will. A political constitution has to assume some forms of sociality based upon a principle of generalised reciprocity, but it cannot assume that of itself this solves the political problem of citizenship. Instead sociality may take the form of reciprocity within the limits of certain social groups, but bounded reciprocity across those limits. Insofar as this leads to the problem of political mistrust, we are back to all the problems associated with the assignment of veto powers within a constitution.

One line of argument here is to take seriously Martin Hollis's insistence on the importance of the inner point of view of the actors associated with the method of *Verstehen* (Hollis 1998: 156). In practice this means that there is only a limited amount that we can or should expect from constitutional design in terms of solving problems of trust and security between social groups. Whatever constitutional devices there are need to be understood from the point of view of the actors who are affected by them, and the commitments and values that those actors bring to their perception may well be decisive. The constitution of the political system of Northern Ireland, for example, is replete with devices based on the principle of concurrent majorities in order to reassure both nationalists and unionists that nothing can be done without their joint consent. Yet, though such assurances may be necessary to create the climate for joint working, they are hardly sufficient. We might even want to go further and say, as Robert Dahl (1956: 134) said many years ago, 'in so far as there is any general protection in human society against the deprivation by one group of the freedom desired by another, it is probably not to be found in constitutional forms'. Even if we do not want to say that much, we surely will not think that constitutional engineering by itself will solve long-standing political problems that have bred mistrust.

This might suggest that a culture of compromise is important to the functioning of democracy, and that is undoubtedly true. An ethic of compromise requires sometimes of actors that they do not useful their rightful powers to the full extent, even perhaps when they suffer wrong or injustice as a result of not using those powers. As Richard Bellamy writes (1994: 436–41), the value of compromise is not that actors stand in a neutral position, but that they seek to stand in a context-bound common position. Where compromise means accepting a collective decision with which you profoundly disagree, conformity to the general will may therefore exact a price.

There is also a twist to the story, however, derived from Martin Hollis's insight that even Rousseau is not enough. A political community requires citizens who are willing both to accept the general will and play their part in responsibly criticising prevalent social practices. In the limit, exercising the responsibility of criticising prevalent social practices may mean conscientiously dissenting from what the general will requires in the form of civil disobedience. Good citizenship requires a norm of stubborn dissent as well as social compromise.

Once we say this we are in the realm of values rather than of rationality. In so far as the tradition of the Enlightenment sought to move away from the assumption that morality could be based upon tradition or revelation, it did a service in stressing the connection between the free exercise of human reason and deliberation about political and personal ends. But it is the naturalistic fallacy to believe that moral choices can be derived from the understanding. How dissent and compromise are to be balanced in the responsible exercise of citizenship is not a theorem from a syllogism of practical reason, but the way in which someone expresses their character. Instrumental rationality is not enough in the conduct of human affairs because rationality is not enough.

Throughout *Trust Within Reason* Martin Hollis returned to the thought expressed by Condorcet that reason shows how 'truth, virtue and happiness are bound together by an unbreakable chain' and the triumph of reason within a moral order always remained his goal and the practice of his personal life. He would, therefore, have been disappointed in my conclusion that there are some moral choices that are beyond the reach of reason, particularly where the practice of citizenship is concerned. I should love to have heard his arguments and to have been defeated by his wit and intelligence. I am deeply sorry this will never happen.

REFERENCES

Barry, B. 1965. *Political Argument*. London: Routledge and Kegan Paul.
Bellamy, R. 1994. '"Dethroning politics": liberalism, constitutionalism and democracy in the thought of F.A. Hayek'. *British Journal of Political Science*, 24:4, 419–41.
Buchanan, J. & G. Tullock. 1962. *The Calculus of Consent*. Ann Arbor: University of Michigan Press.
Calhoun, J.C. 1853. *A Disquisition on Government*. Ed. C.G. Past. Indianapolis: Bobbs-Merrill, 1953 ed.
Dahl, R.A. 1956. *A Preface to Democratic Theory*. Chicago and London: Chicago University Press.
Durkheim, E. 1933. *The Division of Labour in Society*. Trans. G. Simpson. New York: The Free Press.
Hollis, M. 1998. *Trust Within Reason*. Cambridge: CUP.
McLean, I. 2001. *Rational Choice and British Politics*. Oxford: OUP.
Rousseau, J.-J. 1754. *Discourse on the Origin of Inequality*. Trans. G.D.H. Cole. London: J.M. Dent & Sons, 1973 ed.
Rousseau, J.-J. 1762. *The Social Contract*. Trans. G.D.H. Cole. London: J.M. Dent & Sons, 1973 ed.
Scharpf, F.W. 1988. 'The joint-decision trap: lessons from German federalism and European institutions'. *Public Administration*, 66:3, 239–78.
Sidgwick, A. 1931. *History of Ethics*. Enlarged edition by A.G. Widgery. London: Macmillan.
Titmuss, R.M.. 1970. *The Gift Relationship: From Human Blood to Social Policy*. London: Allen & Unwin.
Tsebelis, G. 1995. 'Decision making in political systems: veto players in presidentialism, parliamentarianism, multicameralism and multipartyism'. *British Journal of Political Science*, 25:3, 289–325.

5

Trust, Choice and Routines: Putting the Consumer on Trial

ROBERTA SASSATELLI

'...and he was telling new stories, which, by telling, from true became fantasy and from fantasy, truth'.

Italo Calvino

Trust is a puzzling entity for social and political theory. It is puzzling because it challenges and yet thrives on individualistic views of the subject: half rational, half emotional, always singular and yet defined by its being amidst other individuals. It is puzzling because it draws attention to different aspects of the social bond, procedural and substantive, which may be conflicting. Finally it is also puzzling because it is experienced, conceived and modelled in different, sometimes irreconcilable, ways and yet it often derives its deeper value from a somewhat universalistic flair. What I propose to do in this paper is to start from Martin Hollis' framing of the problem of trust in his last work *Trust Within Reason* (Hollis 1998) and show how his picture may be developed, enriched and, partly, challenged by shaping the agent of trust in the guise of a consumer.

Hollis' book addresses trust within a framework which foregrounds choice and reason, something which has also characterised the social scientific concern with consumer practices. In contemporary society the actor is increasingly portrayed as a consumer. The consumer has also entered the field of ethics as the new biotechnology debate shows; it is not entirely unknown to the sphere of religion, as testified by some forms of sacred tourism; it has become the agent in whose name political action is undertaken. Especially after the Second World War, 'consumer choice' has become the fundamental paradigm to endorse or to oppose for ethical and political choice. In the political arena of the eighties, for example, the term 'consumer' was supposed to give people rights they were otherwise deprived of (Hall & Jacques 1989). Still, translating the Hollisian setting into the vocabularies and scenes of contemporary consumer practices may appear daring to those who are familiar with little more than the dominant neo-classical picture of the consumer as an instrumentally rational, pleasure-seeking individual. Nevertheless, as we shall see, when enriched by sociological and anthropological views, this move allows for a surprisingly rich perspective on trust, choice and the social bond in every day life.

Trust and the Hollisian Trail

In the best English tradition, Hollis saw philosophy not merely as an academic enterprise, but as a way of thinking about the world which is at once involved and detached, like a puzzle to treat with levity only because each move is itself utterly serious. And it is precisely with a puzzle that *Trust Within Reason* begins. With the help of backward induction, one of the classical problems of game theory, Hollis constructs an ideal path which Eve and Adam, ideal actors themselves, are asked to undertake together. They will have to take turns in choosing among alternatives which get progressively better from the perspective of total utility, but which are each marginally worse than the previous for the person who has to choose. Game theory is thereby articulated with a condensed history of the philosophical answers to the problem of trust. This gives way to the 'Enlightenment Trail', a parable which allows one to pose 'the problem of trust both as a precise puzzle about rational strategic choice and as a grand enigma about the bond of a well-ordered society' (Hollis 1998: 128). Eve and Adam could proceed along the trail and reach the last glorious public house, 'The Triumph of Reason', or halt at the first tavern, 'The Rational Choice', which is comparatively much less attractive for both. Equipped solely with different preferences and with the capacity to choose instrumentally, our two prudent travellers will end up eating less well, on the whole, than they could have done in those taverns placed farther along the path of co-operation.

In order to proceed past the first tavern, the two travellers will have to learn to promise. They will have to be provided with progressively tighter forms of trust, so as to correct their purely instrumental outlook.

This is what Hollis proposes to do. Thomas Hobbes figures as the author who set the problem in modern terms, i.e. with a world populated by instrumentally rational actors having to live together and working within a frame of forward-looking, self-regarding reasons. For all their prudence, the sum of the choices of these self-interested beings may well produce an outcome inferior for all. Hobbes resorts to what appears as an obvious remedy, namely sanctions or, more solidly, the creation of a Leviathan through social contract. In this view, fear is the key to trust. Still, fear of sanctions is a poor substitute for genuine trust. It will only marginally work because each member will rationally break the rules whenever it is safe to do so; and the appointed sheriff is unreliable, being endowed with the same basic motives as the supervised. To make these objections convincing, Hollis deploys his sociological palette: free-riding is, he writes, 'a serious matter in a shifting modern society, where people are opaque to one another' while 'policing, informal and formal alike, is both costly and inefficient' (Hollis 1998: 32). Fear is thus no solution to the problem of trust; it does not work. Even when Hobbes declares it a 'law of nature' that 'men perform their covenants made', a Hobbesian couple could not reach past the only marginally better tavern 'The Foole'. Free-riding is always lurking somewhere: the only possibility to prevent it relies on divinely ordained principles of justice, something rather contradictory with a theory of obligation as self-interest mediated by contract.

While, precisely in Chap. 13 of *Leviathan*, Hobbes declares that 'men do not take pleasure in each other's company', David Hume is the philosopher of polished sociability. A lesson in benevolence by Hume may bring Eve and Adam to feel reciprocal sympathy. Their egoism thereby shifts from the psychological to the philosophical level. Still, compassion, benevolence and the other passions which link our pleasure to that of the others work just like egoistic motives: they do not make Adam and Eve trustworthy in 'the normative sense in which we trust people to do what is expected of them even when that would go against their balance of satisfactions' (Hollis 1998: 42). Better-off than the Hobbesian partners, the Humean couple reaches as far as 'The Sensible Knave', a tavern which is still far from offering the best sum of the utilities of the two travellers. Sympathy is, in other terms, no solution to the problem of trust either. Humean philosophical egoism demands that action be guided by how the actor judges its consequences: everything which counts can be expressed in consequential terms and each actor remains a bargain-hunter. As we will later be told, all attempts at refining with technical devices (from utilitarianism to revealed preferences) this model of rationality are deemed to fail. An obstacle persists in the inability to represent promises other than in a consequentialist language.

Reference to the antinomy between consequentialism and trust runs through the whole book, encompassing even Smith's impartial spectator. Hume himself however is portrayed as having fought against such an antinomy: a deficit of trust afflicts every society composed of benevolent speculators and, precisely because of this, we need to resort to 'justice', an 'artificial virtue', a 'remedy in the judgement and understanding'. Hollis' discussion of Humean anthropology is instrumental to dismiss these corrections too. They are written off as untenable in the Humean context: 'in a psychology where reason alone cannot be a motive to any action of the will how can such a remedy bind us in *foro interno*?' (Hollis 1998: 65).

Several times throughout the book Hollis declares the need for a 'radical change in the agent' and for 'a fresh notion of rationality'. These changes are invoked as ways to overcome the shortcomings of a framework – roughly traceable to the anthropological and epistemological views systematised by neo-classical economics (Hollis & Nell 1975) – which remains short of trust precisely because all reasons are translated into satisfactions, thereby being homogenised and treated instrumentally. Later along the trail it will become clear that it is above all the actor, rather than rationality, which is to change. Better, it will emerge that Kantian reason is no substitute for instrumental rationality when we deal in trust. Quite rightly, although surprisingly to some, Kant will be appreciated and dismissed: the German cure may bring Eve and Adam to 'The Triumph of Reason', but it does so relying on duty rather than on trust-within-reason.

Indeed, *Trust Within Reason* is not the conventional broadside of a moral philosopher against rational choice. It is rather a more subtle endeavour, testifying to a dual project. At the beginning of the trail, to try to deliver the best possible outcome, Hollis indicates three possibilities (Hollis 1998: 26–7): the 'simplest is that each of us can do as we think best for ourselves, provided that we do what suits us all'; alternatively, 'a rational person's ends have to be moral in a sense which makes our individual concerns subordinate to those of humanity'; or, finally, 'we need thicker ends which cannot all come from further reflection on our personal advantage'. The first option (contractarian/utilitarian) is immediately branded as less simple than it seems. In the second option (Kantian) trust becomes a sign of our rationality, rather than the bond of society. It is the third option, for all its ambiguity, that we are subtly asked to look at. It is this possibility which responds to the Hollisian dual project: capturing 'the conditional character of everyday trust' and asking 'which social relations generate trust-within-reason' (Hollis 1998: 105).

Now, this possibility requires a complex model of the agent. By definition, some of his or her ends will, and some will not, come from self-interested instrumental calculations. Under these conditions, the reader may consider that Hollis' dismissal of Hume's condemnation of the Knave is too swift. Although it may be right that, given his notion of the self as a bundle of preferences, Hume cannot congruously deploy it, it is still possible to explore the idea that a person, who is incapable of loyalty to him or herself, will soon lose self-respect. This view would fit nicely with what is proposed at the end of *Trust Within Reason*. From the beginning of the book, trust is associated with promise, something which is never fully discussed nor disputed. Among other things, this allows Hollis to conceive of trust not as a continuous state, but as an event which is connected to the specific circumstance in which individuals consciously contemplate alternative courses of action (Luhmann 1988). Still, approaching the conclusion, we are invited to consider Richard Titmuss's well-known work on blood donors (Hollis 1998: 145–9). Blood donation appears to be one of the most striking cases of disinterested trust or, at least, of non-instrumental trust which is far from being irrational. For Hollis we should understand it as a form of 'generalised reciprocity' among '*relative* strangers', 'known members of *our* network', whereby altruism is tempered by the intention to contribute to particular, interdependent networks which demand loyalty and can both offer concrete support and entrench identity. This is 'philosophical egoism in the first person plural, where the 'we' is neither a sum of associated individuals nor all of humanity but a matter of membership'. By pushing this proposal beyond itself, we may consider that, instead of promise, trust could have been portrayed as a self-fulfilling prophecy. As such trust would have been more convincingly defined as a mixture of moral pressure and calculated guess, a cross-breed of the attempt to realise a positive vision of oneself and of the effort to construct the world as one thinks best.

Still, to define trust in the first place as a self-fulfilling prophecy, would have been less compatible with both the contractarian and the Kantian traditions. The notion of promise both mirrors the logic of contract and allows us to conceive of trust as dutiful. In other terms, it works well with the solutions as given within universal reason. And Hollis is surely looking for a fresh practical reason which is universal, although heroically strategic rather than prudent or duty-bound. However, a view of trust as self-fulfilling prophecy may bring us closer to the sophisticated picture of the actor which Hollis is looking for. Certainly, in doing so, it grants wider scope to the sociological context, too. Precisely the latter must have been its shortcoming in the Hollisian context: as a self-fulfilling prophecy, trust locates individuals in social relations so deeply that they become social first and individual only in some context.

Ultimately, for Hollis, this remarkable change in the actor drew the model too close to remedies which entail a local morality and a local rationality. This in turn did not appear to offer a firm (in so far as universal) basis to evaluate how reasonable are the social arrangements which generate local communities of trust. Still, if we start to fill in the rather abstract picture of the trail that Hollis provides, we will have to start precisely by considering the local. Indeed, contextual elements – such as the actual characteristics of the pubs, the nature of the path, the wider environment, and so on – as well as the contingencies of the travel would suddenly become of the essence. If we replace Hollis' Adam and Eve, with two slightly less abstract actors, today's Mr and Mrs Consumer, we may get yet another metaphor for the analysis of trust and choice.

Of course this is a big move. The trail will no longer be intertwined with the history of philosophy; rather, it will depart from a discussion of some of the more influential ways in which consumer choice and trust have been portrayed in the social sciences. Putting the consumer on trial on a trail thus renewed means, as compared to the Hollisian picture, that far greater consideration will have to be given to the characteristics of the taverns presented to our travellers. This may allow us to deviate from the individualistic picture which Hollis adhered to, as one may think that wants or preferences are continuously negotiated – learned and changed – vis-à-vis not only those of one's own travel companion, but also vis-à-vis one's own encounter with the world of goods.

Putting the Consumer on Trial

The widespread usage of the term 'consumer' in public and political discourse in recent times has coincided with neo-liberal precepts – witness Thacherite vocabulary – thereby envisaging the consumer as an isolated self-interested individual. Indeed, this kind of consumer was the model for neo-classical *Homo economicus*, an abstract and universal agent, conceived of as a black box of given preferences constrained by a given budgetary level and linked to the environment, defined as the goods available and their relative prices, through his/her instrumentally rational choices aiming at maximising the utility function, defined as the satisfaction associated with the bundles of goods matching his/her preferences (Hargreaves Heap 1989). It is this model which epitomises rational choice theory. In a brief polemical essay, *Friends, Romans and Consumers*, even Martin Hollis exploits consumers as an emblem for rational choice theory and its shortcomings: 'consumers are individuals related through contracts made to mutual advantage'; they can only contribute to a political community as 'an association of private individuals whose public contributions are instrumental' (1996: 151, 153). Yet, to depart from this image would not have been difficult. There is plenty, in contemporary theories of consumer practices, which suggests that the consumer is far from being the champion of neo-classical instrumentality.

This section, therefore, will explore how we can best conceptualise consumer choices, and how we can re-think the notion of trust. Trust for the neo-classical mainstream economist is a lubricant to exchange, itself portrayed as a non-easily substitutable commodity which may not be bought very easily. Even for sociologists like James Coleman, trust is purposive behaviour aimed at maximising utility under risk, with mutual trust as a form of social capital which cuts down the cost of monitoring activities (Coleman 1990: 306ff.). Yet, as Hirschman (1984) suggested, if trust is a commodity, it is one that increases with use.[1] As we shall see, trust and consumer choices are intertwined in complex ways that cannot be placed on a neat means–end sequence, nor comprehended without reference to the context where consumption takes place.

Goods as Gates and Bridges, Trust as a Self-Fulfilling Prophecy

We take Mr and Mrs Consumer and we place them in a market for pubs and taverns like that with which we are familiar: there are many taverns, subtly differentiated among themselves, each offering a specific combination of characteristics which comprises more than pints and crisps, each enjoyable in some respect and in different manners at different times. In a situation like this, we may figure out that Mr and Mrs Consumer are overwhelmed and paralyzed – no matter what their individual utility or the sum of their utilities might be. This risk was clearly identified by Georg Simmel (1907). Simmel saw consumption in the modern world as a process of 'reappropriation of things' when the subject faces a drawing apart of 'objective culture' from 'subjective meanings', of the conditions of production from the possibilities of enjoyment. In this situation, as 'objects cannot anymore impose their rhythm on the subject', so the 'subject may not be able to impose his rhythm onto objects' (Simmel 1907: 643). Our relationship with objects changes, we change. We become 'consumers', subjects confronted with a specialised and modifying world of commodities which do not determine us, but which have to be continuously appropriated, if we are to make sense of ourselves, the world and our place in it.

Paralysis is a risk, as much as compulsive spending, but we may take it that Mr and Mrs Consumer are part of the vast majority who are too wise or too naive for that. They are more likely to manage their consumer choices nicely: they will go to a pub, often to the very same pub over and over again, often but not always enjoying themselves, very rarely discussing why they have 'chosen' such a venue or questioning (and indeed quantifying) the probably different utilities they may derive from the experience. Indeed, in sociology and anthropology, consumer choice has been discovered not to be a choice about utility at all. Consumers are active, coherent and rational, yet hedonistic explanations relying on individual satisfaction are abandoned in favour of a structuralist view which see goods as the material basis for expressing and reproducing the meanings shaping and bonding the social space. Goods and services express and reproduce distinctions, they are both material and symbolic strategies of inclusion and exclusion (Bourdieu 1979; Douglas & Isherwood 1979). For Mary Douglas, for example, goods are needed as both aids to interaction and indicators for fixing intelligible worlds, they are the material basis for expressing and reproducing the cultural meanings which shape and bond a social space (Douglas & Isherwood 1979).[2]

As soon as the ceremonial and semiotic qualities of goods and services – their capacity to mark out social relationships – are identified, Mr and

Mrs Consumer appear as busily going to pubs to reinforce or shift their relationship, to remark their status among other couples, to get the last bit of information about the association of one particular beer to a valuable lifestyle, and so on. Trust itself becomes the object of choice: the use-value of a meal or a drink is deeply entangled with the many ways in which this very meal is a sign and a practice of trust and distrust, of how people position themselves in the world, being associated with some and dissociating themselves from others. In this picture, trust appears to take on the role of a self-fulfilling prophecy. We trust the preferred product to be able to both mark and construct ourselves, our relationships and the world. Consumer choices, Douglas says, reflect basic choices about what kind of society to live in. Commodities are selected precisely because they are not neutral, because they would not be tolerated within rejected cultural perspectives on the organisation of society, and the pleasure to be gained from them thus corresponds to a 'pleasurable fulfillment of social duties' (Douglas 1982: 16). A mundane practice like shopping is neither determined by fashion or advertising, nor purely instrumental, on the contrary 'wandering round the shop is actualizing a philosophy of life' (Douglas 1992: 102).

Douglas has a strong tendency to portray the consumer as a coherent cognitive operator who is realising a coherent worldview on the basis of a rejection of other equally coherent perspectives. If, from a social-theoretical perspective, the identification/dis-identification dynamic is key, Douglas' underlying philosophy foregrounds duty and responsibility. When choice becomes a fulfilling of social duties, trust (and distrust) may rather mechanically be reproduced through such choices. Perhaps, in the Hollisian context, this gets us too close to Kant on practical reason and too far from him on morality: a duty-bound rationality and community-bound set of morals – which may neither capture the conditional and negotiational character of trust nor offer a safe moral platform to evaluate the different forms of trust. More widely, the critic may say that the coherent worldview realised through consumer choices is in fact an *ex post* rationalisation which masks the variety of meanings and reasons embedded in consumer practices. The critic may also say that this view does not account sufficiently for both contingency (the ongoing negotiation characterising social practical action) and embeddedness (the fact that trust is a condition for action, including action aimed to create or reinforce social groups and their boundaries).

Trust as a Complexity-Reduction Device, Choice as Normative Claim

As suggested, trust is not only the object of action, it is also what allows Mr and Mrs Consumer to make their choices. In this vein, trust should also be understood as a taken-for-granted background which works as a complexity-reduction device: it is a gradually developing inbuilt set of expectations which are located in time and space in the context of specific institutional settings and which are typically deployed to orientate oneself in everyday reality. The point here is not that our two travellers will not spend much time in weighing all options and will instead stay in the first tavern – or in any which fits with the relative social position they happen to occupy. The point is that they will move along the pub trail as a result of the continuous ongoing negotiation among themselves as to what they perceive is normal and natural. Trust in one another, in pubs, in the specific pubs on the trail, in money, and indeed in trails will all have to be there for any move Mr and Mrs Consumer may make. Trust is here thus conceptualised as a background condition for action, a routine structure of expectations: it may also be the object of choice, yet as such it is reflexively linked with choice, being at the same time the necessary ground for it.

Harold Garfinkel (1963) has famously discussed trust along these lines. The father of ethnomethodology turned Parsons upside down. According to Parsons (1937) everyday experience does not appear to have an order until it is organised and classified via a number of analytical constructs. Garfinkel (1988) instead maintains that there is an 'endogenous' order in everyday activities, and that there cannot be a neat separation between this order and the stories – including social-theoretical schemes – which explain it. Experience is not at all chaotic because the actions of which it is comprised are accomplished in so far as they are organised in intelligible ways. We may say, in terms closer to the focus of this paper, that the orderliness of social life is grounded on the mutual trust people display to one another, with the trustworthy person being one who masters the discrepancy of prescribed attitudes with respect to reality 'in such fashion as to maintain a public show of respect for them' (Garfinkel 1963: 238). Garfinkel shows how taken-for-granted assumptions which constitute everyday life produce actions that confirm the individual's expectations and how actors elaborate and stretch the existing rules in order to cover new events. Actors are not reflexive, yet their actions and discourses are, with participants in interaction attributing to one another a reflexive awareness of the normative accountability of their actions.[3] In this sense, while normal social reality is a contingent ongoing accomplishment of competent social actors, routines are of essential importance; they are 'products of the perceived normal values of interpersonal events that members of a group seek through their adjustive activities to maintain' (1963: 188).

Although Garfinkel stresses the emergent quality of routines, he also seems to insist that they help to sustain social reality, which may otherwise culminate in an endless and empty search for ultimate meaning. This is developed further in the thought of Niklas Luhmann (1979). Despite the obvious differences, this parallel is not without truth (Mistzal 1996). Luhmann indeed conceives of trust as a complexity-reduction device. Trust 'reduces social complexity by going beyond available information and generalizing expectation of behaviour in that it replaces missing information with an internally guaranteed security' (Luhumann 1979: 93). However, it is reduction of complexity which combines knowledge and ignorance and resembles induction: 'in the last resort, no decisive grounds can be offered for trusting; trust always extrapolates from available evidence ... Although the one who trusts is never at a loss for reasons and is quite capable of giving an account of why he shows trust in this or that case, the point of such extra reasons is really to uphold his self-respect and justify him socially. They prevent him from appearing to himself and others as a fool, as a inexperienced man ill-adapted to life, in the event of trust being abused. At most, they are brought in to account for the placing of trust, but not for trust itself' (Luhmann 1979: 26). So, like Simmel (1908: 318ff.), he considers that while trust may be based on (some) knowledge, it cannot be explained by it: people who know everything do not need to trust, people who know nothing cannot be reasonably confident. Like Garfinkel, Luhmann also considers that the problem of trust is to be understood in procedural rather than essentialist terms: what is relevant in everyday life and what social theorists will have to address if they want to understand trust is not the actual characteristic of trust relationship, it is rather the beliefs people hold about other people's beliefs about it (Luhmann 1979: 66–9). In other words, people trust on the assumption, and the appearance, that other people trust; they trust on the assumption and appearance of everything being, so to speak, 'in order'.

This picture of trust is compatible with the view that choice is descriptively inadequate to understand what Mr and Mrs Consumer are doing, and yet it might have an important role as a normative claim. Choice is indeed better understood as a normative claim rather than a fully realised practice. On the one hand, the idea of individual and rational choice does not corresponds to the practical modalities by which subjects learn how to consume. On the other hand, it constitutes the normative frame for such processes and a structuring principle for the institutions where they take place. Like all other social action, consumption must also be felt as valuable: and the subject which consumer practices demand is modelled on the notion of choice. Ideal as it may be, it is an autonomous, self-sufficient subject who has some objectives, who strives to get them and who believes that the best way to do so is to act on the basis of a goal-specific, instrumental rationality, following the advice of experts or resorting to specialised agencies. As a category of action, choice relies on a distinctive anthropology: invited to think of themselves as choosers, individuals are asked to make themselves calculable and foreseeable, while promoting themselves as the ultimate and non-substitutable source of value. This requires individuals who are sovereigns of themselves, who have become, as Friedrich Nietzsche would say, the owners of their will (Foucault 1976, 1983).

Our two travellers, Mr and Mrs Consumer, will thereby be seen to go along their trail in an ongoing negotiation which has no ground zero and which is merely reconstructed as a rational enterprise. They will be busy, constantly making small adjustments, such that what they are, as much as what they want, is endlessly produced. Trust and choice will become essentially a matter of presentation: a ceremony and a rhetoric which fixes identities, bonds and worldviews. It is evident that this picture of trust and choice may also be problematic, both within and without the Hollisian context. It may help to understand trust as a disposition, an attitude which is learned. Yet as a subject's attitude to a particular object or person it is not transferable to other objects or people. At the same time, as Luhmann writes, '(t)he relationship of trust to an object ...independent of specific individual interests and contexts of experience, occurs regardless of the particular state of affairs which it becomes relevant. As a typical example, trust in a particular person will be activated wherever the one who trusts encounters this actual person regardless of their respective roles and contexts' (1979: 27). All in all, this concentrates on the function of trust rather than on its - often contingent and situated - conditions. It also draws attention away from how trust is formed through time and practically operates in a variety of socially standardised contexts.

Consumption as a Situated Learning Process, Trust as Calculated Attachment

Considering the situation of today's consumers, we immediately notice that they have to learn and trust not only their fellows, but also those who sell and offer them goods and services, as well as those goods and services themselves. When, with a rather loose metaphorical move, Mr and Mrs Consumer are taken as our travellers in the world of pubs and taverns, then it becomes evident that the profile of each tavern at hand matters greatly, as much as the specific sequence of taverns, and all other contextual elements. We may accept that choice is the normative model people have to confront when they describe and understand themselves as consumer. Still, people *act* as consumers and we will have to find ways of describing their practices.

Consumption can be fully appreciated as a form of *social* action only by leaving behind the idea that such action may be modelled as a purchase decision, itself to be traced back to rational choice – be it a case of utility maximisation or of identity maximisation. Paradoxical as it may seem, consumption is a *productive* activity. First, consumer practices contribute to produce other consumption: they produce capacities, knowledge, and attitudes, circularly, that help choosing. Second, cognitive, affective and normative elements are all intertwined in complex ways; learning to consume often means learning to discard; discerning some characteristics often means wanting to morally evaluate them. Third, in order to avoid conceptualising consumption as a series of abstract and individualistic decisions, we have to consider that consumer practices happen in institutions. If different from those traditionally studied by sociology, these institutions for consumption are, nonetheless, more and more widespread.

In a few words, the process of consumption may best be understood as a prudential learning process, located in time and space (Sassatelli 2001). Certainly, these (institutional) contexts and (social) situations do not create needs from the void, yet they contribute to make real, concrete and specific desires which are often very vague. In this sense, needs only exist in those contexts where people try, more or less successfully, to satisfy them.[4]

Whether we look at pubs, theme parks, restaurants or supermarkets we can see that, as a practice, choice is realised through an interactive learning process. A good example comes from the sociology of dining out (Warde 1997). Only through practice do people learn that they want certain foods, learn to want them in appropriate ways, and learn to make sense of them beyond the immediacy of their enjoyment. Choice of certain foods and restaurants entails a process of learning which is locally sustained by a series of specific and highly codified manners and whose significance goes well beyond the context of consumption, being appropriated as knowledge to be spent in different social contexts. Even when we shop, choice of a particular item is shaped by the organisation of space, time and interaction. Our choices in the cathedrals of immediate satisfaction, the supermarket and the shopping mall, are rooted in daily rituals marking human relationships and will acquire much of their meanings in the subsequent, again specifically situated, display and use (Miller et al. 1998).

With this emphasis on context, rituals and interaction, trust may be appropriately described as a sort of calculated attachment. Here again trust is a mixture of knowledge and ignorance, yet the emphasis is less on the cognitive, time-saving functions of trust and more on its affective qualities when it comes both to the object-subject relation and to concerted action. In Albert Hirschman's classic, *Exit, Voice and Loyalty* (1970), the author reckons that 'loyalty', or 'attachment to a product', as a 'reasoned calculation', is reciprocally interwoven with the (perceived) capacity to influence the producer. As is evident, objects are not taken in isolation. The object–subject relation is instead placed in the wider web of social interactions and institutions which help to define these very relations. Structural characteristics of the market are relevant for the perception of the influence that a consumer may exercise – for example, the influence of consumers will be larger in markets with few buyers than in atomistic markets.[5] To go back to our travellers, it may be, if Mr and Mrs Consumer are alone in the market for taverns, that they will have such a strong influence on all tavern managers, that these will fight to offer ever new levels of satisfaction, both individual and collective. Should they be part of a larger mass of consumers, as is realistically the case, they will still be able to influence tavern managers, asking more or less directly for slight product modifications. This will interact with their own couple loyalty. The fact that they are indeed a couple should not be overlooked. They are likely not to be able to 'exit' their relationship, thus developing both their capacity to negotiate or 'voice' their requests and, with it, their declared loyalty to each other. Rather than settling for inferior joined outcomes, a couple like this, in a flexible and relatively responsive market for taverns, is likely to actively run after increased utility forever – even if as a means to keep the relationship stable.

These arguments are, to some extent, in line with Hirschman's focus. He was mainly concerned with loyalty as an important factor for product quality recuperation provided that 'it can neutralize ... the tendency of the most quality-conscious customers ... to be first to exit ... giving the firm ... a chance to recuperate from a lapse in efficiency' (Hirschman 1970: 79). However, some recent phenomena may help us consider a wider structural picture where consumers may indeed act as a powerful grouping. Let's think about the market of food in the context of European integration, food scares and innovations such as genetic engineering. When a common market is being created as much as when innovations in the technological basis are introduced, the potential scope of the market is enormously enlarged and the fact that we cannot exit from it (but only from specific goods) becomes an issue. Previously obvious boundaries which commanded trust in everyday exchange practices can no longer be taken-for-granted. Yet, distrust might become a resource (Luhmann 1979) and loyalist behaviour assumes a different meaning as the high price of exit may stimulate voice just because one has nowhere else to go: 'the output or quality of ... (its) organization matters to one even after the exit. In other words full exit is impossible' (Hirschman 1970: 100). The market itself may be seen more clearly as a public good which is not only to be preserved from monopolistic tendencies, but also increasingly makes sense only in relation to the 'public' whose 'good' it is supposed to serve.

The exploration of the possibility conditions of market-exit may lead to the overcoming of the 'consumer-exit' model: just as the impossibility – or unbearable cost – of abandoning the labour market has legitimated the formalization of workers rights, so the impossibility of a market-exit *per se*, as compared with specific product-exit, seems to demand 'voice'. In this context, consumers may come to play a more direct political role by responding to their newly visible ascribed status: they may behave as 'consumers-citizens' with mobilisation, boycotts or new buying patterns; or they may behave as 'citizens-consumers', providing the necessary legitimisation for state or regional attempts at protecting/promoting the local and the traditional.[6]

Concluding Remarks

We are often told that modern society is characterised by an alarming deficit of trust. In his own way, Martin Hollis appeared to agree with this view. He posited the problem of trust in modern society as key in so far as we need a renewed form of trust which copes with disembeddedness, globalisation and multiculturalism without losing its soul – which, we are invited to think, is inevitably that of a liberal political community made of autonomous agents. In this framework, consumers are easily taken as a negative benchmark: while the Frankfurt School questioned the very autonomy of the consumer in the chaos of commercial images, Hollis played a different tune. Consumers' lifestyles and private interests are – we are told – so divided that each may well be a stranger to the rest; their collective interests too weak to care for public goods; their reason so instrumental that any concern for the interests of the losers is itself merely instrumental (Hollis 1996). Yet, we have seen that, whilst not irrational dupes, consumers are less instrumentally rational than one is accustomed to think, that they rely on trust as much as construct trust relations through their consumer practices.

Even consumers thus act on trust and produce trust. Modern life, Simmel (1908: 313) wrote in the early days of the twentieth century, 'is based to a much larger extent than is usually realised upon faith in the honesty of the other'. This is also true when we increasingly shape our relationship on the model of 'exchange', 'a sacrifice in return for a gain'. Even consumer exchange, however fleeting and superficial it might be, both creates a bond between people and is predicated on some form of trust: 'without the general trust that people have in each other, society itself would disintegrate, for very few relationships are based entirely on what is known with certainty about another person' (Simmel 1907: 178–9). The functioning of a complex society depends on a myriad of diffuse, mundane forms of trust, including those which we encounter in the supermarket, in the high street shops, in the petrol station, or in pubs and taverns.

Simmel was probably the first social theorist to consider the trust-building function of mundane social relations such as courtesy. Above all, he showed that even money, with all its impersonality, needs trust: cash transactions cannot occur without trust in the state as the agency responsible for the administration of money, which in turn sustains the stability of the monetary system: '(t)he feeling of personal security that the possession of money gives is perhaps the most concentrated and

pointed form and manifestation of confidence in the socio-political
organisation and order' (1907: 179). Indeed, while during monetary
exchange we are trusting the individual agents who operate in the
economy, the functioning of the monetary system illustrates how in
modernity personal trust is partially translated into a generalised trust in
the ability of systems to perform.

The modern monetary system also reveals our willingness to accept
fictions, and to trust them (Frankel 1977). This is important when we
think of how consumers may think of themselves and act. It is clear that
we are all very different as consumers, that very few tastes or preferences
are shared by any two of us. Indeed, as I have suggested, we are pulled
and pushed to incarnate the autonomous, authentic agent – with his or
her original and highly specific wants. Yet, when we are prepared to
accept banknotes or credit cards as if they were valuable, then we might
become capable of accepting and indeed supporting the category
'consumers' as if it were indeed a meaningful and coherent entity. To put
it more sharply, if and when a culture of voice and protest, or simply
conscious boycotts and self-recognition, develops among consumers,
they may indeed find that they have something in common.

According to Hirschman (1970: 126), individualistic exit from an
unsatisfactory product is more likely to occur than interest articulation
because 'the effectiveness of the less familiar mode [of reaction] becomes
not only more uncertain, but tends to be increasingly underestimated'.
Because of this, a culture of 'voice' would be particularly important.
Hirschman himself notices that in this respect 'voice is essentially an *art*
constantly evolving in new directions' (1970: 42). His arguments are
sketchy but penetrating: beyond market-structure considerations 'the
propensity to resort to the voice option depends also on the general
readiness of a population to complain and on the invention of such
institutions and mechanisms as can communicate complaints cheaply and
effectively' (Hirschman 1970: 43). This demands, on the one hand, that
voice be recognised as an important – effective and advantageous –
mechanism and, on the other hand, that institutionalised mechanisms of
interest aggregation and the communication of dissatisfaction be
developed.

Hirschman's observations are, I believe, to be understood beyond
their apparent cognitivism, taking into account the ideological-
normative dimension. In other terms, not only the perception of
influence, but also the development of a belief in a right – or duty - to

influence is fundamental. This has been hampered by a powerful narrative which has contrasted consumption as a private individualistic sphere with work as a public sphere of identity recognition and collective action. The moral superiority traditionally given to production activities has meant that it was assumed that society as well as relative social position could only be ameliorated there. While consumption was, and could remain, an area of the individual's will, production was the right place to make one's voice heard, it was there that rights should be promoted. Yet we may think that the changing perception of the market, of its standing *vis-à-vis* the political and the environment, may come to intersect the tradition which has led to the establishment of a legal framework for consumer protection, thus implying a stronger, if only contingent, capacity to articulate consumers' interests as collective interests.[7] In other words, we may think that people can and will play their roles as consumers in different ways.

Just like we have learnt to be citizens through modernity, so we both are and may learn to be a sort of consumer different from the neo-classical image. Honour, trust, and collective goods are much more known to the consumer than we are invited to think when, for example, positional goods are discussed in rational choice models (see also Hollis 1996: 167ff.). This is due not only to the fact that goods themselves are very different and complex, commanding mixed forms of attachment and calculus, but also and more importantly to the fact that they are never just objects; they always embody social relations.

This circumstance still does not tell us much about how should we evaluate the forms of trust and relationships that grow together with our consumer practices. In other words, Mr and Mrs Consumer may well get to the last tavern and even past it, yet we have not provided a solid ground to judge when their path as well as their final stop are fair and just. This moral concern is ultimately what worried Martin Hollis the most. In *Trust Within Reason*, he repeatedly insists on the duality of his project: to find a form of reason receptive enough to account for every-day trust, and robust enough to distinguish among different types of trust, reasonable and unreasonable. Reason and trust have both descriptive and predictive connotations. The former is associated with probability calculations (what we expect to happen), the latter with normativity (the normal becomes honourable and we expect from some persons some actions whatever the consequences). Normativity is, as we have seen, unavoidable even in the case of consumers. Yet this is still normativity of a sociological sort, i.e. it is embedded in particular social places and histories rather than necessary when observed comparatively and with critical distance. Having demonstrated that we cannot avoid – as social theorists or human beings – some normativity of this sort, Hollis looks for one which would be fair and discerning. He would have demanded Mr and Mrs Consumer not only to co-operate and stretch out to the happiest tavern, but also to be just, their preferences and bonds being both advantageous and reasonably desirable.

This enterprise looks paradoxical enough in the Hollisian framework where little is said about preference formation, standardisation, and the object/subject relationship. It does look particularly arduous if we take a more open and dynamic view of the subject, one where even preferences are learned in interaction. Once we dispose of a notion of individual autonomy as an anthropological given and consider that we are and want, to a large extent, what we learn to be and to want, it may be more difficult to take up Hollis'intimation and ask questions with the 'fighting arrogance' of those who have not renounced universal answers, even if they know that these will not be conclusive. And yet, we may think that only from such a standpoint can we truly incarnate the greatest strength of liberal universalism, namely its utopianism. Certainly to believe in chimeras one must be strong, above all one must trust oneself and the others quite a lot, one must be loyal. But, and this is perhaps more important, one must also always have both the courage to play seriously with the idea of exiting such chimeras, while having the real possibility of doing it.

NOTES

1. Rational choice theory has been the object of criticism from all quarters, not only because of its lack of assumptions about the genesis and nature of individual preferences, but also for being rooted in a single form of cultural rationality – competitive individualism (Wildalvsky 1994). When it comes to trust, rational choice is said to employ too narrow a notion of trust because trust is not a means that can be chosen to a given end (Luhmann 1979), and because it fails to furnish an account of shared meaning, as the condition for trust relations (Rawls 1992).
2. In short the argument goes like this: the rational self cannot behave rationally, unless the world be characterised by a certain coherence and regularity. He/she needs an intelligible reality made of visible signs, and goods provide the material basis for stabilising the categories of culture. Consumer choices are, thus, moral judgements about oneself and the surrounding social reality. Consumption gains momentum as 'the very arena in which culture is fought over and linked into shape' (Douglas &

Isherwood 1979: 57). It is clear that this function of meaning creation is distant from commodity consumption for intrinsic utility correlated to individual a-social needs, while ostentation and conspicuous consumption is just one of the meanings goods can take over. On this argument, Hargreaves Heap (1989) maintains that these authors were able to bring back into the field of economics an expressive form of rationality which points at the use of goods for saying things about ourselves. However, I would reckon that too much emphasis is placed on self expression and, since the subject finds expression through consumption but is not constituted by it, this sort of explanation seems to posit a difference between means and ends which may still reintroduce a new form of instrumental reasoning.

3. According to Heritage (1984: 106–10; see also Csyzewski 1994), ethnomethodology marks a 'new departure' from traditionally phenomenological notions of reflexivity, translating reflexivity from the subject (and his/her individual capacities of thought) to action (the reflexivity of accounts).

4. With the development of material culture and the growth of leisure time a number of institutions for consumption have appeared. These places – restaurants, discos, gyms, malls, etc. – are all the more autonomous from the wider society and differentiated, having an influence on the sedimentation of tastes which is not coterminous with that of other social spheres. Social stratification has indeed become more complex, with belonging and distinction being determined not only from the production side, but also from the consumption side. The ever greater resources spent for marketing studies - which delineate profiles of consumption on the basis of the organisation of purchases into lifestyles - are perhaps the best indicator of this kind of phenomenon. The success of the models based on lifestyles shows that social groups can be defined (as much as define themselves) by recognising similar consumer preferences, without them being directly traceable to relative positions in the productive structure or to formal education.

5. The issue is rather complex. If we consider, for example, the transformation of the distribution system from a myriad of small retailing shops to supermarkets and the reduction of personal interaction to its minimum, we may think that impersonal exit is favoured. At the same time, producers will try to foster loyalty, as testified by the importance of the 'brand'. Product loyalty in this case seems less linked to interaction factors as in the case of traditional retailing systems where it was the shopper as a person to play a decisive role as target of 'voice'. Yet, brand marketing strategies elicit some measure of attachment which may well be the basis for 'voice' actions even if 'exit' is available.

6. Countries across Europe are obviously divergent in the strategies they are likely to adopt. The first response appears typical of countries like the UK where product standardisation is crucial for consumer confidence and powerful corporations are met by a variety of consumer interest groups. The second one is more likely to occur in countries like Italy or Austria where tradition, locality and personal relations are still strong as a basis for trust and where protectionist measures are in place to promote sustainable farming. For a wider discussion, see Sassatelli & Scott (2001).

7. The history of consumer rights from the 1960s may indeed be conceived as the institutionalisation of channels for the expression of 'voice', providing the ideological-normative foundation of consumer interests articulation (Aaker & Day 1982). However, the translation of consumer interests into rights has taken off from the consumer-exit model: the 'consumer rights' approach is addressed to the redistribution of power between producers and consumers within the borders of individualistic market relations. Rather than pointing at the difficulties in combining 'exit' and 'voice', then, the rhetoric of consumer advocates has been that of giving to consumers a measure of political power adequate to their economic capacity, of

recognising the consumer as a political actor *stricto sensu*. Political issues such as the redistributive dimension - what goods and services should be provided to whom - or the solidarity dimension - encouraging consumers to take account of the preference of others - of consumption relations have been left out of the picture (Potter 1988). Still, with the development of issues such as globalisation, ecology and new technology the boundaries of the market and its internal logic are obviously and yet again in dispute.

REFERENCES

Aaker D. & Day G., eds. 1982. *Consumerism: Search for the Consumer Interest*. New York: MacMillan.
Bourdieu, P. 1979. *La distinction: critique sociale du jugement*. Paris: Minuit.
Coleman, J. 1990. *Foundations of Social Theory*. Cambridge: The Belknap Press.
Csyzewski, M. 1994. 'Reflexivity of Actors versus Reflexivity of Accounts'. *Theory, Culture and Society*, 11, 161-8.
Douglas, M. & B. Isherwood. 1979. *The World of Goods*. New York: Basic Books.
Douglas, M. 1982. 'The effects of modernization on religious change'. *Daedalus*, 111/1, 4-28.
  1992. 'In defence of shopping'. Eisendle & Miklautz 1992: 95-117.
Dreyfus, H. & P. Rabinow, eds. 1988. *Beyond Structuralism and Hermeneutics*. Chicago: University of Chicago Press.
Eisendle, R. and E. Miklautz, eds. 1992. *Produktkulturen und Bedeutungswendel des Konsums*. Frankfurst: Campus.
Foucault, M. 1976. *La Volonté de Savoir*. Paris: Gallimard.
  1988. 'The subject and power'. Dreyfus & Rabinow 1988: 208-26.
Frankel, SH. 1977. *Money: Two Philosphies. The Conflict of Trust and Authority*. Oxford: Basil Blackwell.
Gambetta, D., ed. 1988. *Trust*. Oxford: Basil Blackwell.
Garfinkel, H. 1963. 'A conception of, and experiments with "trust" as a condition of stable, concerted actions'. Harvey 1963: 187-238.
  1988. 'Evidence for locally produced, naturally accountable phenomena of order*, logic, reason, meaning, method, etc. in and as of the essential hecceity of immortal ordinary society'. *Sociological Theory*, 6/1, 103-9.
Gronow, J. & A. Warde, eds. 2001. *Ordinary Consumption*. London: Harwood.
Hall, S. & M. Jacques, eds. 1989. *New Times: The Changing Face of Politics in the 1990s*. London: Lawrence & Wishart.
Hargreaves Heap, S. 1989. *Rationality in Economics*. Oxford: Basil Blackwell.
Harvey, O.J., ed. 1963. *Motivation and Social Interaction*. New York: The Ronald Press.
Heritage, J. 1984. *Garfinkel and Ethnomethodology*. Cambridge: Polity.
Hirschman, A.O. 1970. *Exit, Voice and Loyalty*. Cambridge, MA: Harvard University Press.
  1984. 'Against parsimony: three easy ways of complicating some categories of economic discourse'. *American Economic Review*, 74, 88-96.
Hollis, M. & E.J. Nell. 1975. *Rational Economic Man. A Philosophical Critique of Neo-Classical Economics*. Cambridge: Cambridge University Press.
Hollis, M. 1996. *Reasons in Action. Essays in the Philosophy of Social Sciences*. Cambridge: Cambridge University Press.
  1998. *Trust Within Reason*. Cambridge: Cambridge University Press.
Luhmann, N. 1979. *Trust and Power*. New York: John Wiley & Sons.

1988. 'Familiarity, confidence, trust'. Gambetta 1988: 94–107.
Miller, D. et al. 1998. *Shopping, Place and Identity*. London: Routledge.
Misztal, B.A. 1996. *Trust in Modern Society*. Cambridge: Polity Press.
Parsons, T. 1937. *The Structure of Social Action*. New York: McGraw-Hill.
Potter, J. 1988. 'Consumerism and the public sector: how does the coat fit?'. *Public Administration*, 66, 149–65.
Rawls, J. 1992. 'Can rational choice be a foundation for social theory?', *Theory and Society*, 21, 219–41.
Sassatelli, R. 2001. 'Tamed hedonism: choice, routines and deviant pleasures'. Gronow & Warde 2001: 93–106.
Sassatelli, R. & A. Scott. 2001. 'Wider markets, novel food and trust regimes'. *European Societies*, 3/2, 231–63.
Simmel, G. 1907 [1990]. *Philosophy of Money*. 2nd edition London: Routledge.
1908 [1950]. *The Sociology of Georg Simmel*. New York: The Free Press.
Warde, A. 1997. *Consumption, Food and Taste*. London: Sage.
Wildavsky, A. 1994. 'Why self-interest means less outside of social context'. *Journal of Theoretical Politics*, 62, 131–59.

6

Whose Dirty Hands?
How to Prevent Buck-Passing

BARBARA GOODWIN

In his article 'Dirty Hands' (1992), Martin Hollis analysed the train of
events which preceded the 'infamous Massacre of Glencoe' in 1692.
Captain Campbell and his soldiers committed 'murder under trust',
abusing the hospitality of the MacDonalds, whom they killed, and
breaching their own honour. But the murder was explicitly ordered by
the political authorities and the order was passed on through the higher
ranks of the army until the command was given to execute the order.
Hollis's argument initially focuses on the question of 'obedience under
orders' – who among the order-givers was responsible for the massacre?
But his wider theme is the inevitability of politicians having 'dirty hands'
because of the role which they are expected to fulfil, satisfying interest
groups with conflicting demands. The article is fascinating for anyone
working on moral responsibility and the question of how to determine
responsibility where a number of people contribute to a harmful action
or outcome. The latter question arises regularly in complex and
hierarchically structured organisations of which an army is one example.
Whenever a disaster occurs, such as the sinking of the *Herald of Free
Enterprise IV*, there is a clamour to identify who within the organisation
was responsible, not just legally but morally, since disasters and harm
raise moral issues. This is when the buck-passing begins.

I recently undertook a study of how employees of large organisations
feel about their responsibilities, and how organisations determine these
(Goodwin, 2000). This article considers some of the questions raised in
the study in more abstract, philosophical terms. But the abstract
argument is also intended to offer a guide to how organisations might
structure responsibilities internally, and what they might do when
questions of blame arise. In what follows, the focus is on occasions where

minor negligence, omissions or mistakes eventuate in harm, rather than on cases of deliberate wrongdoing or gross negligence, where the question 'whose dirty hands?' can sometimes be answered straightforwardly. The case of people carrying out *immoral* instructions, on which the Hollis article concentrates, raises different and more extreme issues which I will not address here.

Two Meanings of 'Responsibility'

The allocation of degrees of responsibility is important wherever there is division of labour and co-operative activity; in other words, it must happen in most human activity which is not entirely solitary. In thinking about this, we need to clarify what is meant by 'responsibility'. Glover suggests that 'to hold someone responsible for an action of his can be to hold that it is legitimate to praise, blame, reward or punish him for that action, where any of these responses would normally be appropriate' (Glover, 1970: 49). This *ex post* definition of responsibility is common usage. In a different, *ex ante* sense, 'responsibility' denotes 'duty' or 'obligation' or 'area of concern'. It will be better to use 'responsibilities' in the latter sense, to make the difference clear. But these different senses are two sides of the same coin: if you neglect your *responsibilities* you may end up having to take *responsibility* for any harm that ensues. People's responsibilities at work are, I think, moral responsibilities. Performing your job properly is a moral duty to your employer, your colleagues, the 'consumer' and others, as well as a prudential precaution against being sacked.

The Obfuscation of Responsibility

The allocation of responsibilities and the determination of responsibility after any error or accident are especially serious matters for large and complex organisations, whether these are businesses, bureaucracies, governments, trades unions or voluntary organisations. In complex organisations the problems of clarifying responsibility are twofold. First, with a joint activity or a jointly produced product it is not always easy to determine what contribution each agent in the process made to the outcome. It may be unclear who should receive credit for its success, or who is responsible if it goes wrong. The buck may be passed and victims may fail to receive redress. Organisational conventions may be adopted to clarify this but they are more likely to stipulate who should be *held* responsible (e.g. the Board of Directors) than to try to identify who was 'actually' responsible, which may be difficult or impossible with a joint product or outcome. Second, most organisations are hierarchically organised and although the *responsibilities* (i.e. duties) of employees at different levels may be clearly defined, individual *responsibility* after a harmful event may not always fall on the person who brought about the event: a supervisor will often be held responsible for something which a member of her team does wrong even when she had no knowledge of the wrongdoing. This is because ensuring proper performance by team members is one of her responsibilities.

While the convention that people are responsible for their subordinates' errors may present no problem to those operating within such organisational conventions, there is a problem for the philosopher if we start from the premise that before you can feel responsible, or acknowledge your responsibility, for an event or outcome you must feel yourself to have had some free will in the matter. (This pre-condition is captured in the maxim 'ought implies can'.) But this is not always the case. It is unpleasant to be held responsible for another's (bad) actions, all the more so if you were unaware of them or powerless to prevent them. Even though you may be deemed so to be responsible legally or organisationally, you may be left with a sense of injustice. The 'indirect responsibility' which managers are deemed to have for the work of their subordinates is also difficult to conceptualise. We might understand intuitively what indirect responsibility means, but we cannot, for example, quantify it by saying that the manager was only 75 per cent (or 50 per cent) responsible because her subordinate made the error. Nor may the manager in many cases *feel* (morally) responsible for a subordinate's derelictions. Full acceptance of responsibility has a psychological, even an emotional, component. In cases where the manager had no free will in the matter because she could not have prevented her subordinate's conduct (perhaps even because of the intractability of the subordinate) this component is lacking. Also, it is not uncommon for individuals at one level of an organisation to conspire to conceal vital information from people at another level, as was demonstrated by the Scott Report on the 'arms to Iraq' affair and the investigations into the collapse of Barings Bank. Could a manager properly be held responsible for what was done behind her back? The problem is that in structured organisations, where different functions are performed at different levels of seniority, responsibility cannot be easily determined and, by being dispersed, may simply disappear. Those held formally responsible can claim they were not wholly in control, or were left in ignorance. If this is true for managers and supervisors, the same holds for those who work to instruction, acting under orders. As a result, when disaster occurs, the buck may disappear entirely, leaving victims aggrieved.

It might be thought that the law provides a solution to the question 'whose dirty hands?' when something goes radically wrong but, in the United Kingdom, post-disaster trials of large companies have frequently been markedly unsuccessful; for example, the trial of P&O and seven employees for manslaughter some years after the sinking of the *Herald of Free Enterprise IV* was halted by the judge, who ordered their acquittal (Wells 1993: 69–73). The law relating to the criminal responsibility of corporations is complicated and seems defective in determining which person or persons at which level of the organisation should be criminally charged as a result of a disaster.

Towards an Ethical Framework for Responsibility

Clearly, organisations need a framework to provide a method of determining the responsibility for mistakes which led to harm or disaster. But why might organisations require an *ethical* framework when businesses and public-sector organisations are regulated by so many laws and statutes, promulgated with the aim of preventing organisations and their employees from causing intentional or unintentional harm to others? The answer is that, as well as the shortcomings of the law mentioned above, while regulatory laws influence organisational practice, they cannot govern the minutiae of the internal operations of every enterprise, nor should they. Furthermore, the laws relating to the organisation are unlikely to be known in detail by employees. Accordingly, they should be reinforced by organisational rules and codes of conduct which follow the spirit of the law and are made known to employees. Even so, there is often a gap between the rules and what employees actually do in the course of their work. There is scope for interpretation of the law or the in-house rules and for cutting corners. There are escape routes from responsibility for both lower-level employees ('I was acting on orders'; 'nobody told me *not* to do it this way') and for managers ('the regulations were posted in the workshop, but the operatives ignored them'; 'I did not know that the worker was contravening the safety procedures').

Morality, and especially a sense of moral responsibility, must plug the gap between law, codes and daily practice. There is a need for staff at all levels in an organisation, whether it is an army, a corporation, a public agency or some other body, to have a sense of their responsibilities and duties, and to carry them out. Apart from its value for the morale and smooth operation of the organisation, this is important both prospectively – to ensure that mistakes and harmful actions will be averted – and retrospectively – to ensure that, if harm occurs, those at fault can be identified, reprimanded or punished and, if appropriate, can make reparations. As I suggested earlier, in many cases of harm the problem is how to divide responsibility between individuals for a harmful product or event which results from the joint activity of a number of agents – for example, a co-operatively produced artefact such as a car which turns out to have defective brakes. The person who is 'causally' responsible for the defect – the brake fitter – may complain of being given faulty materials or bad information, or say that the work was not properly checked at a later stage. Direct, 'causal' responsibility for the defect of a joint product or service is not always equivalent to full and sole responsibility, because of the nature of co-operative undertakings.[1]

This paper is concerned with moral, not criminal, responsibility. But my aim is to consider whether an examination of some laws which do not relate specifically to corporations can help us to devise models of responsibility which could be adapted to operate inside large organisations to clarify questions of responsibility and assist in identifying dirty hands. The primary reason for adopting such models would be the prevention of harm or disaster but they would do so partly by explaining how blame would be allocated after harm has been caused. If the employees of an organisation are made aware from the outset what share of responsibility is deemed to be theirs, and what their duties are and *why* they have these duties, they are in a position to conduct themselves so as to fulfil their obligations, and have an incentive to do so. Equally, other organisational stakeholders, such as customers or shareholders, are in a stronger position to insist that employees or managers whose actions harm stakeholders are called to account.

In the next section I set out some legal solutions to the problem of evasion of responsibility which might be adapted to organisational practice and ask whether something akin to the strict liability principle could contribute to developing a model of responsibility appropriate to people working in hierarchical organisations, or co-operating in joint enterprises.

The Law, Buck-passing and Models of Responsibility

To resolve cases where negligence or omission have led to harm, the United Kingdom (like many other countries) has laws of strict or absolute liability which do not rely on the presence of *mens rea* (intention). More important for my purposes, the strict liability principle helps to resolve issues of responsibility in certain types of cases where the different parties involved in an illegal act or an accident seek to blame each other and to exonerate themselves by asserting that the other party had *mens rea* whereas they did not. I will examine three typical cases involving strict liability, of which I have had experience,[2] and propose three models for the allocation of responsibility in hierarchical organisations which are based on those cases.

Case 1: Drilling through a High-voltage Cable

A small building firm, 'Builders Ltd', was charged with breaching Health and Safety regulations because a workman on its site had drilled through a live cable. Typically, small building firms in the UK employ few workers and sub-contract skilled workers for tasks such as plumbing and wiring. Even their regular workers usually work on a 'self-employed' basis, so that they are technically not employees of the firm. Evidently, a building company operating like this is in a strong position to claim that none of the workers on site were its agents (i.e. its employees) and that anything which they did wrong was not its fault. It can also claim it has no responsibility for them if something happens to them. Anticipating this defence, the prosecution in this case laid alternative charges, one based on the employer's duty to protect his employees from working on live cables, by proper insulation and warning identification, and one based on a company's general duty to prevent *any person* on a site from harm from electrical installations.

Builders Ltd was renovating two derelict houses and had called in a damp-proofing company to drill and inject the basement walls. The dampproof technician, Smith, had plans provided by his own company, Dampproof Inc., which surveyed the property and told him where to drill. At the corner of a basement, he drilled through a live high-voltage cable which led the electricity supply into the house and was embedded in the brick wall. His wrists and face were badly burned. Smith gave evidence that the foreman (site agent), Brown, had not warned him about the cable, nor had Dampproof Inc. The basement had been poorly lit, some bulbs were missing and the embedded cable had not been visible. Brown, called as a prosecution witness, was the 'self-employed' site agent of Builders Ltd, in control of running the site. He knew the cable was there, and knew that the electricity company had been asked to disconnect the supply to the house and had removed the electricity meters. He stated 'I didn't mention the cable to Smith. I didn't feel it necessary because *you couldn't miss it.*' And, with an implicit contradiction, 'I assumed it was dead'. The implication was that he would have warned Smith had he known that it was live, even though 'you couldn't miss it.' An employee of Electricity Co. attested that Builders Ltd had not specifically requested *total* disconnection of the supply until two days before the accident, and that such a request normally took four or five days to be complied with. He stated that 'some indication of the location of a live cable should be made to advise everyone on site'. A government Electricity Inspector, an expert witness, stated that 'unless there's positive information that a cable is dead, it should always be assumed to be live'. Photographs appeared to show that the cable was visible in part of the wall but was concealed behind rendering in the corner.

The defence was that the builders had done everything reasonable within their control, except for marking the cable with a warning notice. They had requested Electricity Co. to disconnect the supply but it had only removed the meters and sealed off the supply *inside* the house, so the cable remained live. Dampproof Inc. should have noted the cable during the survey and told Smith not to drill near it. Smith should have seen the cable. It was not Brown's task to tell Smith where not to drill, since this could invalidate the dampproof guarantee. Counsel for the defence implied that Electricity Co., Dampproof Inc. and Smith himself were all partly responsible for the accident. The prosecutor responded that Builders Ltd, or their agent Brown, were in overall control and could, and should, have prevented Smith from carrying out work near the cable, or warned him of its existence.

One test of *causal* responsibility for an event, which may also indicate moral responsibility, is to employ counterfactuals. Would the accident have occurred if (1) the basement had been better lit (Brown's responsibility)? (2) if Brown had shown Smith the cable and warned him 'I think it's dead, but be careful just in case'? (3) if Electricity Co. had cut off the supply outside the house when first requested, instead of at the meter inside? (4) if Builders Ltd had been more diligent in marking the cable and ascertaining whether Electricity Co. had disconnected it? (5) if Dampproof Inc. had warned Smith of the cable or marked it on the plan? (6) if Smith had himself examined the basement wall more carefully? The answer is that any one of these counterfactuals, if true, could have prevented the accident. Each omission could in principle be viewed as the entire cause of the accident. However, no omission alone would have sufficed to cause the accident if some of the other omissions had not also occurred. Does this demonstrate that the accident was *no-one's* fault? Surely not. *Everyone's fault in part*? Perhaps. In a civil suit, apportionment of blame would be appropriate in such a case, but criminal courts must establish guilt, or acquit.

The magistrates found the builders guilty on the second charge, founded on breach of their duty to protect everyone on site from injury by live electricity. It seems that, morally, each of the parties involved bore some responsibility for the accident and no-one was wholly responsible for it, but the law dictates that those in charge take the blame, even though there was no *mens rea* on the part of the builders and they defended themselves quite convincingly against the implied accusation of negligence.

Organisational Model 1 – Responsibility at the Top

In this model, parallel to the 'drilling through the cable' case, full responsibility is deemed to reside at the top of the organisation even when harmful actions or omissions occurred at a lower level of the organisation, or outside the organisation. The model equates the responsibility for issuing orders with responsibility for their implementation. But it encounters the problem that the orders may have been carried out improperly, or not at all, in circumstances where the order-giver could not have known or foreseen this. It therefore stretches the order-giver's sense of responsibility to the limits. As the manager of a company, I can issue orders and establish rules about how they should be carried out, but I cannot spend all my time ensuring that they are followed in the way I intended. The axiom 'ought implies can' suggests that I can only have duties which I can reasonably be expected to be able to perform. Constant surveillance over every employee is an impossible duty. If I delegate this to under-managers and supervisors, they must in turn take responsibility for the actions of those whom they supervise. But if I am deemed responsible for everything, will they take their responsibilities seriously?

Holding chief executives and directors responsible for everything that goes wrong is a simple but extreme convention; it says 'the buck stops here' and makes the top manager strictly liable for whatever happens. But applying this model may make top managers responsible for problems they could not have prevented and may allow lower-level employees to feel *less* responsible for their own work. A practical objection is that many top managers, directors, government ministers and heads of public services are expert at circumventing the 'responsibility at the top' convention and hanging on to their positions, and bonuses, no matter what goes wrong. Typically, they blame others: for example, since the creation of semi-autonomous government agencies, Ministers have repudiated responsibility for 'operational' disasters in the agencies, claiming that they themselves are responsible only for strategy. So this is a convention which allows responsibility to dissipate. Giving those at the top an impossibly high degree of responsibility, responsibility beyond their powers of control, will lead them to repudiate it when things go wrong. The regularity of such acts of repudiation casts strong doubt on the usefulness of the model.

Case 2: A Television Inspector Calls
It is an offence in the United Kingdom to install or use a television without a licence. Television Inspectors make surprise visits to premises where no licence is held. Their practice is to interview the person who answers the door and, if there is a working television, to report that person for the offence. In the following typical cases, first the inspector interviews and reports a television owner who admits to having no licence. He then calls at four other premises where there are unlicensed televisions and reports (a) the baby-sitter who is watching television, (b) the adult son watching his mother's television while she is out, (c) the tenant of a flat who assumes that the landlord has licensed the television provided in the flat and (d) an overseas visitor, who knows nothing about the licensing system.

Because the offence is one of strict liability, no intention to commit the offence needs be proved and the people in categories (a) to (d) will often be prosecuted by the Television Licensing Authority, as well as the owner of the unlicensed television. They are usually found at least technically guilty since there is virtually no defence, except where the television does not work. Here is a situation where legal and moral responsibility seem entirely divorced, except in cases where the television owner has dishonestly evaded paying the licence fee. People in the categories (a) to (d) may feel unfairly treated by the strict liability principle of the television licensing law. But the law is formulated to prevent evasion of responsibility and buck-passing by people falsely claiming to be in categories (a) to (d), thereby exonerating themselves and saving the licence fee. In fact, even if someone in categories (a) to (d) is successfully prosecuted, the Television Licensing Authority may subsequently prosecute the owner of the television.

Now take the following imaginary but possible case: five friends, including the television owner, are watching the unlicensed television when the inspector calls. All five are prosecuted for the offence and, necessarily on the strict interpretation of the law, found guilty. It is held that the four friends should have checked whether the television was licensed before watching it. In such a case, there is a multiplication of guilt and punishment which should, surely, be laid at the door of the television owner. Five people, rather than one, are fined. The law seems to have overreached its purpose, the prosecution of unlicensed television owners, in finding all five 'culprits' guilty. It appears draconian. However, this may provide a useful example if we are trying to construct a model of responsibility to cover the situation where two or more people are involved in a joint activity, a model which will prevent them from trying to evade personal responsibility.

Organisational Model 2 – Equal Responsibility

The 'five friends' television case provides the inspiration for this radical model. The model proposes that every member or worker in an organisation should be held equally responsible for any action or omission, and equally to blame for those which caused harm. Its purpose is to ensure that, because no-one can escape the net of blame, everyone will take care that not only he, but also his colleagues, act properly. In other words, each will feel some responsibility for what the others do. The concept is one of collective responsibility: it rarely or never happens, but the British Cabinet should in theory resign *en masse* if one member makes a disastrous policy error which all the others endorsed. Scapegoating is a more likely outcome. A familiar example of the model in action is when a teacher keeps the whole class in detention because no-one will own up to some naughty trick. This is not just a trivial case, because the classroom situation exposes the obvious difficulty with this model of responsibility: the innocent are punished along with the guilty, although they feel no responsibility for the bad behaviour and could not (let us suppose) have prevented it. It is a utilitarian strategy, which uses the innocent as a means to punish and shame the miscreants. It may seem blatantly unjust, but the assumption underlying wholesale detention is that pupils will in future take steps to restrain their mischievous classmates and will develop a sense of collective responsibility for order in the classroom. This assumes a certain *esprit de corps* within the class group.

It is doubtful, however, whether a similar group sentiment could obtain within large, hierarchical organisations, where workers in different departments do not know each other, let alone understand each others' functions. How could they feel responsible for each others' actions if they did not even know what was being done and had no power to prevent it? 'Ought implies can' is violated here, too. Those lower down the pyramid might reasonably feel that the managers were paid more and so should take more responsibility if anything went wrong; managers are, after all, in a more controlling position. The equal responsibility model could also lead to unpleasant reprisals against those who were perceived as 'really responsible' for the actions which caused the harm. In a hierarchy, then, this model runs into practical difficulties as well as moral problems.

The model would, however, be appropriate and may be workable in smaller organisations, especially non-hierarchical organisations such as Co-operatives. In such bodies there exists the necessary condition of an *esprit de corps* and a sense of collective enterprise (c.f. the 'ideal classroom' situation). In the ideal Co-operative, there is a perception of equality between the members so that no-one is thought to be more in command or better paid and so more responsible. People feel entitled to warn or criticise others if their actions appear wrong or liable to cause harm. Because they are jointly in charge of the enterprise and, typically, are its joint owners, they may have the sense of control and free will necessary to satisfy the 'ought implies can' stipulation. It seems that a necessary precondition for the equal responsibility model which is, ideally, a model of collective responsibility, is *equality of status and of power* between the members.

This condition rarely obtains in the business world or in public-sector organisations but there has been movement in some organisations towards greater equality of power and responsibility in the implementation of empowerment policies. Employees are 'empowered' to take decisions, and trained to feel personal responsibility for good customer service. Where emphasis is placed on 'self-managed teams' the principle of equal responsibility can operate within the team. Some businesses operate procedures to create a sense of joint responsibility: for example, on some production lines each task performed is checked and initialled by one or two operatives next down the line, so that every part of the finished machine has been double-checked and vouched for. No-one will vouch for a shoddy piece of work since she will then share the blame. It appears, then, that a collective responsibility ethic could be generated in discrete sectors of large organisations, but that the hierarchical structure of such bodies, and the consequent inequalities of status and power between employees, make the model impossible to apply across the board.

In summary, the equal responsibility model could be effective in improving conduct and standards of moral behaviour and preventing harm, if everyone knew and accepted the rules and the ethical framework for allocation of responsibility. The model could operate in Co-operatives or small organisations where there is at least approximate equality of status and power.

Case 3: The Overloaded Truck

This case provides a possible model for a proportionate sharing of guilt and blame, again on the basis of strict liability. A truck driver taking a load of rubble to the refuse tip is stopped by the police and taken to a weighbridge, where the truck is found to be overloaded. (This could be an offence committed without *mens rea* if no-one intended to overload the truck, but the rubble weighed more than was expected.) The driver states that his employer told him to overload the truck to save an extra journey. The truck owner, when interviewed, claims that the driver received no such instruction, but must have overloaded the truck to save himself the extra journey. He says this happened without his knowledge as he was not even at the site. The same case is brought against each separately and both are found guilty. By prosecuting both, and by not requiring *mens rea*, the law circumvents the typical reaction of drivers and employers, which is to exculpate themselves by blaming each other. The court deems that two people committed an offence which was really committed by only one of the parties (assuming no collusion on overloading). However, the driver is generally fined less than the owner, not just because the latter is usually better off, but also because the employee may indeed have been 'acting under orders' and his job may have been at risk if he refused to overload.

The law is based on a common legal view of authorisation and agency, namely that the author, the truck owner, remains responsible for the driver's action, having made the driver his agent, although the driver is also held responsible for his own actions. This provides a useful ingredient for any model of responsibility: the authorisation by X of Y to be his agent does not absolve X of responsibility if Y transgresses, nor can Y absolve herself by claiming that X ordered her to transgress.[3] The duty of acting rightly or the burden of guilt should be shared between X and Y in some appropriate proportion.[4]

Organisational Model 3 – Proportionate Responsibility

The third model, then, allocates responsibility for the products or actions of an organisation to its different members in various proportions. Although 'allocation of blame proportionate to responsibility' sounds a fair model, there are problems about determining degrees of responsibility for a harmful product or event. Should the manager bear a higher proportion of responsibility because she is in charge, or should the junior employee who actually performed the harmful action or made the mistake? Each option has a certain appeal. Different observers might disagree factually about who was most responsible for a disastrous train of events, as was demonstrated by the investigation into whether incompetent managers were to blame for Barings Bank's collapse rather than the rogue trader, Nick Leeson, whose actions were the immediate and perceived cause of the Bank's downfall.

A practical solution would be to assume that salaries reflect degrees of responsibility. It would then be possible to devise a crude calculus of responsibility for all the members of an enterprise in the following way: total the salaries, wages and bonuses paid annually by the enterprise and then allocate responsibility proportionate to each member's share of the total. Thus, X is 1.25 per cent responsible for any good or harm done by the company because she earns 1.25 per cent of the total. Y, the Managing Director, is 17.3 per cent responsible because she earns 17.3 per cent of the total. Similarly, the law sometimes quantifies proportionate responsibility for the purpose of awarding damages.

Where we are concerned with the negative aspect of responsibility, i.e. its role in the process of blame and penalisation, the calculus could be useful. Suppose that a company agreed to pay £10,000 damages to a customer who had been harmed by one of its products: X could then be required to pay 1.25 per cent of £10,000 and Y, 17.3 per cent. Perhaps X and, even more, Y would be reluctant to accept a job on this basis. But if such a system were established, the awareness of this potential liability would bring home to each member of staff, in the most direct way, the fact that her individual work and her company's products or activities, could harm customers or other stakeholders, and that she had a duty to prevent that, backed by a powerful economic incentive. If the joint actions of a number of workers caused harm or damage, they could be required to take pay cuts in proportion to their percentage of the wage bill. Conversely, proportionate bonuses should reward any exceptionally good workers or managers. At this point, we seem to have reinvented the wheel, since bonuses, employee share-ownership and profit-sharing schemes are now quite common in the private sector: extending such schemes to include *loss-sharing* is more novel. However, profit- or loss-sharing schemes hardly constitute an *ethical* framework for responsibility since actions performed for prudential reasons – increasing your bonus, or covering your back – are not in themselves morally motivated. What the calculus demonstrates, however, is that there are practical ways of determining the *relative* degrees of responsibility of employees.

The main problem with the proportionate responsibility model is that responsibility is something you feel, internalise and act on *wholly*, or to the best of your ability – you cannot limit your moral liability to 1.25 per cent or 17.3 per cent. It makes no sense to speak of 'feeling' 17.3% per cent responsible for an event, but we often say 'I feel partly responsible for what happened' and so the idea of taking a share of blame is one with which we are familiar. I think we can solve this problem by adopting the rule 'everyone is fully responsible for the aspects of the process under her own control'. Defining which aspects of the process were under her control may be problematic, especially when she was acting under orders, but this rule captures the idea of 100 per cent responsibility for what one does, while leaving scope for us to say in mitigation 'but her actions were only a tiny component of the whole operation'.

I suggest that where harm has been caused and dirty hands must be identified, some version of 'everyone fully responsible for the aspects of the process under her own control' would be the most appropriate method of apportioning blame. It is demonstrably more just than the 'all responsibility at the top' model, or the equal responsibility model, which would be unfair in a hierarchy. It also confines individual responsibility to areas in which individuals had some choice and control. If the third model were adopted, the organisation's disciplinary code could be made sufficiently flexible to reflect differing degrees of responsibility for any harmful outcome. A supervisor might be demoted while his subordinate merely loses the annual salary increase as a result of an error for which they were both partly to blame, the subordinate for committing the error and the superior for not having supervised the work properly. There are bound to be attempts at buck-passing wherever joint activity occurs and things go wrong, but these should diminish if an organisation makes its model for determining responsibility proportionately clear to all employees and stakeholders.

Educating for Responsibility

An ideal framework for responsibility should satisfy several criteria: it should be seen as fair by employees, it should prevent the buck from disappearing entirely and it should enhance the operation of the organisation. Model 3, proportional responsibility, satisfies these criteria. It has the advantage of seeming intuitively just, it prevents buck-passing and it reflects and may enhance the way in which an organisation operates. The 'responsibility at the top' convention is widely flouted when things go wrong, and it does not reflect the way in which people in organisations operate. The more radical Model 2, 'everyone responsible for their own and everyone else's actions', could work in a Co-operative or any other organisation of equals, but is not well suited to a hierarchical or bureaucratic organisation. Nevertheless, progress towards the latter model, which maximises the commitment and moral alertness of employees, is being made in many companies via institutional measures such as profit-sharing or share ownership for employees. To commend this may be to conflate moral and mercenary motives in a very un-Kantian manner but it is realistic.

It may seem contradictory to have invoked the analogy of strict liability laws when I have emphasised the importance of holding people responsible only in cases where they can *feel* responsible (in legal terms, this would mean where they had some conscious intention or *mens rea*). They may not feel responsible in the case of an unwitting omission or where others were involved in causing the harm. But it is the role of strict liability in preventing repudiation of responsibility which is important here. It might be objected that I am trying to reconcile the irreconcilable in searching for a model strict enough to prevent buck-passing which nevertheless retains the psychological component of responsibility. Certainly, the allocation of responsibility is ultimately stipulative, and may not square with what people feel about who caused or intended a harmful event, because often a train of events is too complex to analyse and those concerned may each see them from their own perspective. However, I suggest, people can be educated, or can train themselves, to *feel* responsibility in accordance with the organisational framework. Supervisors are not *born* feeling that they must shoulder the blame if one of their team makes a stupid error: they learn to feel that way, to subdue the individualistic voice which whispers 'it wasn't *my* fault' and to ask themselves whether they should have taken measures to prevent such errors. Hollis observes that 'office holders have moral duties which private persons do not' (Hollis, 1996: 142) and this point applies equally to conceptions of responsibility. In our public lives as employees, volunteers or members of a club, we accept the 'public' responsibilities determined by our organisation's framework.

Although no framework can guarantee to identify a unique person who is 'really responsible' for a harmful event, and indeed the idea of 'real' responsibility may be radically misconceived, it can ensure that people are aware of their duties and of the extent to which they will be held responsible if things go wrong. But people can adapt their idea of what constitutes responsibility to whatever system of determining responsibility their organisation adopts, whether it be a top-down 'blame culture', an empowerment culture or a culture of equal status and equal responsibility. That they do this, is the best defence against buck-passing.[5]

NOTES

1. In this context I use 'co-operative' as a synonym for 'joint'; it does not imply the sort of intentional co-operation which animates a co-operatively-owned undertaking. Such undertakings, discussed below, are described as 'Cooperatives' to make the distinction clear. But of course all organisations rely on interpersonal co-operation.
2. These 'typical' cases are based on some that I experienced in a London magistrates' court (lower court) while sitting as a Justice of the Peace (magistrate).

3. This contrasts with Hobbes's view that the people authorise the sovereign to act for them, yet remain responsible for its actions, a prescription for an irresponsible sovereign (Hobbes 1651: ch.XVI)

4. I could also mention the case of the 'caterpillar sandwich', sold in the local grocery store but supplied by a sandwich-making firm: here the co-responsibles are not in a chain of command but horizontally linked and are likely to receive the same level of fine for supplying contaminated food.

5. This article has concentrated on criminal liability; a parallel set of issues concerned with the ultimate burden of compensating a victim of a corporation's civil wrongs deserves a separate study. Suppose the owners of the *Herald of Free Enterprise IV* are sued for personal injuries by a victim of the disaster, why should the company's shareholders carry the liability if the company's loss has (for example) been the fault of the Master of the ship? When a company is successfully sued, it almost never happens that an individual who caused the damage indemnifies the company.

REFERENCES

Glover, J. 1970. *Responsibility*. London: Routledge & Kegan Paul.

Goodwin, B. 2000. *Ethics at Work*. Dordrecht: Kluwer Academic Press.

Hobbes, T. 1651. *Leviathan*.

Hollis, M. 1992. 'Dirty hands'. Hollis 1996.

1996. *Reason in Action*. Cambridge: Cambridge University Press.

Wells, C. 1993. *Corporations and Criminal Responsibility*. Oxford: Clarendon Press.

7

Many (Dirty) Hands Make Light Work: Martin Hollis's Account of Social Action

STEVE SMITH

Martin Hollis's work was characterised by a core conception of social action, based upon a strict individualism underpinned by a notion of the self acting according to reason. In this paper I want to critique his conception of social action, arguing that it fails to take sufficiently into account any notion (either hermeneutic or naturalist) of social structure. I also want to point to some of the hidden traps in his characterisation of the choices facing social theorists (as represented by his famous two-by-two matrix). Let me be clear, however, at the outset that I want to critique Hollis's view of social action precisely because it is one of the most logically coherent and well-worked-out examples of the position in the history of the philosophy of social science. Yet I must also note that it is a view that is often implicit and often has to be deduced from some of the things he does not say. Indeed, in many ways it is a view of social action entirely consistent with the title of one of his books, *The Cunning of Reason*. By this I simply mean that Hollis wrote very skilfully, setting up alternatives and problems in such a way as to come in at the end of the book or article with a resolution to these alternatives and problems that justified his own view of social action. I must also confess that it has taken me many years both to realise this and to develop this critique, so powerful is his model and his associated reasoning. I am also sure that, were he still alive, he would be able to show with his usual mixture of wit and logic just how mistaken and contradictory I was. It is truly tragic that he is not around to continue that conversation.

I am going to start by spending some time outlining Hollis's position on social action, but first I want to say something about my collaboration with him during, and then after, our time together at the University of East Anglia. I need to do this because the argument that follows emerges out of the trajectory of my own thinking resulting from this collaboration. I taught on Hollis's philosophy of social science course for some six years, appearing as a defender of the 'explaining' side of the understanding–explanation divide. Hollis spent a couple of weeks telling them all that was wrong with conceiving of the social world in naturalist terms, and then I had two weeks to convince them otherwise. There are many stories to tell about those teaching sessions, but the important point is that they led the two of us collaborating on a number of projects, most significantly our book *Explaining and Understanding International Relations* (Hollis & Smith, 1990; Hollis & Smith 1986; 1991; 1992; 1994; 1996).

I was trained as a social scientist in the 1970s, when, in International Relations, behaviouralism and positivism ruled the day. Working with

FIGURE 1
MARTIN HOLLIS'S MATRIX OF SOCIAL THEORY

	Explaining	Understanding
Holism		
Individualism		

Hollis caused me fundamentally to re-think that position, and in the last decade I have been increasingly persuaded by a more hermeneutic account of the social world. What has remained is a conviction that individualistic accounts of the social world are flawed and misleading Therefore, although I have essentially moved from the explaining to the understanding side of the divide, I am still holist rather than individualist. Thus, while I have moved from top left to top right, Hollis steadfastly remained in the bottom right box of his quadrant. In the concluding section of this paper I return to the problems of using this matrix to characterise social theory.

Hollis's account of social action underpins virtually everything he wrote, but the main statements are to be found in his books *Models of Man* (1977) and *The Philosophy of Social Science* (1994), as well as in a series of other books and articles (Hollis [1967] 1996b; [1979a] 1996c; 1979b; [1983] 1996f; 1985a; [1985b] 1996d; 1987; 1996a; 1996e; 1998; Hollis & Nell 1975; Hahn & Hollis 1979; Hollis & Lukes 1982; Hollis & Sugden 1993; Hargreaves Heap et al. 1992). There are a number of key themes in his work, and the way I want to introduce them is to look at some of his main writings in some depth. In one sense, the Hollis view of social action is to be found complete in *The Philosophy of Social Science*, but although it is tempting just to look at that book, I think it is more interesting to trace the way in which Hollis's views developed through his career. I am also interested in the ways in which the various themes emerged and matured. It is fascinating to realise, for example, just how late on in his career he developed his matrix of social theory. I hadn't quite realised that it appeared first in book form in our collaborative volume (1990), because he had been using it in teaching for at least six years before that. What is most noticeable when looking at all his writing is just how crucially intertwined are the main themes, and just how precise a theory of social action they lead to. That is not the picture that emerges from looking at any one of his books, because they are all written in a very specific way, with many questions left open for the reader to reflect on. In that sense, his theory of social action almost has to be deduced from his writing; it never really gets stated up front, and is often that which is left after he has demolished the alternatives. Nonetheless, throughout his work there is a set of dominant themes: reason, individualism, a preference for understanding over explanation, and for rationality over relativism. I want to trace the development of these by looking at his major works.

Reason and Ritual

The first main statement that I want to discuss is the 1967 paper 'Reason and ritual' ([1967] 1996b), which, I think, turns out to be particularly illuminating in establishing one of the main foundations of Hollis's social theory, the concept of rationality. In this paper, Hollis starts with an anthropological puzzle: the Yoruba people reportedly carry around with them boxes covered with shells. When asked, they say that the boxes contain their heads or souls, which they are protecting. Hollis argues that when anthropologists attempt to interpret this behaviour, significant philosophical questions arise. If success in anthropology is measured by the ability of the anthropologist to understand what actors in other cultures mean and believe, then this raises the problem of how they would know that they had indeed correctly understood what he terms 'ritual beliefs' (that is metaphysical beliefs which inform ritual action): 'How, then, do we decide when it is more plausible to reject a translation than to accept that a society believes what the translator claims they believe?' (Hollis 1996b: 199) Hollis dismisses one obvious answer, namely that this is an empirical question, such that by learning Yoruba and checking that the answers that the Yoruba give are indeed what they mean. This is because ritual beliefs cannot simply be checked against 'the facts', that is they do not have objectively specifiable truth conditions. Unlike everyday beliefs, facts cannot be used to get to the beliefs, but instead beliefs get us to the facts. Similarly he rejects the notion that ritual beliefs can be understood empirically if they contain words that do admit of objective truth conditions; this runs into the problem that the words involved may be used metaphorically, as in the Aborigine example of describing the sun as a white cockatoo, and as such may admit of several very different meanings (Hollis 1996b: 202). Finally he dismisses the claim of anthropologists such as Evans-Pritchard who, in his study of the Azande, argued that the meaning of Zande ritual beliefs is to be found in their role in social relations, such as, for example, in maintaining the existing power structure. Yet Hollis claims that this move confuses explaining why beliefs come to be held with identifying with those beliefs. Thus 'A Zande, who believes he has been bewitched, surely does not believe that he has offended some social order ... He surely believes, rather, that he is the victim of supernatural interference' (Hollis 1996b: 205).[1]

In place of these attempts to ground ritual beliefs in empirical referents, Hollis appeals to rationality: 'it is my thesis that we can identify a ritual belief only if it is rational by our own standards of rationality ... some assumption about rationality has to be made *a priori*, if anthropology is to be possible; and ... we have no choice about what assumption to make' (Hollis 1996b: 206). Anthropologists have to make a series of *a priori* assumptions to be able to make sense of utterances, for example about truth and falsity, about contradiction, about inference and about identity. Hollis argues that 'these notions set the conditions for the existence not only of a particular kind of logical reasoning but also of any kind whatever' (Hollis 1996b: 211). Thus he accepts Evans-Pritchard's argument that Zande beliefs about witchcraft and oracles are empirically false but rational both for them and for us; the Zande are caught in a web of belief so that although they realise that the failure of an oracle requires explanation, they seek to explain this contradiction between the mystical and the empirical by reference to other mystical notions, such as witchcraft. Hollis cites Evans-Pritchard: 'in this web of belief every strand depends on every other strand and a Zande cannot get out of its meshes because it is the only world he knows. The web is not an external structure in which he is enclosed. It is the texture of his thought and he cannot think that his thought is wrong' (Hollis 1996b: 215). For Hollis, then, rationality, like reality, is not to be defined relative to local conceptual schemes. Instead there is a set of *a priori* assumptions that anthropologists must rely on for their enquiry to be possible, and these relate to a common process of logical reasoning. 'These notions are *a priori* in the sense that they belong to his [the anthropologist's] tools and not to his discoveries, providing the yardsticks by which he accepts or rejects possible interpretations. They are not optional, in that they are the only conditions upon which his account will be even intelligible' (Hollis 1996b: 219).

The importance of this article is that in it Hollis constructs a very powerful foundation for the subsequent development of his social theory. For Hollis, rationality is an *a priori* feature of individuals acting socially. This does not mean that they always act rationally, only that asserting a statement, believing it to be true and then linking that statement to others within a language structure, depends on a deep set of assumptions. If anthropologists do not assume the existence of these assumptions in all cultures then they cannot pretend to understand those cultures; as he entitled one of his later papers, 'The epistemological unity of mankind' (1979b). In that paper he sides with Strawson against Winch over the possibilities of cross-cultural understandings. Contra Winch (1958), who essentially argues for the impossibility of understanding alien cultures from outside, Hollis accepts Strawson's (1959) claim that there is a central core of belief that operates within every culture, and which basically identifies and interprets the objective particulars that surround each society in roughly the same way. As Hollis puts the contrast between the two views: for Strawson 'understanding an alien culture is initially a matter of discovering how to perform the tasks of the universal conceptual scheme in another language ... For the 'Winchian' there is no given core and no theoretical limit to the possible peculiarity of each culture. Enquiry starts by detecting the constitutive rules and thence determines what is real and rational from within (Hollis 1979b: 228). I will return to the problems associated with this view later.

Models of Man

Hollis's major statement of his social theory comes in his book *Models of Man* (1977). In this book Hollis starts with what will become one of the core themes of his life's work, namely his attack on the notion that social behaviour can be a subject for science. That, then very fashionable, notion maintained that political theory relied on conceptions of an essential human nature that were not verifiable and were thus metaphysical. In their place social scientists wanted to develop empirical and value-free accounts of human wants and needs, seeing them as dependent variables. Hollis rejected this view, arguing that these same theories were in fact dependent on implicit conceptions of human nature: 'since textbooks of social science are still confident that we have progressed from religion through philosophy to science, it remains worth saying that older assumptions are not so easily shed. Indeed, they cannot be shed. Every social theory needs a metaphysic ... in which a model of man and a method of science complement each other' (Hollis 1977: 3). Hollis sees two main rival models of man, which he terms 'Plastic Man' and 'Autonomous Man'.

Plastic Man is the account of human nature that developed in the Enlightenment, whereby human beings were seen as 'natural creatures in a rational world of cause and effect ... objects in nature differing from others only in the degree of complexity' (Hollis 1977: 7). He cites approvingly La Mettrie's claim that 'Man is not fashioned out of a more precious clay; Nature has only used one and the same dough in which she has merely varied the leaven' (Hollis 1977: 7–8). Plastic Man, then, is both naturalistic and deterministic. The former implies that there is one natural order, as opposed to the Cartesian distinction between god, mind and nature, with mind and nature distinctly different realms. Mind was the realm of free will, of subjects and of consciousness, whereas nature was the realm of matter governed by deterministic laws. Such a distinction meant that if science was appropriate for the study of the natural world of matter, then it could not be appropriate for studying that which matter was not, that is mind. Naturalism is the view that nature extends to the human mind, and thus that science is just as appropriate a method for the social as for the natural world: 'there is no boundary between inner states and environment or between self and society' (Hollis 1977: 9). Hollis sees determinism as supplying the one form of scientific explanation appropriate for both the natural and the social realms, and he defines it as meaning that 'every fact which has an explanation, together with some other fact, is an instance of a natural law' (Hollis 1977: 10). Thus knowledge emerges from identifying the laws that govern behaviour, and humans differ only insofar as they represent different intersections of these laws. The social world, like the natural world, is a world of cause and effect, and Plastic Man is causally determined save for any random element. Those aspects of the social world that seem to require a more active notion of the human agent are merely areas that have not yet yielded to scientific explanation.

For Hollis the version of causal explanation that is most appropriate for Plastic Man is positivism, Hume providing the account of cause and effect. Hollis defines positivism as having six features; 'a natural law is a regularity in nature holding in specifiable conditions; we know we have found one, when we have a well-enough confirmed theory; a theory is a set of logically-linked, high-order generalisations; the only test of a theory is the success of its predictions; prediction and explanation are two sides of the same and only coin, in that explaining a phenomenon is finding a theory from which it could have been predicted ... the same method holds for all sciences and that normative statements have no place in science' (Hollis 1977: 47).

Yet, Hollis notes that there was another voice in the Enlightenment, a voice that argued that the power of reason allows humans to 'master nature, manipulate society, change culture and, indeed, shape our own selves' (Hollis 1977: 12). This is Autonomous Man, who is distinct from the rest of nature by virtue of rationality. As Hollis describes the differences between Plastic and Autonomous Man, 'whereas Plastic Man, being formed by adaptive response to the interplay of nature and nurture, is only spuriously individual, his rival is to be self-caused. Where Plastic Man is an object in nature, his rival is the "I" of the I and the Me. Where Plastic Man has its causes, Autonomous Man has his reasons' (Hollis 1977: 12). Autonomous Man denies both naturalism and determinism; agents act rather than behave, and they do so in a way that is not governed by the laws of cause and effect. Much hangs on this claim. As Hollis puts it 'a man's reasons for acting can explain his actions, without being the cause of them ... human conduct falls under such concepts of *action* as imply that it cannot be wholly explained by causal laws and conditions' (Hollis 1977: 14-15). Hollis extensively uses the analogy of the theatre, and specifically the concept of role, to illustrate his argument: 'what is our life? The play of action. Informally the earth is a stage where actors play characters and we must seek the man in the mask ... I shall treat roles as sets of normative expectations attached to social positions ... the mark of great acting is that the character lives in the actor and becomes part of his self-image. The actor does not so much impersonate the character as personify him ... For Autonomous Man the notion of role offers an *explanans*. Agents create their roles' (Hollis 1977: 70-73). Hollis's main claim is that roles never fit so tightly that they require only one course of action, so that those that occupy the roles have some role distance which allows them varying degrees of freedom in interpreting how to play the role.

But what is the alternative to a causal account of human behaviour? As suggested by Hollis's previous work, his favoured candidate for the alternative to causal explanation is the notion of rationality. Hollis thinks that there are serious limitations to a causal analysis of action, and that, while the actions of Autonomous Man will have partial determinants of a causal sort, these actions are not undertaken because they are instances of a causal law at work. It is important to note that Hollis has a very specific view of causation, and I return to this later. He sees causation as involving the notion of law so that it holds universally in the same conditions, and he distinguishes it from goal-directed behaviour in his claim that 'goals pull from in front and causes push from behind' (Hollis 1977: 109). Reasons are distinct from causes, claims Hollis, because they do not have the same 'law-like, transitive relation of cause and effect. Knowledge of a fact is not to be analysed as true belief caused by the fact'

(Hollis 1977: 127). Instead, Hollis sees rationality doing the work by linking interests through motives to provide the reasons for action: 'good reasons must be the actor's own reasons and that raises the question of motive ... A motive, viewed for our purposes as a desire defined in terms of its object, can be treated, I shall maintain, as the actor's real reason, defined in terms of his interests' (Hollis 1977: 132). In this light, Hollis restates the actor analogy: role provides reasons for social action, but these are not in themselves the reasons for individual action, and for that we need to know the real reasons for an individual's action. 'In so far as he has calculated well and found the interpretation of the role which best serves his real interests, we have a   complete explanation. In so far as we judge him unjustified, we want a causal explanation of the residue. False consciousness has causes; true consciousness is its own explanation' (Hollis 1977: 139–40). Thus, we understand a person's actions by starting from the assumption that actors exist in role-governed contexts. Their roles give them required or legitimate ways of behaving. So, when we ask why it suited actors to do their duty in the way they did, this involves looking for further goals towards which the immediate goals are means. Hollis stresses that he is not saying that all actors always act autonomously, but he does believe that Autonomous Man should be the starting point and that which it cannot explain should be seen as a departure from that ideal type. In an important statement, which gives an indication of what he is opposed to, he writes 'nor do I suppose that the mass of mankind are so helplessly trapped in ruling ideologies and false consciousness that only a structural determinist can explain their antics ... lack of power is not to be thought of as stupidity' (Hollis 1977: 140–41).

Having outlined the two models of man, Hollis goes about judging between them by turning to epistemology, specifically by focusing on the concepts of rationalism and reason. Specifically he wants to show that the very process of understanding requires an underlying conception of rationality. As he puts it, someone trying to understand what another mind is thinking proceeds by constructing a 'bridgehead from assertive utterances expressing true and rational beliefs, assuming the Other Mind to be a rational man by *the* criteria of rationality.... [this] is not an empirical hypothesis, tested against experience, but a precondition *a priori* of the possibility of understanding' (Hollis 1977: 155). Hollis sees Autonomous Man as the starting point for understanding social action because it is what he terms the 'rational expression of intention within rules' (Hollis 1977: 186). The context that faces an agent may both enable and constrain action, but ultimately fully rational action is its own explanation. For Hollis, Plastic Man is only of use in explaining that which cannot be explained by Autonomous Man: 'an active conception of man always has the first move and causal explanations were needed only when it did not also have the last. Similarly, the actor's own reasons being the alpha of explanation, even when they were not also the omega, explanation in terms foreign to the actor was posterior and applied only to departures from rationality ... the rational [is] prior to the real' (Hollis 1977: 186).

This theme, that rational behaviour is its own best explanation, runs throughout Hollis's work, and is the often unstated foundation for many of his forays into debates with sociologists, economists and political scientists. In the 1996 book of his collected essays (Hollis 1996a) he outlines the centrality of rationality in his work. The book starts with the sentence: 'linking these essays is a simple conviction that people act, for the most part, rationally and that the social sciences depend on it' (Hollis 1996e: 1). Hollis cites approvingly Hobbes's statement in *Leviathan* that 'reason is the pace, increase of science the way, and the benefit of mankind the end'. This remains my motto too' (Hollis 1996e: 1). And, as in his 1977 book, he argues that rationality is not discoverable by observation but is an *a priori* principle of interpretation. He supports this claim by quoting the following passage from Hume: 'Mankind are so much the same, in all times and places, that history informs us of nothing new or strange in this particular. Its chief use is only to discover the constant and universal principles of human nature' (Hollis 1996e: 13). These constant and universal principles are not found by observation, but by rationality. Hollis explicitly opposes relativism: 'the criteria of truth and rationality being universal and objective, relativism yields' (Hollis 1996e: 15).

The Cunning Of Reason

Hollis's most detailed analysis of reason is found in his 1987 book *The Cunning of Reason,* in which he rectifies what he saw as a gap in *Models of Man,* namely that it had little consideration of economic accounts of rationality. Interestingly it is also in this book that Hollis develops for the first time a detailed distinction between science and hermeneutics. This was a secondary theme in his earlier work, but it is only in *The Cunning of Reason* that it takes centre-stage, and it is precisely this distinction that sets the stage for his analysis of reason. Hollis states that it is the meaning that actions have for the agent that is central to the distinction between nature and the social world. As he puts it: 'the guiding imperative here is that action has meanings which can be understood only from within' (Hollis 1987: 3). He outlines four examples of how meaning matters: experience, utterances, actions and ideas all have meaning for people – 'the social *is* what it *means*' (Hollis 1987: 4). By contrast, science takes an outsider's view of nature by finding causes for effects. Despite the problems inherent in this enterprise, especially he notes, after the writings of Popper, Quine, Kuhn, Feyerabend and Lakatos, he maintains that 'we still believe deeply that the workings of nature are a test of belief, not an effect of it' (Hollis 1987: 6). The attempt to produce an outsider's account of the social world is precarious exactly because the agent's inner state does seem to be an important ingredient of any attempt to understand social action. Yet again, as in his earlier work, Hollis sounds a warning against a Winchian interpretation of the social world. This is because Winch's focus on rules and culture seems to Hollis to leave as little room for an active autonomous individual agent as does the outsider account. So, having ruled out both an outsider account that sees behaviour as caused and an insider account that sees behaviour as merely following social rules, Hollis turns to answer the question of what is the best vantage point for assessing insider accounts of social action. His answer, of course, is rationality, and he introduces Weber's four components of an account of rationality: *zweckrational* (instrumentally rational), *wertrational* (expressively rational), traditional rationality and affective rationality. As before, he sees these as ideal types, which can explain a large part of social action, and, following Weber, he argues that these explanations have to be adequate both at the level of meaning and at the causal level. Adequacy at the level of meaning requires *verstehen*, a form of empathy that allows the observer to be aware of what an agent is doing and then proceeds to the rational reconstruction of the agent's thoughts by using Weber's four ideal types of rationality. Adequacy at the causal level requires the use of what Weber termed *erklaren*, the use of social statistics to show that what *verstehen* has found is typical behaviour. Having got this far, Hollis notes that there is an ambiguity in Weber's work between seeing *verstehen* as a distinctive form of explanation, which needs only reassurance from the causal level, and seeing it more as an aid to causal analysis, and 'thus leaves unresolved the deeper puzzle of how an insider's or agent's point of view finally relates to an outsider's or spectator's one for purposes of social science' (Hollis 1987: 9).

Hollis does not share Weber's ambiguity, although he only reveals this some 180 pages later! The route by which he gets to his conclusions about the cunning of reason is via an analysis of economic notions of rationality (also the theme of Hollis 1996f). Hollis argues that economic accounts of rationality paint an incomplete picture because they stress the *zweckrational* at the expense of the *wertrational*. For Hollis, 'the final notion of rationality is one which merges *zweckrational* with *wertrational*. The governing concept is that of a good reason for action, even if the philosophical gain threatens to be at the expense of the economist's tidy mathematics' (Hollis 1987: 201). Hollis sees explanatory understanding (*erklarendes verstehen*) as the best way of characterising social action. In so doing, he rejects Weber's claim that *erklaren* can explain particular cases on the grounds that Weber defined *erklaren* in Humean terms of covering laws, making individual actions explicable as examples of a generalisation for similar cases with similar initial conditions. Hollis says simply, 'I shall risk denying that rational actions have causal *explanations* in this sense or in any stronger one which appeals to a natural law to account for particular instances' (Hollis 1987: 190). He amplifies this claim by rejecting notions such as the laws of supply and demand, seeing them instead as the systematic general result of the decisions of individual suppliers and consumers. Thus 'when an economist hits on a new economic "law", his discovery will prompt him to identify an unnoticed reason which has been moving a number of economic agents to do what is systematic in sum. Having identified this reason, he has explained the "law"' (Hollis 1987: 190). In contrast to natural science, where he does think that there are laws of nature of an explanatory kind, he denies that social patterns are part of an explanatory causal order. Rather, he sees good reasons as their own explanation of action because the reasons are why the agent acted as he or she did: 'The best explanation of action is that the agent did it for good reasons which he recognised to be good ... but the distinction between legitimating reasons and real reasons, coupled with the point that actors are incompletely transparent even to themselves, calls for watchfulness' (Hollis 1987: 192).

The cunning of reason, a phrase originating from Hegel, refers to how a series of individual rational actions can lead to patterns and effects apart from the intentions of the individual agents. This is in part due to the distinction between ideal and second-best examples of rationality. In the former, the agent, knowing that others are relatively similar to him or her, and therefore will act for the same reasons, chooses what is collectively valued by both the agent and other agents. But this is relatively rare in social life, and so the second-best case of rationality exists when a rational agent cannot expect that what he or she would do in the ideal case will produce the best result. This can be because of the imperfect rationality of other agents, because roles do not harmonise or because power may distort perfect rationality. The result, which Hollis admits is the stuff of the social world we live in, is that ideal rationality may well cost an agent a good solution, since the best can be the enemy of the good. But while he feels that this leaves rationality with some problems, he feels that these are less problematic than the problems associated with other conceptions of rationality, and certainly of the standard economist's account of rational choice and game theory. The effects of the cunning of reason apply where unintended consequences of action are 'found to be the collective efforts of individually rational decisions … In other words a theory of social action can be credited with being able to account for social change, provided that the changes result determinately from choices by agents' (Hollis 1987: 205). This is a very individualist account of the social world, as illustrated by Hollis's statement that 'I rest my case for a revised individualism. In a sentence, Adam (singular and plural) is the prime mover of social life, enabled and constrained by rules which evolve in response to the combined effect of choices. Since the prime mover is only partially sighted, the combined effects are full of surprises sprung by the Cunning of Reason' (Hollis 1987: 206).

All of this leaves open the tantalising question of what Hollis means by individualism. He says that the individual is not the kind of individual assumed by rational choice theory, nor the kind of individual assumed by theories of organisations and collectives. The individual is neither a free-floating rational chooser nor someone responding to external causal forces. He follows Pico della Mirandola, who, in 1484, wrote of God speaking to Adam, saying 'I have given you, Adam, neither a predetermined place nor a particular aspect nor any special prerogatives in order that you may take and possess these through your own decision and choice … You shall determine your own nature without constraint from any barrier … I have placed you at the centre of the world … I have made you neither heavenly nor earthly, neither mortal nor immortal, so like a free and sovereign artificer you might mould and fashion yourself into that form you yourself have chosen' (Hollis 1987:1). For Hollis the individual is at the centre of the social world. But Hollis means something very specific by the self. It is not, for him, the sum of its roles nor the sum of roles, body and psyche. Instead Hollis has a very specific view of agency, a view dealt with in several places, notably in Hollis [1979a] 1996c and [1985b] 1996d, but in most detail in *The Cunning of Reason* (1987).

Despite the cultural variations in the world, Hollis sees the self as having a core, which is not the entirely free-floating self of Sartre (Hollis sees this as not a portrait of the self at all), but is instead a self able to act intelligently in a world of social positions, a self able to act for reasons, which need no further reasons. In contrast to the self postulated by economic theories of rationality, which Hollis sees as abolishing the individual (reducing it to consistent desires plus an information processing device), he sees the self as 'a social agent ... not an empirical "me" but an active "I". It stands outside its knowledge of its (agent's) place in the social system, and is known transcendentally, in that understanding presupposes it. Its activity is what makes social life possible' (Hollis 1987: 211). Thus, contra Durkheim, Hollis sees the self as much more than the clay moulded by social forces, but also as much less than an independent self that 'vanishes into darkest privacy' (Hollis 1987: 212). Turning to Rousseau, Hollis sees the self as created by the very social contract that they themselves make. He cites Rousseau: 'for to be subject to appetite is to be a slave, while to obey the laws laid down by society is to be free' (cited in Hollis 1987: 212). Note that Hollis interprets what it means to 'obey the law' in terms of selves consulting their reason and acting according to their duties as subjects.

Hollis ends the book by contrasting the world described by Sophocles in *Antigone*, written in the fifth century BC, with the contemporary world, and argues that the modern world has greater scope for self-creation. This is because 'we are now born into fewer of the roles which come to constitute us and choose more of the partners with whom we play and change the game. In part it has become possible because we have learnt that it is possible. In part it has become possible because we now believe it is possible' (Hollis 1987: 213). However, there is a dark side to this freedom: whilst a modern Antigone might have avoided the choice of duties (obey her ruler or bury her brother) that marks

Sophocles's play, Hollis notes that 'she might be marked down for motiveless killing by strangers on the streets of an impersonal city. The Cunning of Reason can make as much mischief in the new world as in the old' (Hollis 1987: 213)

The Philosophy of Social Science

Hollis's main statement of his view of the social world is contained in *The Philosophy of Social Science* (1994), but all the main themes in that book have been introduced in the work already discussed, and extensively previewed in the book he and I wrote in 1990. International Relations always struck him as an excellent coat peg on which to hang his concerns about structures, explanation, rationality and agency, as well as a stark version of the Other Minds problem. As mentioned above, it was only in our book that he had outlined the infamous matrix of social action as an organising strategy (Hollis 1994: ix). This matrix structured the 1994 book, and amplified considerably on Hollis & Smith (1990). In that book we introduced the debate between explaining and understanding by using the two approaches in an introductory chapter to set up the contrast between outsider and insider accounts of the social world. Hollis then wrote two wonderfully concise chapters in which he outlined the main features of explaining and understanding. In the 1994 book, the structure is very explicitly on explanation versus understanding with a secondary debate between holism and individualism. The matrix formed by these two debates led to four views of social action: namely systems (top left), games (top right), agents (bottom left), actors (bottom right). In each case these views entail ontological, epistemological and methodological commitments.

The bulk of the book consists of three chapters on explanation, then two on the holism–individualism dispute on the explanation side of the matrix; then there are two chapters on holism–individualism on the understanding side. Finally, there are three chapters in which Hollis looks at the familiar themes of combining the two approaches, value neutrality, rationality and relativism, and then a conclusion that loudly proclaims that in the social world there are always at least two stories to tell.

The main moves made in the book are entirely consistent with the picture of Hollis's view of social action that has been outlined above. It will come as no surprise that Hollis finds explanatory accounts of social action unconvincing, for the by now familiar reason that the kind of causal analysis appropriate to the natural world simply does not fit the social world. He offers as an example what was his favourite illustration of the weakness of positive social science, namely Przeworski and Teune's 1970 discussion of voting behaviour (an essay I passed on to him in the early 1980s). They simply ask, 'why does Monsieur Rouget, age twenty four, blond hair, brown eyes, a worker in a large factory, vote Communist', and give as an answer that 'to explain the vote of M. Rouget, one must rely upon general probabilistic statements that are relevant for voting behaviour and have been sufficiently confirmed against various sets of evidence' (Hollis 1994: 40). Thus explaining his voting behaviour is achieved by showing that he is predictable. Hollis will of course have none of this, and argues that to account for M. Rouget's vote, we need to know something about how he saw his vote. This leads to a discussion of understanding from both a holistic (Winchian) position and from individualistic (active self) perspectives. Of these, Hollis sees holism leaving too little room for individuals, and he thus prefers to see the social world as one where rational actors can interpret their roles. As he puts it, 'the holism of the top right box would be well served if persons in the public arena always acted in accord with clear directives issuing from their social positions, and triumphantly so if there were norm-governed social positions to annex all social relationships, however apparently personal and intimate' (Hollis 1994: 180). But Hollis thinks this is a misleading picture of the social world because 'there is still great latitude in interpreting roles, especially for anyone playing several. Role conflict unmasks the self caught in it ... the actors refuse to be absorbed by the interplay of medium and outcome. They have their exits and their entrances and, crucially, their reasons for doing what they think rational and right' (Hollis 1994: 181-182).

In his concluding chapters, Hollis spends considerable time attacking the relativism of the Winchian view that social rules are comprehensible only in their local cultural context. He quotes Winch's statement that 'the criteria of logic are not a direct gift from God, but arise out of and are only intelligible in the context of ways of living and modes of social life' (Hollis 1994: 239), and then disagrees fundamentally with such far-reaching relativism. In this sense relativism is just as much his target as is naturalism. He uses the Azande and witchcraft as an example to show that such relativism leads to a hermeneutic circle. Evans-Pritchard argued that the Azande believed that witchcraft was real, yet Hollis believes that this claim leads anthropologists into dangerous waters: 'to discover the rules governing thought among the Azande, we need to know that they take witchcraft for real; to discover this, we need to know some of their words for everyday objects; to discover these words, we need to know the rules governing thought among the Azande ... To put it simply, we need to know what is locally rational before we can know what is locally real; and we need to know what is locally real before we can know what is locally rational (Hollis 1994: 240). As a result, 'all interpretations become defensible but at the price that none is more justifiable than the rest. If this is indeed the upshot, the circle turns vicious and the hermeneutic imperative to understand from within leads to disaster' (Hollis 1994: 241). But of course, Hollis does not want to reject hermeneutics, only the top-right version of it. He offers four ways out of it (understanding is piecemeal; realism, leading to some causal theory of perception; anchoring beliefs in social structures; and, his preferred choice, Strawson's central core of human thinking). Thus, directly contrary to Winch, he believes that 'The criteria of logic may or may not be a direct gift from God, but, as an indispensable piece of conceptual equipment, they are presupposed by any attempt to make coherent sense out of modes of life' (Hollis 1994: 244).

In his conclusion, Hollis makes the same move as was made in our joint book (the idea of course was his): he runs through each of the four versions of social action (systems, agents, games, actors) after likening them to a dance round a maypole. Starting with the top left (systems) he critiques each in turn, showing that it is open to critique from the next view (agents, then actors, then games, then systems again). One tempting reaction to this is to see all four merging with one another, as the ribbons around the maypole do when the may dance takes place. Thus explanation, understanding, holism and individualism would become entangled: 'the result would be an all-embracing social theory where structure is the medium in which action reproduces structure and where this dialectical interplay evolves in a dynamic synthesis' (Hollis 1994: 249). Yet Hollis rejects this possibility as too chaotic, and so he offers four possible resolutions to end the dance around the maypole: these are the intersections between the four quadrants (systems and agents; systems and games; games and actors; and actors and agents). Whilst he sees a lot to be gained from mixing holism with individualism (games and actors, or systems and agents) he does not see understanding and explaining as combining well (systems and games, or agents and actors).

But by mixing he does not mean blending. He accepts that combining individualism with holism has problems, but he is far more willing to countenance this than to combine explanation with understanding. This is because he sees explanation and understanding (whether in holist or individualist mode) as entailing distinctly different ontologies, epistemologies and methodologies. As he puts it, writing about combining agents and actors, 'each version of individualism has more in common with one sort of holism than with the other sort of individualism' (Hollis 1994: 257). Hollis sees combination of the diagonal pairs as simply incoherent.

His final conclusion is that there are always two stories to tell about the social world: 'the stubborn contrast is still that between Explanation and Understanding, with naturalism and hermeneutics still in dispute over ontology, methodology and epistemology' (Hollis 1994: 257). Ontologically, where naturalists see functional systemic pressures, hermeneutics sees a world constructed by meanings. In the former, the natural and social worlds are constructed from the same dough; in the latter they are fundamentally different worlds. Methodologically, though both accounts can start by looking at meaning from within, they treat this differently, with naturalism stressing the causes of meanings, and hermeneutics arguing that reasons and meanings do not have causes thus conceived. Finally, epistemologically, the two approaches differ enormously, with a direct tension between the foundationalism of explanation and hermeneutics having problems both dealing with the Other Minds problem and of avoiding the hermeneutic circle leading to a dangerous relativism. Hollis ends the book by saying that the aim has not been to find final wisdom, but he calls for 'a notion of autonomy which links the good life, the free citizen and the norms of a just society' (Hollis 1994: 260).

Critique

I want now to turn to offer a critique of Hollis's view of social action, and I will do so by making seven related points. Whilst, of course, he would have answers to them, I do feel that they add up to a robust critique of his position, but his is a position that I believe repays serious engagement. His is a call for an active version of the individual, opposed to holism in both explanatory and understanding forms, and particularly opposed to the kind of individual portrayed by explanation in either holist or individualist guise. His is a view that is firmly anti-relativistic, hence his opposition to Winch, and yet it is a view that rejects an appeal to science as arbiter of claims over the best account of the social world. His ultimate criterion is human reason, the core of which he sees as both common and considerable. Yet, this seemingly rarefied, ultimately epistemologically based account of the social individual hides deeper and profound commitments both to human freedom and to reason as the surest path to human improvement. Hollis's view of the individual is fundamentally a moral commitment, as an active and responsible actor, rather than a puppet, slavish role player, or rational fool. This is above all an Enlightenment view of knowledge, reason and the individual, and this is why Hollis was always keen to argue that whilst structures and roles, or holism of any kind, might constrain actors they also enable them.

Nonetheless there are problems with his account of social action. First, and most fundamentally, there is the significant level of agency that Hollis gives to the individual and the correspondingly limited role he sees for structures of any sort. Hollis is opposed to any form of holism, be it of a structural-functionalist kind on the left hand side of the matrix, or a Winchian kind on the right hand side. In my view, although now for slightly different reasons than when we wrote the book together, he underestimates the impact of structure on actors, and correspondingly overemphasises the room for agency. It is not that he does not have a notion of structure, only that he ultimately sees it as the sum of both intended and unintended consequences of individual action. Consequently he sees agency having a much larger role than I think it has. As I mentioned above, when we wrote the book together, I felt this for top-left reasons, now I feel it for top-right reasons. When we wrote and taught together, it was clear that his strong preference was for bottom-right accounts of the social world. One of his favourite analogies was of playing a hand of cards: while he accepted that one could draw a poor hand, he nonetheless felt that our emphasis should be on how to play the hand as skilfully as possible. Thus even the most tightly fitting roles gave the actor some room for manoeuvre and even the most powerful structures gave space for agency. In this light, there was a political economy to his work, in the sense that it was true that if one was as clever and adept as he, then one might indeed be able to play one's cards skilfully, but I was always concerned that this could never apply to more than some of the highly educated and wealthy in society.

I realise that Hollis felt that anyone could play their hand well or poorly, and that this was a democratic impulse, but I still feel that many, probably the vast bulk, of people in the world have structures that sit heavily on their shoulders, and that these significantly limit their agency.

Second, his view of science is a very specific one, namely the naturalist notion of a positive science whose methods are applicable to both natural and social worlds. Hollis was of course aware of the wide range of approaches in the philosophy and practice of science, but it definitely does suit his purpose for science to be presented as positivist. This is because positive science is the version of science most opposed to hermeneutics, and thus it enables him to claim that if science is like this, and hermeneutics is like that, then the two cannot be combined. Were he to work with other conceptions of science, such as conventionalism or realism, then the contrast with hermeneutics could not be so starkly drawn. In this sense Hollis could be criticised for basing his work on a version of science that most accurately characterised classical physics before the advent of relativity and quantum theory. Bohr's notion of complementarity and Heisenberg's uncertainty principle seem to me to suggest that the overlap between the epistemological, and even ontological, entailments of much contemporary science are by no means as diametrically opposed to hermeneutics as Hollis suggests. In short, his clear-cut contrast between the two is as much a product of his definitions as it is a reflection of any defining and intrinsic features of science. Similarly, his treatment of social science relies on an accurate, but nonetheless partial, view of what it is. He is on his strongest ground when criticising the kind of social science popular in the behavioural revolution of the 1950s and 1960s, as reflected by his delight in the example about M. Rouget's voting, and the massive literature on rational choice theory, which still dominates economics and increasingly dominates political science. So, in one sense he is right to focus on positivist social science, but in another sense this does skew the analysis so as to create a slightly misleading version of the alternatives.

Third, Hollis sees causation in a very restricted way. Although in some places he points to alternative versions of causation (Hollis 1977: 107), the version that he returns to time and time again is the Humean account. For Hollis, causes are prior to the effects they produce, they are separated from them, and they are law-like. In my view, although he is well aware of other conceptions of causality, the Humean version fits his purposes a little too well for him to abandon it. This strikes me as important, because Hume's notion of causality is scarcely cited in the contemporary philosophy of science literature, with the current vogue being for more realist notions of causal powers. Yet, no other notion of causality would serve Hollis's purposes as well as does the Humean version. This is because Hume's definition is most obviously contrary to Hollis's position that hermeneutics cannot be combined with science; Hollis needs to establish that the actor's reasons cannot be explained by science, and it is therefore enormously helpful for him to be able to point to Hume's notion of causation as something diametrically opposite to his own notion of the reasoning self. Other conceptions of causation are less obviously incompatible with hermeneutics.

Fourth, Hollis's notion of rationality could be critiqued for being rather ethnocentric, despite the fact that this was exactly the claim that he constantly rebutted. This is because of his acceptance that there indeed was a central core to rationality. Of course, he needed to substantiate this claim because without it there was always the danger of relativism, as represented by Winch's work on language games. But the doubt remains that this belief in a central core of rationality and reason could well be an ethnocentric, culturally specific and masculine account. What, for example, if the Azande simply did not recognise the concept of a contradiction, and thus could not see a contradiction between their claim that every offspring of a witch is also a witch, and the fact that this would imply that all Azande were therefore witches? Think also of feminist work on the philosophy of the mind and on the differences between male and female thinking patterns. It is simply not clear to me that the central core of rationality that he relied on is as universal as he claims. The recent dispute in anthropology between Obeyesekere (1992) and Sahlins (1995) over the killing of Captain Cook is a good example of a dispute that ultimately is one about the thought processes and categories within which different cultures operate. A more contemporary example is the differences between the mindsets of those who planned and carried out the 11 September 2001 atrocities and the mindsets of Western leaders: I am not sure that they share much of a common core of reason and rationality, so much so that the groups seem to live in different worlds.

Fifth, although Hollis could contemplate a mixture of holism and individualism in the understanding, if not in the explanation, column, he was ultimately either unclear or deliberately evasive about the precise mixture he would tolerate. Towards the end of *The Philosophy of Social*

Science, he writes about the possibilities of having a mixture of the two, but he never offers much in the way of detail as to what he has in mind. In his writing he presents this as leaving the reader with a puzzle, but in my view it is because in the end he wanted to leave the self with as much room for manoeuvre as possible. Therefore, although in theory he saw room for a mix between games and actors, in practice he always wanted to leave the last word with the active self. His view of social action was, therefore, less related to a balance between holism and individualism, on the understanding side of the matrix, than it was based on an ultimately individualistic account of the world.

Sixth, Hollis's style of argumentation and presenting alternatives was testimony both to his view of roles enabling as well as constraining, and to his belief that language could serve as the language of manoeuvre as well as the language of description. His books are masterpieces of design, whereby the alternatives are presented in such a way that his resolution seems to be the only logical choice, and of course that is exactly what it was for him! The same feature was present in his teaching: he would seize upon some unsuspecting student and ask for their view, or even their academic discipline. They would answer and he would reply that being, say, a sociologist, meant that they were committed to the following view of agency, science, causation, rationality and so on. The student would then, in subsequent weeks, be asked to defend their commitments as a sociologist. This was a brilliant technique, though for some students it proved too much! But although all writers construct their accounts so as to present their preferred resolution to a problem as logical or natural, I do feel that Hollis was so skilful at it that one had to be a very attentive reader to see the moves he was making. His standard move was to posit a binary opposition, between, say, *homo economicus* and *homo sociologicus* and then to show that each had a series of problems that required a notion of the individual that just somehow managed to fit into his model of a reasoning agent. In other words, a lot of the power of his writings comes from the way he structures the choices and alternatives.

Finally, this is nowhere clearer than in his matrix of social theory itself. I cannot pretend that I either thought of this problem when we were working together or that I wish to suggest that the matrix should be abandoned, but I do believe that the way the matrix constructs alternatives is a very powerful piece of agenda setting. Put simply, there are many views of social action that just do not fit in his matrix, and do not fit precisely because they challenge his binary oppositions between explaining and understanding and between holism and individualism. Giddens and structuration theory does not fit into one of the boxes, nor does Bhaskar and scientific realism. In each case they see the posed dichotomies as false, and thus Giddens sees no simple distinction between structures and agents, since each constitutes the other. Likewise, scientific realists do not accept the distinction between explanation and understanding. Now, although Hollis, and I, might think that there is an answer to this (basically that Giddens reduces explanation to understanding, with structures as roles, norms and resources, while Bhaskar sees understanding as reducible to explanation) it remains clear that significant approaches do not accept Hollis's starting point of framing alternatives in terms of the matrix. Since we published the matrix in 1990, this has become much clearer still with the rise in popularity work of postmodernists such as Foucault, Derrida and Lyotard, none of whom would posit the choices as between either explanation or understanding, or between holism and individualism. Hollis's matrix sets up the problems and the alternatives in such a way as to provide him with the justification for saying that, while holism and individualism might mix, explanation and understanding cannot. Again, put at its most straightforward, what if the choices are not those he posits, what if we imagine not a two-by-two matrix but a continuum of explanation/understanding and one for holism/individualism? Much depends on the way in which he defines the choices available, and sets up the combinations that can and cannot work.

Conclusion

In this paper I have tried to outline the evolution of Martin Hollis's account of social action. I have focussed on his main writings, and have distilled from these the core components of his position. I have then offered a series of criticisms of his position, the most significant of which are his reliance on a specific (and disputed) model of science set up as the alternative to hermeneutics, and his preference for treating the actor as one with considerable agency. Hollis's twin targets were naturalism and relativism, and these led him to a strong commitment to understanding and individualism. In my view it led him to underestimate structures and to see individuals having more room to manoeuvre and interpret their roles than the vast bulk of humanity possess. To repeat, he felt this because he was deeply committed to human freedom and emancipation, and therefore whatever the structural forces bearing down on an actor, he still looked at how they could exercise agency, because to accept the contrary view would ultimately diminish human freedom and potential. In this sense his was a very moral social theory.

Hollis developed his theory of social action over some thirty years, and in its most important aspects it never underwent major revision. The earliest papers are based on an almost identical model of the world to that presented in his last works, a model itself based on Enlightenment thought, and featuring the same heroes. His writings were uniformly well written and argued, and consisted not only of his major forays into the philosophy of social science, but also his considerable interdisciplinary work with economists, political scientists, sociologists and political philosophers. In this sense he did an enormous amount to show that his theoretical position had significant payoffs in the social sciences. While I still maintain that there are problems with his view of social action, I want to end by simply saying that he was the most generous and unpretentious of people to work with, a man genuinely fascinated by the puzzles that the social sciences threw up, even if he resisted the answers that most social scientists gave to them. In his work, he personified his theoretical commitments by using reason, by attacking naturalism and holism, and by using the structure of a debate or a text to play his theoretical cards as skilfully as possible. His work was indeed reason in action, and his account of social action remains one of the most powerful calls for an actor-centred account of the social world. However much I now think it has flaws, I have no doubt that it adds up to a remarkably consistent and strong account. But, Hollis's account ultimately derived much of its force from the way he drew up the alternatives and presented the choices. His claims that there are always two stories to tell in the social world, and that the two by two matrix contained the range of possible choices in social theory, performed major functions in his work, so that if they were accepted then his preferred options appeared as almost literally logically necessary. Nonetheless, Hollis has left us with an elegant and persuasive account of social action, one that we cannot ignore. His is a significant contribution to the theory of social action, and my aims in this paper have been to distil its main themes and to begin the task of critiquing it. It remains only to say once again that it is such a pity that he is not still alive to dispute my reading of his position and to turn his formidable mind to the weaknesses of my own position.

NOTES

1. Like most philosophers of his time, Hollis used 'he' throughout his work, changing only in the late 1980s. I have not changed any of the quotations, but of course this does raise a deep issue about male and female reason. Hollis clearly believed that there was no difference in the reason of man and women, and this reflected his commitment to emancipation by reason. But as I will note later, feminist work on the philosophy of mind does call this assumption into doubt.

REFERENCES

Brown, S.C., ed. 1979. *Philosophical Disputes in the Social Sciences*. Brighton: Harvester.
Carrithers, M. et al. 1985. *The Category of the Person*. Cambridge: Cambridge University Press,
Hahn, F. & M. Hollis, eds. 1979. *Philosophy and Economic Theory*. Oxford: Oxford University Press.
Hargreaves Heap, S. et al. 1992. *The Theory of Choice: A Practical Guide*. Oxford: Blackwell Publishers.
Harrison, R., ed. 1979. *Rational Action: Studies in the Philosophy of Social Science*. Cambridge: Cambridge University Press.
Hollis, M. ([1967] 1996b. 'Reason and ritual', *Philosophy*, 43, 231–47, reprinted in Hollis 1996a: 199–220.
1977. *Models of Man: Philosophical Thoughts on Social Action*. Cambridge: Cambridge University Press.
[1979a] 1996c. 'Rational man and social science'. Harrison 1979: 1–15. Reprinted in a slightly amended form as 'Three men in a drought' in Hollis 1996a: 19–39.
1979b. 'The Epistemological Unity of Mankind'. Brown 1979: 225–32.
[1983] 1996f. 'Rational preferences'. *The Philosophical Forum*, 14, reprinted in Hollis 1996a: 40–59.
1985a. *Invitation to Philosophy*. Oxford: Basil Blackwell.
[1985b] 1996d. 'Of masks and men'. Carrithers et al. 1985: 217–33. Reprinted in Hollis 1996a: 91–108.
1987. *The Cunning of Reason*. Cambridge: Cambridge University Press.
1994. *The Philosophy of Social Science: An Introduction*. Cambridge: Cambridge University Press.
1996a. *Reason in Action: Essays in the Philosophy of Social Science*. Cambridge: Cambridge University Press.
1996e. 'Prologue: reason in action'. Hollis 1996a: 1–15.
1998. *Trust Within Reason*. Cambridge: Cambridge University Press.
Hollis, M. & S. Lukes, eds. 1982. *Rationality and Relativism*. Oxford: Basil Blackwell.
Hollis, M. & E. Nell. 1975. *Rational Economic Man*. Cambridge: Cambridge University Press.
Hollis, M. & S. Smith. 1986. 'Roles and reasons in foreign policy decision-making'. *British Journal of Political Science*, 16/3, 269–86.
1990. *Explaining and Understanding International Relations*. Oxford: Clarendon Press.
1991. 'Beware of gurus: structure and action in international relations'. *Review of International Studies*, 17/4, 393–410.
1992. 'Structure and action: further comments'. *Review of International Studies*, 18/2, 187–8.

1994. 'Two stories about structure and agency'. *Review of International Studies*, 20/4, 241–51.

1996. 'Why epistemology matters in international theory'. *Review of International Studies*, 22/1, 111–16.

Hollis, M & R. Sugden. 1993. 'Rationality in action'. *Mind*, 102, 1–35.

Obeyesekere, G. 1992. *The Apotheosis of Captain Cook: European Mythmaking in the Pacific*. Princeton: Princeton University Press.

Sahlins, M. 1995. *How 'Natives' Think: About Captain Cook, For Example*. Chicago: University of Chicago Press.

Strawson, P. 1959. *Individuals: An Essay in Descriptive Metaphysics*. London: Methuen.

Winch, P. 1958. *The Idea of a Social Science and its Relation to Philosophy*. London: Routledge and Kegan Paul.

8

The Bond of Society:
Reason or Sentiment?

ROBERT SUGDEN

I first met Martin Hollis in the autumn of 1984. I was being interviewed for a professorship at the University of East Anglia, and he was on the interviewing committee. He questioned me about a paper I had just written, proposing a new theory of the rationality of voluntary contributions to public goods. He wanted to know whether my account could explain a person's being willing to contribute to a public good when not every beneficiary contributed, but *enough* of them did – an issue which, as I discovered later, he had thought a lot about. Fortunately, my theory could indeed explain this. As far as I could tell, he was impressed by what he took to be my theoretical facility, while being sceptical about the philosophical value of economic models of rationality. At any rate, I was given the job. This cross-examination turned out to be the opening exchange in a debate about rationality and sociality which we carried on until his death at the beginning of 1998.

Over these years, we both kept on trying to understand the logic by which individuals act within social structures. Each of us was convinced that this logic could not be fully captured by the received theory of rational choice, and each tried to pin down exactly what was missing in that theory. It sometimes seemed to us that our ideas about some part of this enterprise were converging but, whenever we considered writing a paper together, we were unable to reconcile differences between our philosophical positions.[1] In the course of these running debates, I learned a lot about philosophy and Hollis became more confident about working in rational choice theory. But our fundamental differences remained.

Just after Martin Hollis's death, I read his final book, *Trust Within Reason* (Hollis 1998). In some respects, particularly the idea that the 'bond of society' might be modelled in terms of the rationality of acting as a member of a team (1998: 137–42), the similarities between his ideas and my own were very close. I felt a sense of pleasure and pride about this: I had been working on the idea of team reasoning for several years, and I think it was I who had introduced Hollis to this way of thinking. Yet the philosophical framework within which he put these ideas to use seemed as diametrically opposed to my own as it had ever been.

This essay is the result of my subsequent attempts to understand how our positions could be so close on some issues and so far apart on others. As it was no longer possible to resolve the matter through coffee-break discussions, I read as much as I could of Hollis's work, in the light of what I recalled of our previous debates. I began to see how our disagreements stemmed from two quite different understandings of the nature of social science: a rationalist understanding (his) and an empiricist understanding (mine). In this essay, I try to elucidate these two understandings, using Hollis's idea of a 'liberal community' – a central motif in *Trust Within Reason* – as my focus. Aware of the unfair advantage I now possess in Hollis's inability to reply, I argue that his arguments for rationalism and against empiricism in social science do not succeed.

The Liberal Community

One of the recurring themes in Hollis's work is the problem of understanding the nature of individuals' obligations to the social groups to which they belong. The essential features of Hollis's thinking on this subject can be seen in his allegory of three men in a drought (Hollis 1979). Even by Hollis's standards, the essay is informal – it was obviously written before he became interested in rational choice theory – but the issues it explores are at the heart of his later, and theoretically sharper, discussions of trust and reciprocity.

The story is of a temporary water shortage. The Water Authority appeals for restraint in the consumption of water. In response to this appeal, 10 per cent of the public (represented by Hollis's character Lock) do just what the Water Authority asks of them; 40 per cent (represented by Stock) make minor economies; and 50 per cent (represented by Barrel) carry on just as before. As things turn out, this pattern of restraint is sufficient to allow water supplies to be maintained. (In a typical touch, Hollis tells us that the drought ended suddenly with a period of exceptionally heavy rainfall; we are left to guess whether the self-imposed restraints would have been sufficient in the absence of this good fortune.) We are asked to judge which of the three characters is the rational man. The surprise of the essay comes when Hollis concludes in favour of Stock. Why Stock? '[H]e alone is a rational citizen. He is detached enough from the norms to make place for economic calculation but not so detached that he ceases to be essentially a citizen'. And, explaining the meaning of 'essentially a citizen': 'Stock sees a duty not to let the side down' (1979: 37–8).

The idea is that Stock recognises an obligation to play his part in a collective activity that is for the good of the community to which he belongs, even though it would be in his self-interest to take a free ride on other people's efforts. It is important for the story that a significant proportion of the population recognise some such obligation while another significant proportion do not, and that the collective activity of those who do is sufficient to make an impact. Thus, Hollis is telling us, the fact that some people do not contribute to the collective activity does not excuse other people from their obligations. But at the same time, one person's obligation to do his part arises only in the context of a collective activity in which sufficient others can be relied on to do their parts too. That, presumably, is part of what makes Lock irrational: Lock is sacrificing his own interests when he is under no obligation to do so. It is important too that Lock, Stock and Barrel are represented as *citizens* – as co-members of some pre-existing community, and not just as individuals who happen to be jointly involved in certain kind of public good game. It is because of this that Barrel can be said to be letting *the side* down: if there were no pre-existing community, there would be no side to be let down.

Clearly, Barrel stands for the instrumentally rational pursuit of self-interest, or (which Hollis in 1979 seems to have thought of as the same thing), 'economic calculation'. True rationality, we are asked to conclude, can impose constraints on the pursuit of self-interest. But what is so wrong about Lock? We know that Lock isn't acting alone (10 per cent of the population act like he does), and there is a hint that the efforts of this particularly public-spirited minority would have made a difference if the drought had lasted longer. Hollis's real criticism of Lock is not that he is more public-spirited than strict obligation requires. It is that he has obeyed the instructions of the Water Authority uncritically: he has failed to leave 'a distance between the himself and the role the Water Authority has scripted for him' (1979: 37). In contrast, Stock leaves enough distance to make place for economic calculation. The implication is that a rational person identifies with the public interest of the communities to which he belongs, but not so far as to eliminate the individual viewpoint from which he can ask whether the demands that those communities make of him are reasonable.

In *Trust Within Reason*, Hollis (1998: 143–50) outlines a concept of *generalised reciprocity* which is intended to represent the mutual obligations of a liberal community. Relations within a society are ones of generalised reciprocity to the extent that each member (or enough members) of that society recognises some obligation to act so as to benefit the others, and is confident that the others (or enough others) recognise the same obligation. It is essential that the relation of reciprocal obligation is between *members of a particular society*, and not between abstract rational agents. And it is essential that each member has confidence in the others: otherwise we would not be talking about reciprocity. But it is also essential that the expectation of benefits from the others is not the *reason* for each member's willingness to benefit those others. Blood donation provides an example of generalised reciprocity at work:

> There is a logic of 'enough', I submit, which can overcome the dominance of defection, provided that a sense of membership is in play. Donors cooperate if confident that enough blood is being provided by enough members. Thus, public goods which depend on creative altruism are a matter both of a large enough total to secure the good and of enough contributors for mutual reassurance that contributing is a worthy activity. Enough is then enough. (1998: 147)

As a way of representing the logic of generalised reciprocity, Hollis offers the idea of *team reasoning*. A person who takes herself to be a member of a team and who reasons as such does not act as an individual agent. She does not act as an individual seeking her own interest; but neither does she act as an individual seeking the good of the team. She seeks to do her part in the joint action of the team that will best achieve the team's objective. She does her part in the confidence that enough others will do theirs: if this confidence did not exist, there would not be a team to be a part of. But her contributions to the joint effort are not made *as a means of* securing other people's contributions; nor are they *conditional on* other people's contributions. Each member of the team has an unconditional reason to do her part, alongside an assurance that other members have corresponding unconditional reasons (1998: 137–42). This seems to be a sharper model of the mode of reasoning that Hollis attributed to Stock in his earlier story.

However, Hollis's worry about the submergence of individual identity remains. In *Trust Within Reason*, he presents a new variant of the Lock, Stock and Barrel allegory: the Enlightenment Football League. We are told about three teams. The Marketeers are organised on the principle that each player is paid according to the number of goals he scores, and is motivated only to earn money; team play has to depend on contracts negotiated between the players. They are bottom of the league. Königsberg Universal, whose players act out of pure duty, does rather better. But the most successful team is the Musketeers, whose players have a sense of obligation to one another based on 'complete identification' with the team. Apparently the Musketeers' success derives from their ability to engage in team reasoning. Hollis gives them a partial endorsement, saying that they 'come closest [of the three teams] to illuminating the bond of society'.

Clearly, we are supposed to see that the instrumentally rational self-interest of the Marketeers is not enough to ensure social co-operation. The medicore performance of Königsberg Universal stands for the limitations of a socially abstracted morality of ideal rationality. Kantianism, Hollis tells us, is 'too high-minded to serve as the bond of society' (1998: 102). For human beings as they are, social co-operation has to be grounded in their sense of belonging to *particular* communities: there has to be loyalty and team spirit of the kind we find among the Musketeers. But Hollis is uneasy about this team too. He is concerned that, at least on one interpretation of what the Musketeers stand for, the secret of their success is that

> they obey the norms which put their team first blindly and untroubled by critical doubt. It never troubles them, for instance, that the loyalty which gives them their collective strength is essentially bound up with contempt for outsiders. They are, in some ways, more like ants obedient to the demands of the ant colony than humans intelligent about the values which inform their lives. (1998: 106–10)

The message, I take it, is this. In a liberal community, individuals' obligations to one another have the logical structure of team reasoning.

But individuals maintain a critical distance from the community's demands on them, and are able to recognise and to reject demands which are unreasonable or immoral.

The idea that team reasoning can be malign comes out more sharply in Hollis's discussion of the honour code of the Mafia. He quotes Thomas Nagel's claim that one cannot acquire a duty to murder someone just by taking a job as hit-man for the Mafia. Hollis want to agree with this claim; but he recognises that, viewed from within Mafia society, a hit-man does indeed have a duty to murder. Within that society, failure to fulfil this duty is taken to be an act of dishonour and cowardice (1998: 116). At the level of human sentiment, it seems, there is no categorical difference between the mafioso's abhorrence of dishonour and Nagel's abhorrence of the trade of hit-man. And the mafioso's loyalty to his social group seems at least as well modelled by team reasoning as does the public-spiritedness of blood donors. Hollis wants to say that a person who maintains the right kind of critical distance will recognise the moral difference between the two cases. He is confident that there *is* a difference, which a truly rational individual will perceive; but he never quite specifies what that difference amounts to, or how rationality allows us to perceive it.[2]

Team Reasoning

Although the idea of team reasoning has not yet been accepted as part of mainstream choice theory, it has been around for some time. The idea that such reasoning allows people to solve co-ordination problems that are intractable even to the most altruistic of individually rational agents was noticed by D.H. Hodgson (1967) and developed by Donald Regan (1980). These two writers were specifically concerned with the distinction between act utilitarianism (which is compatible with the conventional account of individual agency) and rule utilitarianism (which is not, but which can be understood as a form of team reasoning). Later, Margaret Gilbert (1989) and Susan Hurley (1989) proposed more general accounts of team reasoning. From the beginning of the 1990s, Michael Bacharach and I, working in a very loose collaboration, developed game-theoretic formulations of team reasoning (Bacharach 1993, 1999; Sugden 1991, 1993, 2000). Team reasoning was a common topic of discussion between Hollis, myself, and other economists at the University of East Anglia, and it featured in the survey of rational choice theory that Hollis and I wrote together (Hollis & Sugden 1993). So it is not surprising that Hollis's account of team reasoning has similarities with my own, and with those of other philosophers and decision theorists.[3]

However, there is a fundamental difference between the role of rationality in Hollis's account of team reasoning and its role in mine. For Hollis, rationality is a normative concept: a theory of rational choice is a theory which tells us *what rationality requires of us*. My interest is not in rationality in this normative sense, but in actual human reasoning, understood in much the same way that cognitive psychologists speak of 'mental processing'. That is, I am concerned with the mental events that occur when human beings *take themselves to be reasoning*. For me, the theory of choice encompasses whatever modes of reasoning people in fact use when making choices. Whether these correspond with generally accepted normative standards of *valid* reasoning is, for me, an open question, to be investigated empirically.[4]

Thus, in my analysis, team reasoning is nothing more than a mode of reasoning that people may sometimes use when interacting with one another. In itself, the analysis of this mode of reasoning does not tell us the circumstances in which people will use it. Team reasoning is reasoning about the most effective means by which a team, understood as a collectivity, can achieve its collective ends. The conclusions of such reasoning have relevance only for individuals who take themselves to be members of a team, and who know what their team's ends are – just as conclusions derived within conventional rational choice theory have relevance only for individuals who take themselves to be acting alone, and who know what their individual ends are.

Think of the top and bottom teams in the Enlightenment football league. In deciding what to do in the course of play, each Musketeer asks 'what combination of moves by all the members of the team would have best results for the team?', and treats the answer as giving him a reason to play his part in the optimal combination. In contrast, each Marketeer asks 'what move by me would have the best results for me, given what the other players can be expected to do?', and treats the answer as giving him a reason to play that move that is optimal for him. The Musketeers consistently win and the Marketeers consistently lose. Does the Musketeers' success give the Marketeers a reason to switch to team reasoning? If we assume that each of the individual Marketeers would prefer to be in a winning team, then it is true that all of these individuals would be better off if *all of them* played like Musketeers. But is that a reason for any one of them to change his style of play? As long as each construes himself as an individual agent, it does not. For each such agent, the only relevant question is: Would *my* aims be more effectively achieved if *I* changed my style of play, given what I can expect the others to do? To which, the answer is: No.

Of course, if we are to explain social co-operation, we must be able to explain how groups of individuals come to identify themselves collectively as teams. But should we expect this explanation to be a branch of rational choice theory? I think not. The received theory of rational choice takes individuals' preferences as given – not because the question of how preferences are determined is unimportant, but because this is not a question that can usefully be addressed by a theory of rational choice. I suggest that the same is true for the question of how group identities come about.

I cannot pretend to be able to offer a fully-fledged theory of group identity. For my present purposes, it is sufficient to say that my preferred approach is to treat an individual's sense of belonging to a team as a *sentiment* – an affectively charged psychological state – and not as the product of a process of reasoning. My hunch is that the concept of *fellow-feeling*, as developed by Adam Smith in *The Theory of Moral Sentiments* (1759/1976), would offer a useful starting point for a theory of the emergence and persistence of group identities. Smith's essential idea is that human beings have an innate tendency to feel pleasure from the consciousness that their own sentiments are aligned with those of others; this tendency is the basic building block of a spontaneous order of sociality and morality. On this account, the bond of society is ultimately a matter of sentiment.

Hollis rejected this approach. Despite his insistence the importance of loyalties to actual communities, he wanted an explanation of social co-operation which was grounded in rationality. Sentiment was not enough. To understand the significance of rationality in his thinking, we need to consider how he conceived the project of social science.

Rationality as its Own Explanation

Hollis's conception of social science is encapsulated in the quotation which he uses to open *The Cunning of Reason*. This is from God's message to Adam, as imagined by Pico della Mirandola in his *Oration on the Dignity of Man* in 1484:

> I have given you, Adam, neither a predetermined place nor a particular aspect nor any special prerogatives in order that you may take and possess these through your own decision and choice.... I have made you neither heavenly nor earthly, neither mortal nor immortal, so that like a free and sovereign artificer you might mould and fashion yourself into that form you yourself shall have chosen. (quoted in Hollis 1987: 1)

This humanist vision places man apart from the natural world. Human beings are self-moving agents in a way that the other inhabitants of the world are not. Thus, if there are to be sciences which explain human behaviour, these must be categorically different from the natural sciences. Hollis is convinced that social science *is* possible: as he puts it in *Models of Man*: 'I shall maintain that rational man is both a free agent and a proper subject for science' (1977: 107). Or, in relation to his object in *The Cunning of Reason*: 'the book is intended both to secure a robust sense in which Adam can be the sovereign artificer of his own life and to leave him the subject of a social science which respects the logic and power of decision theory' (1987: 92).

The problem, then, is to find a way of representing human beings simultaneously as self-moving agents and as the objects of an explanatory and predictive science. Hollis claims that this problem can be solved only by interpreting human action as *rational*. In the words of one of his favourite epigrams: 'rational action is its own explanation' (1977: 21). The idea is that when we discover that a person's action is rational, nothing more is required in the way of explanation. We do not have to refer to social or psychological forces lying behind the action: we can construe the actor as having made a free choice, guided by reason. But because we too are guided by the same reason, we can predict the behaviour of free and rational individuals.

As a model of this kind of explanation, Hollis offers chess theory (Hollis & Nell 1975: 89–94).[5] Chess theory is an interesting case study for methodologists of social science, because its methods are wholly *a priori* but it has explanatory and predictive power. An important feature of chess (a feature not shared by all well-specified games of strategy) is that, starting from any legal position for one of the players, there is in principle a best move (or set of equally good best moves). There are only three possibilities. *Either* there is a move which wins against best play (i.e. which, if correctly followed up in subsequent moves, leads to a win whatever the opponent does); *or* no such move exists, but there is move which draws against best play; *or* every possible move loses against best play. It would be relatively easy to write a computer program which, if executed on a machine with sufficient memory, could find the best move in any given chess position; the only problem is the memory space required and the length of time the program would take to run. In this respect, chess is not essentially different from noughts and crosses; the game is interesting only because, for many positions (and, most importantly, for the opening position), the 'line' of best play is not yet known. The task of chess theory is to discover lines of best play, in much the same sense that a mathematician tries to prove or disprove a putative theorem.

However, most chess theory falls short of the standards of game-theoretic proof. Theorists make different judgements about which lines are best, and give reasons for their judgements. This allows an interplay between theory and practice. On the one hand, chess theory can often be used to predict – with reasonable but not absolute reliability – the moves of strong players. On the other, observations of games between strong players can be treated as partial tests of theoretical hypotheses. (For example, a claim that a certain opening is sound would be called into question if grandmasters who played it against grandmasters consistently lost.) In these respects, chess theory is indeed a science. But, unlike in the natural sciences, the final court of appeal is not the facts of the world, but *a priori* truth.

It is significant that chess theory is not at all concerned with the psychology of human players. In particular, it is not concerned to explain why some people reliably play good moves, while others frequently play bad ones. Chess theory recognises a categorical distinction between the explanation of good play and the explanation of bad, and confines itself to the former. And its 'explanation' of good play does not go beyond *a priori* analysis. For chess theory, we might say, best play is its own explanation. Hollis's contention is that the social sciences should be scientific in the same sense that chess theory is scientific.

Now on the face of it, there is an obvious disanalogy between chess and social life. The rules of chess are well defined and are taken as given, both within the community of players and within the community of theorists. Thus, although the truth-value of a particular hypothesis (say, that a certain move constitutes best play from a certain position) may be unknown, there is no ambiguity about what that hypothesis *means*, or about how, in principle, its truth or falsity could be established. (Think of the computer program.) This is surely not true of social life. There is no standard of success, analogous with the scale of win/draw/lose in chess, accepted by all social actors and by all social scientists. If social scientists are to act on Hollis's proposal, the best they can do is to assert that a well-defined standard of success *exists*, even though they do not yet know – or at least, do not yet agree about – what it is. I take it that this is how Hollis intends us to interpret his metaphor.

Now consider what this approach to social science implies for Hollis's account of the liberal community. Remember that Hollis is offering team reasoning as a model of the rationality of individual participation in collective action. If we are to treat the individual as a self-moving agent, we must allow it to be possible that he acts as rationality truly requires, *because rationality truly requires it*.

It is an essential part of Hollis's understanding of 'community' that our belonging to particular communities can be determined by factors that are outside our individual control. We are born into families, language communities, social classes, and nations, from which we can exit only with difficulty. As we go through life, decisions made with limited foresight generate new ties, to lovers, spouses, children, workmates and so on. That human identity is embedded in social relations is axiomatic for Hollis: he explicitly rejects the kind of liberalism that claims, with Rawls, that 'the self is prior to the ends which are affirmed by it'.[6] Thus, Hollis's endorsement of team reasoning commits him to the claim that what rationality truly requires of us can depend on the particular communities to which we belong, while the fact that we belong to those communities is not the product of our own rational choices.

Now there need be no conflict here with the idea of human beings as self-moving agents. As a rational, self-moving agent, an individual acts as rationality requires; if the requirements of rationality are different in different social settings, then so too is the behaviour of rational agents. But it *is* necessary that the rational individual is conscious of, and motivated by, the requirements of rationality. It is not enough that rationality truly requires her to participate in some collective action, and that she in fact so participates: she must *endorse* her own participation, from a standpoint that acknowledges the possibility of her not participating. This is the requirement of critical distance.

Further, Hollis's methodological position commits him to the claim that there exist principles of rationality, *not* embedded in social relations, which can tell us which social demands we are rationally required to fulfil, and which not. If rationality is to be its own explanation, we have to suppose that, for any given individual in any given social situation, the question of whether it is rational for him to participate in a particular collective activity has a determinate answer. Yet Hollis does not tell us, except in the most general terms, what the relevant principles of rationality are, or how they are to be discovered.

In his early work, he seems to suggest that an answer might be found by developing the concept of *expressive rationality*. The idea is that social obligations are associated with *roles*. In taking on a role, we take on corresponding obligations. The space for rationality comes when we reflect about whether or not to identify with a particular role. This is the realm of expressive acts – acts through which 'the actor affirms his identification with the character'. Expressive acts are rational to the extent that the 'real interests' of the actor coincide with the requirements of the role. But, apart from saying that the concept of real interest is connected with 'that ancient problem about the nature of the Good Society', Hollis does not tell us what people's real interests are, or how we are to identify them (1977: 136–7).

In the closing pages of *Trust Within Reason*, Hollis seems to be suggesting a different approach, in which obligations to particular communities are licensed by team reasoning by individuals who take themselves to be 'citizens of the world'. Reasoning at this highest level, we discover that some kinds of local obligation work to our collective good, as citizens of the world, while others do not; the former obligations but not the latter are then taken to be requirements of rationality. But this requires a concept, not embedded in any particular community, of the collective good of all human beings; and this is left undeveloped (1998: 154–63).

In his last writings, Hollis describes his own position as 'fighting liberalism' (1998: 156; 1999). I take him to be saying that a fighting liberal thinks and acts on the conviction that certain liberal tenets are universal principles of rationality, even if there is no known method of determining what the universal principles of rationality really are. I can see that, when one takes a personal political or moral stand, some such act of faith may be necessary. But what is at issue – for Hollis as well as for me – is how social science should be done. Hollis is proposing that social science recognises a fundamental distinction between the rational and the irrational; but he can give us little concrete guidance about where to draw the dividing line.

Hollis's final line of defence for his methodological position is the claim that social scientists have no choice but to start from *a priori* principles of rationality. This gives him a companions-in-guilt argument: it is true that his kind of social science is grounded on principles of rationality that cannot be fully justified, but so too is everyone else's. In his later writings, this argument is merely alluded to, often enigmatically. Thus, almost at the end of *Trust Within Reason*, Hollis recommends that we accept 'a strongly rationalist account of the *a priori*':

> This is one which takes it that we have a priori knowledge or, more subtly, that our needing it is sufficient for our knowing that we have it. Either way, the case is that otherwise all our thinking becomes incoherent, since it becomes stuck in a self-refuting relativism. We would then be landed with wondering whether what we take for *a priori* is truly so in a language which presupposes it. (1998: 158)

To understand what Hollis means in passages like this, we have to go back to some of his earliest work, in which he discusses what he calls the 'other minds' or 'other cultures' problem. The original analysis is framed in terms of the problem faced by an anthropologist who is trying to understand an alien culture and to translate its concepts into English.[7] According to Hollis, the anthropologist's first step must be to establish a *bridgehead*: a minimal 'class of utterances whose situations of use [she] can specify'. She must then suppose that these utterances are correctly translated by whatever English sentences have corresponding situations of use. This supposition requires her to make two assumptions: that 'the natives perceive more or less what [she] perceives' and that 'they say about it more or less what [she] would say'. Hollis insists that these are *assumptions*, not *hypotheses*. That is, all subsequent translations are justified only by virtue of the truth of the original assumptions about the bridgehead. Thus, those assumptions cannot be refuted by anything that is discovered as a result of later translations: 'no successful translation can destroy [her] bridgehead, since all later translations depend on its being secure'. Nor does the apparent success of later translations vindicate the assumptions, since without those assumptions, the claim that later translations are successful is ungrounded (1967: 191–2).

The significance of this account of translation emerges when Hollis considers the problem of dealing with native sentences that, translated literally, seem to be nonsense. (One of his examples is the supposed belief of some Australian aborigines that the sun is a white cockatoo.) The anthropologist makes sense of such sentences by interpreting them as metaphors or myths. But (Hollis claims) if she is *always* free to deny that a sentence has its literal meaning, as given by her proposed scheme of translation, there are no constraints on 'translation' at all: anything goes. Hollis's conclusion is that translations depend on assumptions about common rationality: 'the *sine qua non* is a bridgehead of true assertions about a shared reality' (1967: 193). And: 'the only way to produce justifiable accounts of other cultures is to make the natives as rational as possible' (1967: 196).

Thus, Hollis argues, there are *a priori* truths of rationality which we have to presuppose if we are to understand other cultures – and hence if we are to do social science. Specifically, we must assume that all cultures 'share our concepts of truth, coherence and rational interdependence of beliefs' (1967: 196). In another paper, he argues that his anthropologist must assume that the natives 'share (at least partly) [her] concepts of identity, contradiction and inference' – that is, that they use a logic which includes the axioms P → P, ~(P & ~P), and [P & (P → Q)] → Q (1968: 211). We still seem to be a long way from the sort of universal principles which could tell us that the loyalties of mafiosi are irrational; but if the argument is correct, Hollis has established an essential bridgehead of his own.

In Defence of Empiricism

I have tried to present Hollis's arguments for rationalism in social science as sympathetically as I can; but I think they do not work. Responding to such an intricate web of philosophically subtle arguments, it is difficult to know where to start. Let me begin with a profession of lack of faith. I am not a humanist. I am not inspired by the Enlightenment vision of Adam as the free and sovereign artificer. The idea that our species can claim some kind of semi-divine status by virtue of our self-attributed rationality – that this rationality gives us the power to 'hover between heaven and earth', as Hollis (1999: 40) puts it in his final paper – strikes me as overweening. We are no one's chosen species. We are just one species of great ape, distinguished from the others by a limited amount of additional mental capacity, by greater facility in language, and by the vastly greater use we have collectively made of the division of labour. How great the differences really are between our mental capacities and those of other species is, I maintain, a question for scientific investigation. It should not be closed down by *a priori* claims about the nature of rationality.

As a social scientist, I do not find it useful to make Hollis's categorical distinction between the rational and the irrational. I stand by the empiricist principle that a science should not assert the existence of differences between observationally equivalent phenomena. Hollis's methodological principle that rational and irrational acts should be explained in fundamentally different ways contravenes that principle. Or, more accurately, it contravenes that principle unless there is a criterion for distinguishing between rational and irrational acts on the basis of observation and experiment. And no such criterion has been offered.

Why shouldn't we make distinctions between observationally equivalent phenomena? My answer is that such distinctions are likely to obstruct our vision as social scientists, looking for better explanations of the social world. Hollis's example of the Mafia illustrates the point. On the face of it, as Hollis recognises, the behaviour of mafiosi who kill according to codes of honour is just as open to explanation in terms of team reasoning as is, say, the behaviour of a firefighter who risks his life in a rescue operation. On the face of it, too, the sentiments of approval that such killings evoke in Mafia society are not different in kind from the sentiments of approval that the firefighter's actions evoke in a liberal society. The apparent similarities between the two phenomena ought to suggest to us the possibility that there are common elements in their explanations. A good social scientist must be constantly on the alert for unexpected similarities and correlations among social phenomena. The more *a priori* distinctions we impose on our conceptual schemes, and the more rigidly we subscribe to them, the less likely we are to discover unexpected truths about the world.

I must concede that in closing the gap between the rational and the irrational, this empiricist methodology opens up a different gap: the gap between social scientist's own viewpoint on his subject matter, and the subject matter itself. As a social scientist, I take myself to be an autonomous agent, seeking to discover truths about the social world. I work within a community of social scientists, whom I take to be autonomous agents too. And I take it that our explanations must satisfy certain standards of logic and of scientific method. Doesn't all this amount to *a priori* assumptions about rationality? So am I being inconsistent in refusing to make *a priori* assumptions about the rationality of the actions I am trying to explain?

Some philosophers – for example, Jean Hampton (1998) in her posthumous book, *The Authority of Reason* – have claimed that empiricist social science is guilty of exactly this inconsistency; and Hollis may have something similar in mind when he talks about 'self-refuting relativism'. Hampton's argument would certainly have force against a social scientist who claimed that the activities of social scientists were exempt from social-scientific investigation – that, as Hollis might have put it, the discovery of scientific truth is its own explanation. But that is not my position. As far as I am concerned, *all* social practices, including the social practices of the scientific community, are potential subject matter for social science. The distinction that my approach forces on me is between the *investigator of* social life and the *participant in* social life. For any social practice, there is a view from within – the practice as seen by the participants – and a view from without – the practice as seen by the investigator. When, as a social scientist, I investigate some particular form of social behaviour, I view that behaviour from without, while participating in the practice of social science. At the same time, my own behaviour as an investigator could be subject matter for a sociologist of science, viewing it from without. I remain unpersuaded that such an understanding of social science is incoherent.

Still, I have not yet responded to Hollis's central claim: that, as social scientists, we have no option but to assume that the actions of the people we investigate satisfy certain universal principles of rationality. So let me say why I think this 'bridgehead' argument fails.

I agree that, in order to begin to understand an alien language or culture, we need to begin from some bridgehead of percepts or concepts that we take to be common to the two languages – 'ours' and 'theirs'. But I do not agree that this bridgehead must be made up of fundamental assumptions that can be neither validated nor invalidated by subsequent discoveries – that these are the axioms on which the whole of our subsequent understandings are grounded. Nor do I agree that the common concepts of the bridgehead must be *a priori* principles of rationality.

It seems to me that all that is required for a bridgehead is a *hypothesis* or *hunch* about some regularity in 'their' language, which we understand by analogy with some regularity in 'ours'. If that hypothesis is successful, it will lead us to discover new regularities in their language. In discovering these new regularities, we are guided not only by the assumption that the original hypothesis is true, but also by our alertness for *new* analogies between the languages – the same kind of alertness that gave us our first hunch. Our confidence in the bridgehead helps us to *recognise* new regularities, but having recognised them, our justification for believing that they are genuine need not depend on the truth of the bridgehead. With the right mix of luck and imagination, we will end up with a system of grammar and vocabulary that allows us to translate their language into ours in a way that makes sense (to us) of what we hear them say. For us to have confidence in this final product, it is not necessary that the translation that we used as the bridgehead has survived intact.

Of course, there is another possibility: using the original bridgehead hypothesis, we may fail to discover new regularities. Then we should try a different hypothesis.

As an analogy, think of the problem (which in my youth was a mainstay of children's puzzle books) of cracking a simple code, in which the set of the letters of the alphabet is mapped onto itself. You are given a reasonably long piece of encoded text, which you assume is English. With a basic knowledge of English, you can make various initial conjectures: for example, that the most common letter in the decoded text is probably 'e', that one-letter words are either 'a' or 'I', that each word contains at least one vowel, and that certain very common words (such as 'the') are likely to occur somewhere in the text. Using these conjectures imaginatively, and with a sense of what constitutes a meaningful message, you should be able to decode the text. In the process, you will form provisional hypotheses, only some of which turn out to be true. But although you could not have succeeded without those hypotheses, your confidence in the final decoding does not depend on them. The fact that you have generated a meaningful message is justification enough for your confidence.

At this point, it might be objected that I am helping myself to a notion of 'meaningfulness'. Isn't the problem of 'other cultures' precisely that of determining whether apparent regularities in the social life of another culture are meaningful? Yes, it is. Hollis is surely right when he argues that, if our translations are to succeed, there must be some overlap between our notions of meaningfulness and those of the culture we are trying to understand. But that does not entail that what we have in common must be *principles of rationality*.

Recall Hollis's slogan that 'the *sine qua non* is a bridgehead of true assertions about a shared reality'. It is significant, I think, that Hollis's example of a bridgehead is a native sentence which translates into English as the assertion 'yes, this is a brown cow' (1967: 192). This is a simple, well-formed proposition, that can be analysed according to the kind of rules of logic that Hollis takes to belong to the *a priori* core of rationality. If the anthropologist is still at the bridgehead stage, and if her informant appears to be asserting simultaneously both 'yes, this is a brown cow' and 'no, this is not a brown cow', then her would-be translation is clearly in trouble. But where did the idea come from that the bridgehead must be an *assertion*? Why should we suppose that the bridgehead is any kind of well-formed proposition?

I have suggested that the bond of society might be understood as a matter of sentiment rather than of rationality. In the light of this suggestion, it is natural to ask whether overlapping *sentiments* could provide us with the bridgeheads we need in order to begin to understand alien cultures. Of course, this approach can work only where there is in fact an overlap of sentiments between the relevant cultures. But that is hardly a problem for an earthbound social science. All human beings belong to the same biological species, and so share a repertoire of genetically encoded dispositions to respond affectively to the world in predetermined ways. Perhaps the ability of human cultures to understand one another *is* an indirect consequence of this fact of biology. I have the sense that Hollis would be unsatisfied with the thought that mutual understanding between rational beings might be 'merely' contingent on natural facts; but for an empiricist, there would be nothing to be unsatisfied about.

Consider a real example of establishing a bridgehead. In the middle of the eighteenth century, the British navigator James Cook commanded three great voyages of exploration to parts of the world that no Europeans had visited before. Exceptionally humane by the standards of his time, Cook made great efforts to cultivate friendly relations with the native populations of the lands he visited. Here is one typical incident, which occurred in 1769. Cook's ship has anchored off the coast of Tierra del Fuego. So far, there has been no contact with the native Fuegians. Cook records in his journal, in a typically matter-of-fact way, that 'after dinner I went on shore, accompanied by Mr Banks and Dr Solander [the naturalists of the voyage], to look for a watering place, and speak to the natives, several of whom had come in sight'. How, we might wonder, is

Cook expecting to *speak to* people whose language is entirely unknown to him? The Europeans land at one end of a bay. Thirty or forty native Fuegians appear at the other end of the bay, and then retreat. Banks and Solander advance, holding out trinkets, intended as gifts. Two Fuegians then step forward, sit down, stand up again, display large sticks, gesture with them, and then ostentatiously throw them away. The Europeans interpret these gestures as signalling the renunciation of violence. Soon the two groups are exchanging what are apparently mutually intelligible gestures of friendly greeting (if 'uncouth' to European sensibilities – it seems that penis gestures were somehow involved on the Fuegian side), and the Fuegians are being entertained to bread and beef on board ship (Hough 1994).

It seems clear that, within a matter of hours, some degree of mutual understanding has been established between people from two human cultures that are about as distant from one another as it is possible to be. Notice that the bridgehead does not involve the translation of words, but of gestures. These gestures seem to be communicating affective states – particularly those of friendship – rather than asserting propositions. The successful translation of these gestures seems to depend partly on common understandings about certain universals of human social life (gifts, greetings, peace, war) and partly on an ability to 'read' emotional tone (notice how, despite the peculiarities of the Fuegians' gestures, the friendly intent behind them was recognised by the Europeans).

Clearly, the process by which this mutual understanding becomes established depends on hypotheses and hunches about the likely repertoire of sentiments and practices within the other society. It might be said that this amounts to an assumption of some minimal degree of rationality in that society. But notice how naturalistically 'rationality' must be interpreted if it is to be applied in this context. As far as we can tell, Cook established his bridgehead without having to discover whether the Fuegians used a system of logic satisfying the laws of identity, non-contradiction and inference. By the time he was in a position from which he might have investigated this question – say, over the bread and beef – he already had grounds for confidence in a set of translations between Fuegian and European expressions. By then, I suggest, he was in a position to entertain the possibility that the Fuegians did not use 'European' logic. That is, he could formulate that hypothesis without invalidating his bridgehead of provisionally accepted translations. Notice that what is at issue here is not whether the Fuegians really did recognise the fundamental axioms of logic. It is whether Cook *had no option but to assume that they did*. My claim is that Cook had other options. One such option, and the option he actually used, was to start from the hypothesis that certain kinds of sentiment – certain affective responses to the world – were common to the Fuegians and the Europeans. If this is right, then what I take to be Hollis's argument for the necessity of rationalism in social science does not succeed.

Conclusion

In Martin Hollis's writings we find repeated sketches, drawn with brilliance and panache, of how social science might be made consistent with Enlightenment humanism and rationalism. Nothing in the present essay denies the *possibility* of such a social science, founded on claims to *a priori* knowledge about reason. Hollis's concept of 'fighting liberalism' seems to acknowledge that such claims are contestable, and will continue to be contested. His aim, then, is not so much to explain the bonds that hold actual societies together, as to show us how societies of free and rational human beings *might be* held together. Hence the model of the liberal community, in which the bond of society – although construed as a bond between socially embedded individuals – is ultimately a bond of reason.

Throughout the years that Hollis and I worked together and debated with one another, I upheld a different conception of social science, in the philosophical tradition of Hume's *Treatise of Human Nature*. This is a social science which seeks to explain social facts are they are, in terms of human nature as it is. Running through all Hollis's work is a strand of argument which, if I have understood it rightly, aims to expose a fundamental incoherence in the project of Humean social science. In this essay I have argued that there is no such incoherence. The bonds of actual societies, I still maintain, are bonds of sentiment.

ACKNOWLEDGEMENTS

A previous version of the paper was presented to a meeting of the East Anglian Philosophical Triangle at Newnham College, Cambridge. I am grateful for comments from participants in that meeting. I have also benefited from discussions with Nick Bardsley, Shaun Hargreaves Heap, Timothy O'Hagan, Angus Ross and Roberta Sassatelli. My work was supported by the Leverhulme Trust.

NOTES

1. We managed to write only one substantial paper together, a critical review of the literature on rational choice (Hollis & Sugden 1993). We always found it much easier to agree on what was wrong with existing theories than on how to improve them.

2. Hollis's last word on the matter is the claim 'we are embedded in games of social life but not lost in them, as the examples of honour and cannibalism show' (1998: 161–2). I take him to mean that culture-independent principles of rationality rule out Mafia-like honour codes and cannibalism. But he hasn't told us how he knows this.

3. Hollis may also have been influenced by another theorist of team reasoning, Raimo Tuomela. It seems that there was some exchange of ideas between the two while Hollis was writing *Trust Within Reason* (see the preface to this book, p. viii). Tuomela's theory is presented in Tuomela (1995).

4. As an example of such investigation, consider 'positive confirmation bias'. Faced with the experimental task of judging the truth of a proposition of the form 'all Ps (in some well-defined class) are Q', many individuals believe that it is useful to test whether objects that are already known to be Q are also P; a positive result from such a test is treated as if it made the truth of the proposition more likely. By the normative standards of logic, such reasoning is erroneous. Nevertheless, it is possible to construct theories of reasoning which track the invalid inferences that human beings actually make in such cases (Jones & Sugden 2001).

5. This discussion, in a self-contained aside entitled 'a mini-science of chess', appears in a co-authored book. But everything about the passage – style, content, the knowledge of chess – mark it out as the sole work of Hollis.

6. The quotation is from Rawls (1971: 560). Hollis (1998: 103) uses this quotation to represent a position he rejects.

7. To allow me to distinguish easily between what Hollis says on his own account and what he says on behalf of the anthropologist, I take the liberty of changing the original male anthropologist into a female one.

REFERENCES

Bacharach, Michael. 1993. 'Variable universe games'. Binmore et al. 1993: 255–75.
  1999. 'Interactive team reasoning: a contribution to the theory of cooperation'. *Research in Economics*, 53, 117–47.
Binmore, Ken et al., eds. 1993. *Frontiers of Game Theory*. Cambridge, MA: MIT Press.
Gilbert, Margaret. 1989. *On Social Facts*. London: Routledge.
Hampton, Jean. 1998. *The Authority of Reason*. Cambridge: Cambridge University Press.
Harrison, R., ed. 1979. *Rational Action: Studies in the Philosophy of Social Science*. Cambridge: Cambridge University Press.
Hodgson, D.H. 1967. *Consequences of Utilitarianism*. Oxford University Press.
Hollis, Martin. 1967. 'The limits of irrationality'. *Archives Européenes de Sociologie*, 7, 265–71. Page references to reprint in Hollis 1996.
  1968. 'Reason and ritual'. *Philosophy*, 43, 231–47. Page references to reprint in Hollis 1996.
  1977. *Models of Man*. Cambridge: Cambridge University Press.
  1979. 'Rational man and social science'. Harrison 1979: 1–15. Page reference to reprint (with title 'Three men in a drought') in Hollis 1996.
  1987. *The Cunning of Reason*. Cambridge: Cambridge University Press.

1996. *Reason in Action: Essays in the Philosophy of Social Science*. Cambridge: Cambridge University Press.

1998. *Trust Within Reason*. Cambridge: Cambridge University Press.

1999. 'Is universalism ethnocentric?'. Joppke & Lukes 1999: 27–44.

Hollis, Martin & Edward Nell. 1975. *Rational Economic Man*. Cambridge: Cambridge University Press.

Hollis, Martin & Robert Sugden. 1993. 'Rationality in action'. *Mind*,102, 1–35.

Hough, Richard. 1994. *Captain James Cook: A Biography*. London: Hodder & Stoughton.

Hurley, Susan. 1989. *Natural Reasons*. Oxford: Oxford University Press.

Joppke, Christian & Steven Lukes, eds. 1999. *Multicultural Questions*. Oxford: Oxford University Press.

Jones, Martin & Robert Sugden. 2001. 'Positive confirmation bias in the acquisition of information'. *Theory and Decision, 50*, 59–99.

Rawls, John. 1971. *A Theory of Justice*. Cambridge, Massachusetts: Harvard University Press.

Regan, Donald. 1980. *Utilitarianism and Cooperation*. Oxford University Press.

Smith, Adam. 1759 [1976]. *The Theory of Moral Sentiments*. Oxford: Clarendon Press.

Sugden, Robert. 1991. 'Rational choice: a survey of contributions from economics and philosophy'. *Economic* Journal, 105, 1269–1302.

1993. 'Thinking as a team: toward an explanation of non-selfish behavior'. *Social Philosophy and Policy*, 10, 69–89.

Sugden, Robert. 2000. 'Team preferences'. *Economics and Philosophy*, 16, 175–204.

Tuomela, Raimo. 1995. *The Importance of Us*. Stanford, California: Stanford University Press.

9

Collective Reasoning:
A Critique of Martin Hollis's Position

NICHOLAS BARDSLEY

'Games' in the sense of *game theory*[1] are situations in which, for each
agent involved, the outcome of their decision depends jointly on what
they and the others decide. Game situations are important for social
science, since interdependence of this kind is ubiquitous. Games are also
of philosophical importance since they render the analysis of rational
action problematic. A simple instrumental conception of rationality, as
employed in rational choice theory (RCT) and game theory,[2] leads to
counterintuitive conclusions in many games. Most notoriously, it would
make it a requirement of practical reason that agents perform acts which
are collectively self-defeating in prisoner's dilemma games[3] – a problem
of 'counterfinality'. These problems are commonly held to characterise
situations of great practical importance, such as problems of pollution
and depletion of common pool resources, and at least one of great
theoretical importance, namely the imposition of government in a state
of nature, as analysed by Hobbes (1651) and subsequent social contract
theorists. Martin Hollis was committed to the view that the concept of
rational action is of primary analytical importance both for positive and
normative social science. His critique of certain structuralist sociologists
in *Models of Man* (hereafter MM), for example, was based around the
observation that they could not accommodate the notion that something
can be done 'purely and simply because there is good reason to do it',
which leaves the theorists unable to account for their own enquiries.
Whilst he appears to have thought economists irresponsible for positing
that only defection is rational in the prisoners' dilemma.[4] He was
consequently interested in revising the analysis of rationality in an
attempt to resolve such game theoretic puzzles.

In early works, he considers a contrast between instrumental and 'expressive' rationality as a possible remedy to counterfactual problems. This paper concentrates on a different problem: 'co-ordination' games, in particular 'impure' co-ordination games (defined below). These games are distinctive in the key respect that they do not involve any conflicts of interest. They seem to call for a different revision to the analysis of practical reason, namely what might be called either 'team thinking', following Sugden (1993), or 'collective reasoning': certain reasons for action can be expressed in the first person plural; there are, as it were, 'we-reasons'. Whilst Hollis' discussion of this matter is brief and he appears to have been a late convert,[5] it occupies a key role in his final work, *Trust Within Reason* (hereafter TWR), where the notion is to have important repercussions for other games. For collective reasoning is to hold the secret of trust between rational beings, enabling them to overcome counterfinality problems as well.[6]

Collective reasoning is likely to be anathema to many economists because they typically espouse some form of methodological individualism. I argue that there is only an apparent conflict here, since collective reasoning is just a particular way of thinking by individuals. However, it does seem to rely on a strong notion of plural subject agency, philosophical analyses of which Hollis invokes in its defence. I show some problems raised by the details of these analyses. The second section discusses alternative rationality concepts which feature in Hollis's work, introducing team thinking. I examine the question of methodological individualism in the third section, which also examines the notions of collective intention-in-action, belief and goal cited by Hollis. This discussion leads into a question about how reasons valid for groups can move individuals to act, and the problem of explaining the possibility of an individual's moving between two distinct modes of action.

The Insolubility of the 'Trivial' Hi-Lo Co-ordination Problem

A pure 'co-ordination game' can be defined informally as a situation in which two or more agents must all independently choose the same action, from a set of available actions, in order to share some prize.[7] If they choose differently, they each receive nothing. For example, two agents might both have to choose, without communicating, between 'heads' and 'tails'; if both choose 'heads' or if both choose 'tails', both receive a prize of five pounds, but if one chooses 'heads' and the other 'tails' each receives nothing. Another stock example is two drivers approaching each other along a road; it does not matter if both drive on the left or both on the right, so long as they make the same choice. An *impure* co-ordination game has the property that the various same-choice combinations are not all equally good.

Suppose two people face the following 'problem', for example: each must specify one of two sums of money, a: £50 or b: £30. If they state the same sum they each receive this amount, otherwise each receives nothing. They cannot communicate. Both prefer more money to less. Payoffs in pounds are therefore as in Figure 1, where the number on the left in each cell is player 1's payoff and that on the right player 2's. Call this the 'Hi-Lo' game, after Bacharach (1999). Hi-Lo is an impure co-ordination game, in which one 'equilibrium' (see below) is better for everyone than the other one (it is 'Pareto superior').

Suppose there is common knowledge of the following:[8] first, that each chooses from the actions available the one leading to the best consequences, given their beliefs about what the other player will do,[9] that is, common knowledge of rationality (CKR), second, the payoff structure and third, any theorem that can be proved about the game. These assumptions amount to a characterisation of *perfectly* rational and well-informed actors. Given these assumptions, in equilibrium each player will choose a strategy that is a best response to the actions of the others. Such a combination of strategies is known as a 'Nash equilibrium'. There are *two* Nash equilibria in Hi-Lo: (a, a) and (b, b), but as (a, a) is Pareto superior the problem *seems* trivial; obviously both

FIGURE 1
THE 'HI-LO' GAME

Player 2

		a	b
Player 1	a	50 50	0 0
	b	0 0	30 30

players ought to choose strategy *a*. However, it is rational for player 1 to choose *a* if *and only if* expecting player 2 to choose *a*, because if she expected 2 to choose *b* the utility maximising choice would be *b* (in our example, £30 is better than nothing).

The problem is this: how might the expectation that the other will choose *a* be grounded? Player 2 is a rational agent and so will only choose *a* if it is rational to do so; it is only rational for 2 to choose *a* if he expects 1 to play *a*. But player 2 knows that 1 is a rational agent and so will choose *a* only if it is rational to do so. Therefore, to solve 1's decision problem: 'is it rational for me (1) to play *a*?' 1 must first solve 2's decision problem: 'is it rational for 1 to play *a*?'. 1 and 2 are in exactly the same position, so all that player 1 can conclude is that it is rational to choose *a* if it is rational to choose *a*. By a parallel argument, it is rational to choose *b* if it is rational to choose *b*. All that player 2 can deduce is the same, and neither are any nearer to knowing what to play after deducing all that can be inferred from common knowledge of rationality and the strategic structure of the game.

The impure co-ordination game is clearly puzzling. One can increase the payoffs under (*a, a*) as much as one likes without changing anything in the logic just given; the individually instrumentally rational choice remains indeterminate, even if millions are at stake. This is a blow both to the positive and normative aspirations of RCT, for not only can real people be expected to co-ordinate on (*a, a*) in H-Lo,[10] but they do better by doing what is 'obviously right' than by consulting RCT which here gives them no advice. Hollis argues further, correctly in my view, that Schelling's (1963) 'focal point' concept, the tendency for one equilibrium to stand out from the others, is of no relevance for the agents of RCT.[11] Accepting the indeterminacy problem as a motivating premise leads one naturally to question the conception of rationality that has given rise to it.

Alternatives to Individual Instrumental Rationality: Expressive Rationality

Another problem faced by RCT is explaining why people vote in large elections, since an individual's probability of affecting the outcome is practically zero. In response to this 'paradox of voting' it has been suggested that the rationality concept formalised in utility theory is too narrow because it focuses only on consequences, excluding the expressive dimension of behaviour. Benn (1978: 3) offers a clear definition of *expressive rationality*: 'an action can be rational for a person regardless of its payoff if it expresses attitudes or principles that it would be inconsistent of him not to express under appropriate conditions, given the character which he is generally content to acknowledge as his own. This is what is called being true to oneself.'

Hollis invokes expressive rationality at key points in various works (1977: 135–41; 1998: 147) but not in the context of co-ordination. To see why it is impotent in Hi-Lo, consider what playing *a* could express. One might want to argue that if either strategy showed, say, trust in others or a co-operative nature or virtually any desirable characteristic, it would have to be *a* rather than *b*. To say that *a*-playing manifests a desirable characteristic *simpliciter*, however, would presuppose that *a* is the better strategy, and this would amount to a circular argument. The supposed good connotation must instead be accounted for. One problem is that, in contrast to voting, the labels attached to the strategies in our Hi-Lo game are purely arbitrary; what is definitive of *a* is simply that it leads to the better equilibrium if both choose it. Therefore any expressive feature of *a*-playing must also arise through the structure of payoffs. We would presumably have to say that as the consequences of widespread *a*-playing are better than those from *b*-playing, this feeds back into an expressive 'payoff'.

In our Hi-Lo case, though, even if we accept that playing *a* says something desirable about the character of a player, regardless of the play of the other, we cannot conclude that it is therefore more rational to play *a*. For if either expects the other to play *b* he will be faced with a choice between an expressive consideration and an instrumental one. There is no reason to presuppose the former to be decisive. Indeed, the instrumental consideration can be arbitrarily enlarged if we specify a greater difference between the outcome under (*b*, *b*) and that under (*b*, *a*), since the co-ordination problem does not depend on the specific values of the payoffs in the equilibria (so long as those under (*a*, *a*) surpass those under (*b*, *b*) which in turn exceed those under (*a*, *b*) or (*b*, *a*)). The indeterminacy problem posed by Hi-Lo is therefore insoluble with each agent concerned only with the *ramifications* of their own act, even with these covering expressive concerns in addition to consequences as usually conceived.

Collective Rationality (CR)

Whilst the notion of expressive rationality takes issue with the *instrumental* character of RCT, reflection on Hi-Lo has led many, including Hollis, to question its *individual* aspect. To give an account of the rationality of *a*-playing in Hi-Lo, it is necessary to account for the relevance of the better outcomes in the (*a*, *a*) equilibrium. Some writers (such as Regan (1980)) have used Hi-Lo to demonstrate the inadequacy of Act Utilitarianism; we can paraphrase their reasoning to show the indeterminism of Act Consequentialism[12] in general. In Hi-Lo, so long as each player plays the same strategy as the other, each has produced the best consequences possible by his/her action given the behaviour of the other. If we wish to have some reasons why *a* should be played, then, we need to abandon Act Consequentialism.

One way of doing this, which is still consistent with a kind of consequentialism, is to cease taking others' acts as given, on a par with the other 'circumstances' in which the agents find themselves. Instead, the agents are to conceive themselves as *acting together* – being together the subject of (that is, the entity which performs) an action. The fact that (*a*, *a*) is better for both is relevant to *us both* but not to *each* of us separately. An Act Consequentialist would conclude that this fact is not relevant; proponents of CR resist this conclusion by insisting that we may see ourselves as constituting a group agent or team. The reason on which the individuals are to act, then, is *a reason addressed to a group not to individuals*. The departure from Act Consequentialism lies in the consideration of the consequences of *sets* of acts, rather than individual acts.

Essentially, the advice to play *a* is the answer to the question 'what should *we* do?' rather than 'what should *I* do?'. On a basic analysis of instrumental reasons, 'A ought to *θ*' means that *θ*-ing is necessary to achieve some goal, where A is an agent and *θ* is an action.[13] Since we may talk of rational action without taking a position on the rationality of goals, and allowing agents to be imperfectly informed,[14] a minimal, 'subjective' conception of rational action amounts to selecting efficient means to A's ends, judging by A's beliefs. This schema leaves open the question of the composition of A; if A is a group, the relevant goals and beliefs would appear to be those of the group.

As Sugden (1993: 86) notes, acting as a team thinker is a far stronger notion than merely acting to fulfil a shared goal. For *this* behaviour is not inconsistent with Act Consequentialism, and so does not get us over Hi-Lo. For if a player accepts a group's goal as his own and asks 'how can I best further this goal?' this will depend on what his partner does and he will be back into the indeterminacy problem of Hi-Lo. This shows that accounts of what is involved in collective action ought to go further than specifying the 'internalisation of the group's goals' (and therefore beyond a mere multiple-utility conception of conflict between personal and group perspectives, such as posited by Sen's famous (1977) 'Rational Fools' essay).

At this point CR may seem to have strong and unpalatable implications. One can reasonably argue that there can only be legitimate reasons for action addressed to groups if there really is a 'we' – if groups are in fact agents. The concern is that group agency implies 'groupish' counterparts to all the factors normally cited in the analysis of action – group mind, group belief, group goal and group intentions-in-action.[15] Reverting to the driving example of a pure co-ordination game, Hollis writes: 'to prevent conditionals from re-surfacing, team membership needs to be a stronger relation than membership of a mere association. One way to make the point is to say that members of teams have 'we-intentions': each, if asked 'what do you intend to do?', replies 'we intend to keep left'. This will be no small innovation, if *we*-intentions presuppose *we*-desires and *we*-beliefs, in short if teams or groups can be agents only if they have the relevant attributes of individual agents. But that is not a *nolle prosequi* and persuasive attempts have been made to work out the apparatus needed for group-agency' (Hollis 1998: 138).

Note that he is careful not to explicitly endorse this implication, but he mentions some philosophical accounts of group agency as being defensible *if necessary*. However, we are told nothing of the actual analysis. One aim of the following sections is therefore to examine some of the details. I start with the question of whether CR commits one to the notion of a group mind, then examine the accounts Hollis mentions of collective intentions, goals and beliefs.

Collective Agency And Methodological Individualism

Methodological Individualism in social science is usually understood as a prescriptive thesis about explanation. A classic statement is that of Hayek: 'there is no other way toward an understanding of social phenomena but through our understanding of individual actions directed toward other people and guided by their expected behaviour' (1949: 6). Yet it involves ontological commitments; it is clearly inconsistent with the existence of a 'group mind', for example, controlling the movements of its members. Methodological individualists sometimes state an ontological thesis, as with Mill (1843: ch7) 'human beings in society have no properties but those which are derived from and may be resolved into the laws of the individual man', and one can find examples of the connection made explicitly – as in Diesing (1971), who describes methodological individualism as 'the doctrine that only individuals are real, societies and groups are not, and therefore all explanation must be based ultimately on statements or laws about individual behaviour'.

Whatever the merits of such general theses, the specific stricture that only individuals have minds seems correct. This may be because, (i) after accounting for the individuals who are thinking and acting in unison in any purported case of collective action, there is nothing left over to think or act (Searle 1990: p.402), or (ii) a group does not have a full-blown mental life (there is 'nothing it is like' to be a group, as opposed to being *in* one),[16] or (iii) unlike individuals' brains, in the case of the group there is no unified material substance of a kind capable of supporting these phenomena.

A way round this problem as Searle (1990)[17] and Gilbert (1989) argue, is to accept that group agency is entirely constituted by individuals' agency (denying the existence of any group mind) but not by the agency of individuals acting *as individuals*. An analogy may help here. Consider the notes making up a piece of music. After considering each individual note or chord there is 'nothing else left over' to constitute the music, but the (individual) notes and chords in series have different properties than they do in isolation: this short G natural in a Bach fugue has a bright, sprightly character. A G natural of the same length sounded alone has no comparable characteristics. Similarly, the acts of individuals acting in groups may have a different character from those of individuals acting as individuals. The analogy is strained because we shall want to claim that it is possible for individuals to have the mental states involved in collective agency in isolation, whereas the notes can only have their musical properties in combination: what is special about group agency is the character of the mental states of those engaged in it, and the character of a mental state is not affected by the matter of whether or not another person also has that state. For further discussion see the section on collective intentions below.

In the absence of a group mind, group agency will consist in the fact that individuals exhibit a different form of agency (they think and act in different ways) when acting in a group than when acting alone. It is a reasonable demand, though, that it be *shown* that no reference to a group mind is involved, and for this we need to turn to the details of the analyses.

Collective Intentions-in-Action à la Searle (1990)

Hollis refers to Gilbert (1989) and Searle (1990, 1995) with approval (Hollis 1998: 138, n.7). Their accounts of collective agency are anti-reductionist in the sense outlined above. On other views such as that of Tuomela (1984), Tuomela and Miller (1988) or Bratman (1992), there is no collective action that is not reducible to that involved in singular agency. These accounts leave unclear how co-ordination problems could be resolved. Tuomela's analysis in particular involves a description (albeit a very precisely drawn one) of what goes on in cases involving successful co-ordination, in which the individuals see themselves as providing the finishing touch to a collective act, apparently without awareness that this raises a game theoretic puzzle.[18] (Similarly, French gives an account of collective *responsibility* which at a crucial point explicitly *assumes* people can co-ordinate (French 1984: ch.5)). The non-reductionist view also gives rise to a problem, however, to which we now turn.

The problem concerns the intentions-in-action of participants in collective acts. For (1) the acts in which we are interested require the action of more than one person. Therefore, one might argue, (2) it makes no sense to say of any individual that their intention-in-action has the collective action as its propositional content. No individual intends to play Strasvinsky's *Rite of Spring*, for example, except on a hi-fi system, because of an uncontroversial constraint: one cannot attempt to perform the bodily actions of others. Therefore there is no possible location for any collective intention; the intentions that actually move people have a different content from any putative collective intention. Therefore there is no collective intentionality and no qualitatively distinct collective action. If there are no acting groups, it is unclear why any individual should act on a reason valid for a group.

Searle (1990), though not writing from a game theoretic perspective, starts from an intuition that there *is* collective action in a strong sense, and tries to show how this can be accommodated within a general theory of intentionality, proposed in Searle (1983), in a way which resolves this matter. For Searle, human actions have privileged descriptions governed by intentions. This is said to be a matter of the particular intentions-in-action held by the agent. Such intentions are *propositional* and *self-referential* – the intention is characterised by a proposition, and succeeds if the action depicted by the proposition is caused by the intention itself. So, in walking down a corridor, if I am successfully acting, I might have the intention (in Searle's notation):

> i.a. (this i.a. causes: I walk down the corridor) CAUSES: I WALK DOWN THE CORRIDOR.

The lower case characters depict mental states of the agent, the upper case ones depict physical events. This notation can be rendered as the standard English sentence: there is an intention in action which has as its content that the intention itself causes it to be the case that I walk down the corridor, and the intention actually does cause it to be the case that I walk down the corridor.

Searle maintains that in collective action, the reference to a group in the members' intentionality must 'lie outside the brackets specifying the propositional content of the intention'; one might have the intention-in-action expressed loosely by 'going for a walk' in two modes, a solo mode and a together-with-another mode. This is in line with the requirement of a distinctively collective form of action. However, he apparently violates the uncontroversial constraint above by arguing that in collective action, the individuals attempt something collective by means of something individual. For if that constraint is correct, the individual cannot attempt 'something collective' at all, unless perhaps suffering from some kind of delusion. But that this is indeed how Searle should be interpreted should be clear from the following passage, comparing the intentionality involved in a single person's firing a gun and two people's mixing Hollandaise sauce (one stirring, the other pouring ingredients).

> '[in the case of my firing a gun] I have an achieve-B-by-means-of-A sort of intention whose content is that that-the-trigger-pulls-as-A causes it to be the case that -the-gun-fires-as-B. And we can represent this as follows:
>
> > i.a. B by means of A (this i.a. causes: A trigger pulls, causes: B gun fires).

Similarly in the case of collective action, there is only one (complex) i.a. and it isn't just any old type of i.a.; it's an achieve-collective-B-by-means-of-singular-A type of i.a. ... :

> i.a. collective B by means of singular A (this i.a. causes: A stirred, causes: B mixed).' (Searle 1990: 412)[19]

However, it seems to me that there must be *something* right about Searle's account. For there are many examples of actions performed by many persons in which the contributions made by individuals are guided by an objective, but which cannot be understood in terms of singular agency to achieve that objective. Consider again the voting case. Voting is often debated as if it is an instrumental act (hence the commonplace 'throwaway vote' argument against voting for a minor party, one which is so small it is certain not to win the election). Taken severally, it is true that votes are effective instruments. However, the flip side of the throwaway vote argument is quite curious; the 'useful' vote would be one for a party which was certain to win, in which case any given individual might as well *not* vote, so far as the victory is concerned. What is right about Searle's formula, if the throwaway vote argument indicates how people actually conceive of voting, is that the individual targets the end-to-be-achieved-with-others (here, electoral victory) through their own act; the former is guided by the latter, but not in the manner of a finishing touch to the collective act. Another simple example is joining in to push a bus up a hill; one does not necessarily think that the goal will not be achieved but for one's own contribution. In both a finishing touch *and* Searle's proposed collective act, though, individuals see their own action as decisive.

I propose that what an individual *can* attempt is his part in a collective act, *done as a part*. This satisfies the constraint that individuals can only attempt their own acts, because the object of the attempt (what it is that is attempted) involves no bodily movement or thinking other than that of the agent himself; it is the manner of the attempt which differs, 'as' meaning here 'in the manner of'. This is not attempting 'something collective' but attempting something, collective-*ly*, as a participant in some group or group action (so it does involve beliefs that others are doing their parts as parts, which will need grounding). Regan (1980) attempts to clarify participation using the example of singing in a chorus:

A Chorus can make a fairly decent sound, and even sing moderately expressively, if the individual singers are adequate, if each individual knows his part, and if each hews to his part to the best of his ability, more or less ignoring everyone else. But ... if the chorus is really to work as a chorus, it is necessary for each individual to listen to all the others, to tune with them, to breathe with them, to swell and diminish with them and so on.... Everybody just has to listen to everybody else and feel themselves part of a community. (Regan 1980, p209).

The passage just quoted is suggestive but hardly amounts to an analysis. The responsiveness invoked here seems mysterious because, on the one hand, co-ordination problems demand that we do not analyse this in terms of conditional behaviours and on the other, one cannot simply say it involves *singing together* because an individual cannot do something 'together'. Concerning the details of the analysis of collective intentionality, then, the crucial issue is how to clarify the notion of doing one's part *qua* part. Sugden (1993) suggests that it means doing it as one's *role in a plan*, designed to bring about the right consequences, rather than doing it aiming at consequences of the act itself.[20] It also involves a belief that others are likewise performing their parts (*qua* parts). The question of the basis for this belief is discussed below.

Group Beliefs and Goals à la Gilbert (1989)

Hollis cites Gilbert's (1989) account of collective beliefs and goals, in which the collective mentality can override that of the individuals. Gilbert introduces this via examples of everyday interpersonal interaction. For instance, in conversation two people might agree that 'Xavier Yawls is a louse'. If one of them then beams and sighs 'Dear Xavier!', her behaviour, according to Gilbert, is irrational because in agreeing that Xavier was a louse a social group of sorts was set up in which each had committed themselves to defending the agreed view. Having parted company, though, each may express whatever view they wish, with impunity, regarding Xavier's character.

According to Gilbert there is a collective belief if and only if a set of persons (not necessarily identifiable independently as a social group) 'openly* manifest joint quasi-acceptance' of that belief. The 'quasi' here is attributable to the fact that one cannot individually do something 'joint', the 'openly*' is a common knowledge condition: each must know that the other knows that they know (and so on ad infinitum) that the belief has been jointly accepted. In brief, the persons must show willing to accept the belief, in conditions under which this expression will be common knowledge. Similarly a group may be said to have a goal if all 'openly* manifest joint quasi-readiness' to further that goal. In this account once the commitments have been made, each incurs a set of rights and responsibilities to the other group members to play their part in actions rational in the light of what has been jointly accepted / volunteered. This done, they together are the subject of that goal or belief; the individuals become members of a 'plural subject', set up to behave collectively.

This account of group belief seems questionable on the grounds that the set of people may jointly commit themselves to a belief that *no* group member has individually. Then on Gilbert's account there would be a group belief which is believed by nobody in the group! This sits uneasily with the fact that beliefs aim at truth; if an individual has a 'we-belief' that is inconsistent with a personal belief, they can deduce that at least one of the two is false. However, whether there are or not such cases is an empirical matter; it would be wrong to rule them out 'from the armchair'.[21] Perhaps we can defuse this problem in any case by distinguishing between belief proper and what a set of people jointly commit to for various purposes,[22] which we might simply call a 'group acceptance'. The case of collective goals which are at odds with private ones seems less unnatural, as there are goals which may not even make sense for individuals – winning the UEFA cup, for example, is essentially a football team's objective. Moreover, conflicting goals are, arguably, an unfortunate fact of life rather than a problem which logically compels a revision.

More pertinent to co-ordination problems, though, is the fact that Gilbert's concept is based on *association* prior to the behaviour which manifests plural subject agency; there is an *explicit* pooling of wills. Nothing in our original description of Hi-Lo, however, relied on 1 and 2 acknowledging to each other either the payoff structure of the game or a joint objective. To insist on such a process is to undermine the motivational force of team reasoning; the Hi-Lo game provides a powerful intuition that co-operation can occur *spontaneously*. The extant formal economic versions of team reasoning, Bacharach (1999) and Sugden (1995), are both theories of collectively rational co-ordination which depict independent team reasoning on the part of individual team members. Whilst we might accept, then, that her conception provides clear cases of group beliefs and goals, thus demonstrating their possibility, the advocate of team thinking as a solution to co-ordination problems should not assent to its being a definitive conceptual analysis.[23] The point needing to be addressed is the relationship between matters of common knowledge and coincident interests, on the one hand, and group beliefs and goals on the other.

Team Membership

Recall that acting according to CR meant accepting we-reasons; 'we should play a' is to produce act a from each, and this is derivative from the fact that (a, a) is the best set of strategies for the team. Why is this not simply fallacious reasoning of the type 'it would be best if I run at the door and Bill opens it. Therefore I ought to start running at the door'? It seems the answer must lie in the proposition that there really is supra-personal agency; if Bill and I really are members of a team, and it is common knowledge that this is the best team plan, and so on, *then* I ought to start running at the door. Moreover, people cannot be genuinely 'members of the same team', as Sugden notes (1993: 87), unless they have common knowledge of this fact.

We *can* now get over Hi-Lo like this:

(1)   It is common knowledge between 1 and 2 that they are a team, and therefore that they both think as team members: there is common knowledge of collective rationality (CKCR).

(2)   Thinking as a team member involves being prepared to do one's part without having to anticipate consequences of one's individual act.

(3)   Because (a, a) is clearly best for the team, both players deduce that a is their part and therefore play a.

In this process, collective reasoning produces an effective collective intention in action, and the expectation that the other player is performing their part will be a by-product of individuals' (collective) intentions rather than their foundation. Hence the rationale for playing a is conditional on *membership*, not on an expectation about the other's strategy choice. (1) and (2) together imply that the possibility that either expects the other not to do their part cannot arise. Sugden (1993: 87) concludes that it is not the case that CR implies that members ought to do their parts even if they expect others not to do theirs. However, we should now raise the awkward questions of how common knowledge of team membership first is formed and second, can persist over time.

One way knowledge of team membership can come into being is through an agreement (explicit or tacit), as in a marriage. Given a plan of action which is in some sense agreed on one can also, it seems tempting to add, posit the existence of less formal associational obligations (à la Gilbert) to explain the persistence of groups over time, for agreements can create such obligations. Both Gilbert (1989: ch.7) and Hollis (1998, ch.8) liken the concept of a plural subject to that of Rousseau's 'Pool of Wills' notion; once one has volunteered one's will, one cannot unilaterally withdraw it without violating other members' rights. Those who act on this obligation do so on a backward looking reason, not one based on the consequences of the act, so it seems we could explain a group's persistence over time by members' acting on their obligations. These obligations are *not* 'ought' statements of the form 'A ought to θ to retain benefits of membership in group G' (which would bring us back to individuals calculating the consequences of their own acts based on expectations of others' behaviour).

It seems, though, that any *reasons* for joining or remaining in a group must either be reasons addressed to the individual as group member or the individual as individual. This raises an acute problem, considered below. Also, we face again the problem of the spontaneity of co-operation in Hi-Lo raised in the previous section. For if we insist that prior interaction underlies rational co-ordination, as in the case of a process of agreement, we licence individualistic reasoning and therefore *b*-playing amongst the unacquainted.

A Problem for Collective Reasoning Within Reason

There is a problem of perspective when we ask how it is that teams are formed. For, if there are reasons for belonging to teams, to whom are these reasons addressed? In giving a reason one would have to appeal to a perspective that is neither that of the person as individual nor that of the person as group member. For the question 'should I ask myself "what am I to do" or "what are we to do?"?' presupposes a first person singular point of view; reasons appear to *presuppose* an agent and therefore a unit of agency. If there is no such neutral point of view, it would appear to be problematic explaining how people in fact move between these two modes, especially if we wish to give a *reason*. If such movement cannot be rational, neither, it seems, could *remaining in* one mode or the other.

Hollis does not raise the problem in this form, but it underlies his discussion of exploitation of team reasoners by individualists (1998: 140–41). One would expect Hollis to look for a solution 'within reason', given that team reasoning *is* 'trust in miniature', and that the work is entitled *Trust Within Reason*. Earlier in TWR, when exploring a contrast between socialised actors and the agents of RCT, the reader is told that '[reason] needs to discriminate with a steady hand if reasonable persons are to differ from rational individuals without acquiring a wholly local identity and source of reasons for action' (1998: 128). In like vein the discussion of team reasoning concludes with an injunction to search for 'social relations that reason can endorse'. Yet the question of explicit arguments to choose between units of agency is not taken up.

It is probable, though, that no such argument can be given. Susan Hurley seems to be searching for one when she writes 'an adequate theory of rational choice should address the question of what the unit of agency among those possible should be' (Hurley 1989: 145). However, in her own account she does not indicate what standpoint can be used to answer this question. At one point, Regan's (1980) decision procedure for co-operative utilitarians is invoked; as she puts it 'collective action does not calculate consequences from a fixed unit of agency; rather it involves first identifying those willing to act collectively and then together doing what is best given what the non-co-operators do (or are likely to do)' (Hurley 1989: 146). However, I think that a distinction between the unit of agency and the number of co-operators is being obscured here. For at no point do Regan's co-operative utilitarians ask themselves 'should *I* be a co-operator?' or 'should *we* be co-operators?', though they may behave *as if* they are not co-operators in the Hi-Lo game if they ascertain that they are the only co-operator of the two. His theory is addressed to the 'Community of cooperators', each 'identifies his fellow cooperators' and proceeds from there, without questioning their own status (Regan 1980, ch.12).

Hurley makes two further suggestions. First, 'whatever makes an individual as opposed to some collectivity the wrong unit of agency in particular cases is whatever makes cooperation with the members of some group beneficial with respect to whatever shared or separate goals are specified, in the circumstances at hand...' (Hurley 1989: 147). This simply gives the group perspective priority over the individual. The other suggestion is that the correct unit of agency 'will vary according to one's substantive goals and ethical views' (Hurley 1989: 147). With regard to the last suggestion, though, we also need to ask: 'why the *person's* goals and views and not the group's?' The problem here is that an overarching perspective will either be equated with the individual or collective one, or constitute a third layer of agency to mediate between them. For this to operate, it too will need to assess the options using *its* beliefs and goals. Adding another layer of agency makes it no clearer how mediation between layers could occur.

We can summarise where the discussion has brought us with reference to Sartre's discussion of the plural subject (1943: pt 3, ch.3, III). Scepticism is expressed there about the reality of the 'we', apparently on the grounds that one can make mistakes about whether or not one is in a plural subject, in normal consciousness.[24] Sartre is working from a Cartesian perspective, in which consciousness is held to involve a revelation of the self to itself. Searle (1990) also notes this tension, but seems inclined to reject the Cartesianism. Such scepticism is not a source of concern in itself, since we have already accepted that there is not a real fusion of consciousnesses (no group mind) in collective agency. It is also clear that the possibility of mistake implies the possibility of not being mistaken as well; this appears to be Sartre's position, since he accepts that the 'we-subject' is real at the level of a psychological experience. However, the fact that we may be mistaken in our experience of plural subject membership raises the question of how we can know if we constitute such a group agent or not. A Gilbertian answer would presumably refer us to obligations based on past interaction, but this is at odds with cases of spontaneous co-operation. Hurley thinks that rationality should tell us, but this seems to be an impossible demand.

Hollis thinks that an assumption of CKCR is problematic, given that individuals may use two modes of reasoning, but remarks that CKR was a 'curious abstraction' in any case, since real people are 'necessarily somewhat opaque to each other' (1998: 141). This would appear to be correct, given the above, but for someone looking for an explanation of why *b*-playing is *ir*rational in Hi-Lo, it is irrelevant; that real agents do not have CKR does not say anything about the ideal case. CKR captures a situation in which instrumentally rational agents are prefectly informed; it would be odd if *b*-playing were irrational only given a degree of ignorance, such as, for example, a false belief that only team reasoning is possible. If we start by assuming CKR, we can reason to indeterminist conclusions; if we start by assuming CKCR, we can reason to the unconditional advice to play *a*. Without a reason to assume CKCR, the task is incomplete.

Hollis' overall position regarding the determination of the unit of agency is set out rather opaquely across chs 7–8 of TWR, but appears at least to involve the following elements. On the one hand there are 'team games' involving perfectly coincident interests, such as co-ordination games, where the lack of scope for opportunism gives rise to co-operation. There are also games where there is a conflict between individual and team rationality, such as the PDG and centipede. Here it is rational to trust, that is, to play as a team member, given a suitable social tie between the participants. This can be a very local tie, as in bonds between neighbours, or a more general, looser tie, as in the inter-relatedness of members of a (passably functional) political community. The latter account for co-operation between 'relative strangers' as in the example of blood donation in the United Kingdom. Such bonds provide reasons which are 'normative features of a situation which [the agents] have partly inherited, partly created' (1998: 141). Trust between socially bonded individuals is rational partly because agents can and do believe it to be so, whereas the counterintuitive conclusions of RCT imply that it 'breaches the limits of what can be consistently believed' (1998: 159).[25]

The unresolved matter of the apparent spontaneity of co-ordination leaves a question mark over the analysis, since it suggests an important factor in rational co-operation may have been overlooked. Without some prior, spontaneous co-operation there is a danger of circularity in the above analysis of counterfinality problems, for co-operation is necessary for there to be such things as good neighbours and workable political communities. It may be that 'simple co-ordination is a team game, free of temptation to exploit the team' (1998: 140), but unless the individuals already have a sense of team membership it is not clear how they could know which action to play, even if they both wish to further the good of the team.

Conclusion

Hollis' treatment of collective reasoning is distinctive in two respects. First, he sees the relevance of notions arising in economics for philosophy and vice versa, and so explicitly (if guardedly) invokes conceptual analysis of collective agency in support of collective reasoning. Second, he reads very great significance into the concept, since it is held to provide the secret of rational trust quite generally. The accounts of we-intentions, beliefs and goals Hollis cites in support of the notion of collective reasoning are not unproblematic, but are at least consistent with the reasonable demand that they do not involve a reference to a group mind. Some other binding force appears to be necessary in its place, though, to generate assurances that team spirit is not one-sided.

I argue that since two modes of rationality are admitted, team and individual, rationality alone cannot provide it. Perhaps the remark about reasons deriving from social relations being 'normative features of a situation' is intended to offer a way out, since if some relations imply that one is involved in a plural subject, perfectly informed agents would know this. Yet if such relations always arise through prior interaction, as Hollis implies, the example of the Hi-Lo game is double-edged, for it shows both the need for the notion of team reasoning and that it can occur spontaneously. This points to a serious omission in the analysis, raising the possibility that the key to trust has been missed. I would not like to claim that my interpretation of TWR is definitive, however. There are hints in ch.8 of TWR that the 'we' perspective is in some way primary, which could account for this spontaneity, but it is easier to glean this impression from the text than it is to find an argument which would establish this priority.

Whilst this discussion takes issue with Hollis' analysis, I would like to end on a more positive note. The notion of collective reasoning represents progress; we need a sense in which b-playing in Hi-Lo is irrational. Also, without it, it is difficult to see why the prisoners' dilemma game has been thought by intelligent people to pose a puzzle.[26] For if rationality consists in individual utility maximisation there is no dilemma at all; each player has *one* lemma to solve, which because of the symmetry of the game is exactly the same as the other player's. Moreover, because each has a dominant strategy, it is an extremely easy lemma to solve. Collective reasoning may indeed, then, have a wide ranging significance. The more positive conclusion is that the problems identified surrounding the notion of collective reasons need, but also deserve, further attention.

NOTES

1. For an accessible modern introduction to game theory see Hargreaves Heap et al. (1992).
2. Henceforth I use the term RCT to refer both to the individual instrumental account of rationality in economics, worked out for non-interactive settings, and its extension to interactive settings which constitutes game theory.
3. In the original 'prisoner's dilemma' story, two partners in crime are given the opportunity to confess. If both decline each receives y years in prison, if both confess each will be sentenced to x years. If only one confesses, the confessor will be inside for w years and the other z. If $w < y < x < z$, then given either choice by the other, confession pays; both confess and both spend longer inside (x years) than under joint silence (y years).
4. See Hollis (1998: 159).
5. Earlier proponents include Regan (1980), Hurley (1989) and Sugden (1993).
6. Such as the 'centipede' game, which exemplifies why trust between rational agents is problematic. See Hollis (1998: 15–18, 55–8).
7. Formally, it is a game for which the matrix of payoffs contains the same payoff for each player in each cell of its leading diagonal, with zero payoffs elsewhere.
8. Something is common knowledge in a population if and only if everyone in the population knows it, knows that everyone knows it, knows that everyone knows that everyone knows it, and so on ad infinitum. See Lewis (1969: 52–6).
9. Or, in economists' language, each player chooses so as to maximise their expected utility taking the actions of the others as given. Utility is a measure, variously defined in economics, of the desirability of outcomes. The expected utility of a strategy is the weighted sum of the utilities of its possible outcomes, where the weights are their associated probabilities.
10. The author has recently completed an experimental study of co-ordination which included Hi-Lo games. 96 per cent of subjects chose 'High'. The results over a range of co-ordination games were consistent with collective reasoning. Details are available on request.
11. I would add that there cannot be an 'odd man out' from a set of only two equilibria, as in Hi-Lo.
12. I define Act Consequentialism analogously to Act Utilitarianism, the only difference being that no specific content is given to the goal; a theory of rational behaviour is Act Consequentialist if and only if it says that an agent's act is rational if (and only if) the agent produces by this act at least as good consequences (relative to the agent's goals) as any other act available in the circumstances.
13. See Aquinas (1980: section 17.3) on inducement.
14. For a discussion of the possibility of irrational 'desires' see Parfit (1984: 120–26). Parfit accepts that a desire is a necessary condition for the existence of a reason for action. Since projects motivating action may be dispositional, rather than occurrent with the action, a statement in terms of goals seems preferable.
15. By intention-in-action I mean what it is the individual is *aiming at* through his action (Searle's conception (1983, 1990)). This need not be a goal understood as an ulterior motive for which the act is undertaken (as when one gives someone a gift in order to make them happy); it can just be the *intrinsic* aim of an act which (partly) explains why this movement of my arm, say, is waving goodbye, rather than exercising my arm muscles.
16. Though if Parfit (1984) is right, everyone is a group – that is, their consciousness is composed of two streams which can be separated by severing certain links between the brain's hemispheres. In this case though, there is a substance underwriting this

'group mind' – the (composite) brain – which is not the case for groups of people. More precisely, then, there is nothing it is like to be a group of people, ordinarily understood.

17. Hollis refers to Searle (1995) but the analysis, which Searle himself refers to, is given in Searle (1990).
18. Tuomela (1995) is recommended by Hollis, which moves closer to Gilbert (1989).
19. The terms outside the brackets specify the kind of intentional state involved, those inside the content. 'i.a.' means 'intention in action', ':' translates as 'it to be the case that', and the comma means 'which'.
20. In my PhD thesis submitted to the University of East Anglia I attempt to incorporate this notion into an improved version of Searle's (1990) analysis.
21. Firms' environmental claims and policies may provide real examples of companies' beliefs which are not believed by any individual manager. I owe this suggestion to Alan Malachowski.
22. I take this suggestion from a review of Gilbert's On Social Facts by Fellows (1991).
23. Swindler (1996) also criticises Gilbert's account for being too narrow; it excludes social structure and vicarious agency.
24. 'The "we" is experienced by a particular consciousness; it is not necessary that all the patrons at the café should be conscious of being "we" in order for me to experience myself as being engaged in a "we" with them. Everyone is familiar with this pattern of every-day dialogue: "We are very dissatisfied." "But no, my dear, speak for yourself."' (Sartre 1943: 414).
25. It is a distinctive feature of Hollis' philosophy that he accepts a certain dualism between natural and social science, premised on the proposition that the truth about the social world is in part dependent on agents' beliefs about it. See Hollis (1998: 156-–7). See also Searle (1995) for an elaboration on this theme.
26. See Binmore (1992: 310) for the view that this does not, indeed, set a puzzle.

REFERENCES

Aquinas, T. 1980. 'Debated questions on truth'. Potts 1980.
Bacharach, M. 1999. 'Interactive team reasoning: a contribution to the theory of cooperation'. Research in Economics, 53, 117–47.
Benn, S., ed. 1978. Political Participation. Canberra: Australian National University Press.
Binmore, K.G. 1992. Fun and Games. Lexington, MA: D.C. Heath.
Bratman, M. 1992. 'Shared cooperative activity'. Philosophical Review, 101/2, 327–42.
Cohen, P.R., et al. 1990. Intentions in Communication. Cambridge, MA: Massachusetts Institute of Technology Press.
Diesing, P. 1971. Patterns of Discovery in the Social Sciences. Chicago: Aldine.
Fellows, R. 1991. Review of Gilbert 1989. Philosophical Quarterly, 41, 100–104.
French, P.A. 1984. Collective and Corporate Responsibility. Columbia University Press.
Gilbert, M. 1989. On Social Facts. London: Routledge.
Hargreaves Heap, S. et al. 1992. The Theory of Choice. Oxford: Basil Blackwell.
Hayek, F.A. 1949. Individualism and Economic Order. London: Routledge £ Kegan Paul.
Hobbes, T. 1651. Leviathan. Ed. R. Tuck.. Cambridge University Press.
Hollis, M. 1977. Models of Man: Philosophical Thoughts on Social Action. Cambridge: Cambridge University Press.
    1998. Trust Within Reason. Cambridge: Cambridge University Press.
Hurley, S. 1989. Natural Reasons. Oxford University Press.
Lewis, D.K. 1969. Convention: A Philosophical Study. Cambridge, MA: Harvard University Press.

Mill, J.S. 1843. *A System of Logic*. London: J.W. Parker.
Parfit, D. 1984. *Reasons and Persons*. Oxford: Clarendon.
Potts, T.C. 1980. *Conscience in Medieval Philosophy*. Cambridge: Cambridge University Press.
Regan, D. 1980. *Utilitarianism and Cooperation*. Oxford: Oxford University Press.
Sartre, J.P. 1943. *Being and Nothingness*. Trans. H. Barnes. London: Methuen. 1976.
Schelling, T.C. 1963. *The Strategy of Conflict*. London: Oxford University Press.
Searle, J.R. 1983. *Intentionality*. Cambridge: Cambridge University Press.
  1990. 'Collective intentions and actions'. Cohen et al. 1990: 401–15.
  1995. *The Construction of Social Reality*. Harmondsworth: The Penguin Press.
Sen, A. 1977. 'Rational fools: a critique of the behavioural assumptions of economic theory'. *Philosophy and Public Affairs*, 6, 314–44.
Sugden, R. 1993. 'Thinking as a team: towards an explanation of non-selfish behaviour'. *Social Philosophy and Policy*, 10, 69–89.
  1995. 'A theory of focal points'. *Economic Journal*, 105, 533–50.
Swindler, J.K. 1996. Social intentions, aggregate, collective and general'. *Philosophy of the Social Sciences*, 26, 61–76.
Tuomela, R. 1984. *A Theory of Social Action*. Dordrecht: Reidel.
  1995. *The Importance of Us*. Stanford, CA: Stanford University Press.
Tuomela, R. & K. Miller. 1988. 'We-intentions'. *Philosophical Studies*, 53, 367–89.

10

A Quick Peek into the Abyss:
The Game of Social Life in
Martin Hollis's *Trust Within Reason*

ALAN SCOTT

Homo economicus attracted and *homo sociologicus* repelled the rationalist in Martin Hollis. The former knows what he/she wants and acts to get it. The latter is really only clear about what the community desires and is over-scrupulous whenever sensibilities may be offended. From the former we can at least expect a decisive and reasonably predictable course of action, while the latter dithers unless unambiguously directed by the *conscious collective*, and, where thus directed, loses our respect as an autonomous agent. All the more disturbing then that the heroic individualism of *homo economicus* should produce such paradoxical results; that those actions should so systematically misfire as soon as the priorities of others interfere. Just as his rationalism attracted Martin Hollis to the figure of the rational self-regarding subject, so too it lead him to a sober recognition of the limitations of the methodological individualism and rational actor models in which *homo economicus* finds a natural home. He would have preferred these problems to have been resolved within the kind of rational framework that a game-theoretical or rational choice approach promises, and much of *Trust Within Reason* is taken up by the search for and probing of solutions within this frame. But the book is also about people not getting what they want and having, if they are lucky, to settle for second or third best. And Hollis too must at least examine a sub-optimal 'solution', namely that offered by sociology. It is with this solution, and his treatment of it, that I shall be concerned. While accepting his reservations about what Dennis Wrong once dubbed the 'over-socialized' model (Wrong 1961), I want to question Hollis's equation of sociological accounts of agency with the holier-than-thou figure of *homo sociologicus*. Before that, it is necessary to say something about what drove Martin Hollis to consider the social model in the first place and about his principle objections to it.

The reasons for Hollis's dissatisfaction with both contracterian/ utiliterian and Kantian/universal attempts to move Adam and Eve along the Enlightenment Trail are so elegantly expressed in *Trust Within Reason* (and will be discussed elsewhere in this volume) that only the briefest scene setting is necessary. The contracterian approach, even when enriched with sentiment or a degree of impartiality, fails to propel Adam and Eve much beyond The Rational Choice, while the latter, Kantian, approach appears to solve the problem too quickly. In a sense the journey is never made since the Kantians already sup at The Triumph of Reason, rendering trust redundant. Furthermore, the Kantian solution is insensitive to the 'conditional' and 'strategic' element in trust (Hollis 1998: 100). However, while contracterians and Kantians disagree about the nature of autonomy, both camps are individualistic. Given that Kantianism, the most philosophically respectable alternative to contracterianism, is not fully to his taste, Hollis is (I think slightly reluctantly) forced to try something else: the idea that people are 'social before they are individual, and plural before they are singular' (1998: 106). So Chapter Six, in particular, appears to break with what has gone before.

Hollis's aversion to what that alternative, non-individualistic, approach has to offer soon becomes evident. It does so in the form of an analogy, the football game. This analogy allows him to try out three versions of the social story: norms as the basis of action, the dramaturgical metaphor and the rule-governed account of action. These too are to be found wanting, though the last of them will at least be incorporated into the final story. Among the football teams neither the 'Marketeers' (contracterians) nor the 'Köningsberg Universals' add anything to the foregoing arguments. The Marketeers' position at the foot of the league is due to the now familiar failure of self-regarding action to resolve co-ordination problems, while the still modest success of the Köningsberg Universals is ascribed to their inflexibility; to their attempt to apply universal rules to unique and (fast) changing conditions. Only the 'Musketeers' add a new dimension. The complete identification of each with each and each with all (the team) produces footballing success, but also intellectual puzzlement. How do they choose their preferences in the first place? How do they come to be loyal to this rather than that team? Are the truly, deeply, blindly loyal indeed animals capable of promising? After all, their loyalty to each other is bought at a cost: disregard for the outsider towards whom they presumably have little obligation, and certainly not that of keeping their promises.

The dramaturgical metaphor and games where formal regulation 'shades into custom and habit' (1998: 111) and where 'the fertile Wittgensteinian analogy between games and social practices ... makes us think of people as participants by posing deep questions about the players who follow the rules' (1998: 113) fair little better, each failing to address Hollis's key reservations about non-individualistic approaches. Here we find ourselves in the world of the 'quasi moral' where 'the morality of action, like its meaning, is internal to context' (1998: 115). Whatever insights this may bring, it is said to make us uneasy. In the dramaturgical metaphor, is it the script or the interpretation which matters? Is there sufficient leeway for us to speak of a self behind the roles, or is the role everything? If the latter, we are back to the Musketeers who are so trapped in their local loyalties that the sense of self is lost, subordinated to the social group. In such a case the quasi-moral becomes too quasi for Hollis's taste and we are in danger of acquiring a moral duty to kill merely by joining the Mafia:

> The bonds of clan, race, creed, class and gender often bind insiders in ways which are morally neither neutral nor, from an Enlightenment point of view, laudable. They often depend on a sense of belonging upheld by contempt for outsiders, who are treated as inferior or even as less than fully human. (1998: 117)

These are the 'dark forces, which flourish only in the shadows where the light of reason does not reach' (1998: 117). The liberal plea – 'Not too much *Gemeinschaft*!' – that I suspect prompts Hollis's observation here is perfectly understandable in light of what has been proposed and what has been done in the name of 'community', but Hollis also tells us not to give up on the notion of rationality as rule following just yet because neither the instrumental nor the moral point of view has furnished us with an adequate way of distinguishing the rational from the irrational and because 'to understand what people are doing is, at least a first step, to reconstruct their reasons for doing it' (1998: 118).

If we can accept the Wittgensteinian dictum 'what has to be accepted, the given, is, so to say, forms of life' (1953: II, 226) yet another option opens up and the problem of trust once again appears to have been resolved: 'the players of most or even all games of social life can be counted on to follow the rules, since their actions are always essentially rule-governed ... [I]t becomes rational to trust anyone following a rule which makes them reliable' (1998: 119). But this conclusion too we are told is muddled and contains an illegitimate blocking move. If we ask whether it is right or rational for a member of the Mafia to honour his contract to kill we need not be satisfied with an answer cast exclusively in terms of local Mafia rules since it is precisely the rightness and rationality of those rules that trouble us: 'yet to dissolve some kinds of question is not to dispose of all and we can still ask whether rules are finally their own warrant or can fail an enduring test of their rationality' (1998: 120). To follow a rule is not necessarily to subscribe to it we are told (1998: 121) and not all empirical grounds for trust are acceptable to the Enlightenment thinker for whom the task remains to search for a spot and a means to 'dig in to prevent making a genuine virtue of whatever is deemed a virtue somewhere or other' (1998: 122); in other words, to find an account which 'suits trust-within-reason' (1998: 123).

It has now become clear why Hollis believes the rule-governed account (like all other social stories) merely holds a flickering candle (1998: 115) up to the problem of trust: 'the original question was not why people do trust one another but whether and why it is rational for them to do so' (1998: 123–4). Rule following does not relieve the rational self from responsibility for its actions nor guarantee that empirical grounds for trust are rational grounds. 'I was only following a rule' is no better than 'I was only obeying orders' as grounds for the abnegation of personal responsibility. Like all social, non-individualistic accounts, rule following fails the test Reason sets. Even where some insights may be usefully incorporated into the final story, the game of social life – whether in a normative, dramaturgical or gaming guise – largely turns out to be a distraction. Lacking both 'arrogance about questions' and 'proper humility about answers' (Hollis 1998: 163), it fails to do the hard work that Reason demands. Hollis accordingly reverts back to the Enlightenment Trail where alternative individualistic options are played out against each other. But perhaps he should have pursued the social option just a little further.

Discussion

In the UEA reading group in which *Trust Within Reason* was discussed after Martin Hollis's death, Rüdiger Bittner observed that Hollis tended to criticise Kant for being too universalist where he was talking about the universal and too particularist where he was talking about the particular. This tendency is indicative too of his approach towards human agency. It is difficult to see what could satisfy someone for whom each solution is either too universalist or too particularistic, and yet whose rationalism is such that he will always push an argument to either its most universalistic or most particularistic conclusion. One specific expression of this tendency is his habit, manifested in the discussion summarized above, of pushing the sociological account of action to its logical (but absurd) conclusion.

The Marketeers and the Köningsberg Universals are, of course, theories as well as fantasy football teams. But what kind of theory is represented by the Musketeers? The obvious candidate is Durkheimian sociology. Actors are norm- rather than interest-driven and social not only before, but also during and after they are individual. 'Every consciousness beats as one' wrote Durkheim (1984 [1893]: 106). Even remembering that he is referring here to a pre-modern (mechanical) form of consciousness, the thought that the individual could be so absorbed into the *conscience collective* seems outrageous. Exactly the same outrage appears again and again in sociological thought (broadly understood). In the Althusserian Marxism of the 1970s, for example, the agent is a mere 'bearer' (*Träger*) of the social structures into which he/she is 'interpolated'; prompting a joke attributed to Zygmunt Bauman: 'the problem with the new Marxism is that it is just the old functionalism'. In contrast, Hollis wants, at most, to defend a view of the social in which the individual is 'embedded but not lost in the games of social life' (1998: 121). I do not wish to call into question Hollis's concerns about the recidivist tendencies of sociology to fall back on radically holistic models of the social in which agency becomes lost, but nor do I want to 'defend' sociology by meekly pointing to counter tendencies (e.g. Weber's, perhaps superficial, commitment to methodological individualism, or Simmel's attempt to wrestle – in a rather Hollisian spirit – with the tensions between individualization and sociation (*Vergesellschaftung*)[1]. Rather, I want to argue that there is a much more differentiated account of agency to be found exactly where one would least expect it, in the Durkheimian heritage itself. While sociologists have frequently been duped by their own tendency towards 'sociologism' into treating the actor as mere 'role player', this tendency is based, I want to suggest, upon a misreading of the sociological model of action which they themselves have inherited.

Even Durkheim, particularly in latter works such as the *Elementary Forms of Religious Life*, did not argue straightforwardly for a *homo sociologicus* model. The whole point of his distinction between the sacred and the profane is precisely to acknowledge that much of the time something like an egotistic account of human actions and motivations is close to the mark. Only when we come together in collective acts (and in our memories of those acts) are we fully social beings (even the Musketeers cannot be playing football all of the time). Here Durkheim offers a dualistic account in which we necessarily vacillate between being Marketeers and Musketeers: 'on ordinary days, the mind is chiefly occupied with utilitarian and individualistic affairs ... When the Australians hunt or fish in scattered small groups, they lose sight of what concerns their clan or tribe' (Durkheim 1995 [1912]: 352). Mary Douglas puts the point well when she notes that Durkheim transferred the conflict between individual and society 'to warring elements within the person' (Douglas 1987: 10). Durkheim might be said to share Hollis's view that 'the Musketeers come closest so far to illuminating the bond of society' (1998: 109), but not in such a way as to imply that the social bond demands that we are always and everywhere Musketeers. As Durkheim remarked, 'society cannot revitalize the awareness of itself unless it assembles, but it cannot remain continuously in session' (1995 [1912]: 353); nor, we might add, can it remain in a state of permanent solidarity demanding unquestioning loyalty. On such a view, which seems to me closer to the spirit of the sociological tradition than does an oversocialized view of action, the one thing that Adam and Eve are not going to be on their pub crawl is consistent. The struggle between self- and other-regarding action is both eternal and internal.

We can make the point with reference to one of Hollis's own favourite examples, giving. Hollis takes Richard Titmuss' s account of blood donation as a paradigmatic case of giving as an expression of the altruism of *homo sociologicus*. The gift, blood, is a donation not only to a particular (unknown) individual, but also, symbolically at least, to the community; it is something approaching true altruism. The individual, as a 'globule of desire' (Veblen), is nowhere to be found in this small selfless

act.[2] However, there is a competing classical account of giving from
within the Durkheimian school which offers a quite different, more
sociologically 'realistic', account of its social function namely, Marcel
Mauss's *The Gift*, first published in 1925. For Mauss, giving has less to
do with altruism than with the assertion of power – ' the gift necessarily
entails the notion of credit' (Mauss: 1990 [1925]: 36) – and with status
competition: 'the unreciprocated gift still makes the person who has
accepted it inferior' (1990 [1925]: 65). Giving is an inherently
dangerous activity which is just as prone to destabilize as to stabilize
social relationships: 'the obligation to give is no less important. ... To
refuse to give, to fail to invite, just as to refuse to accept, is tantamount
to declaring war; it is to reject the bond of alliance and commonality'
(1990 [1925]: 13). A correctly executed act of giving and receiving can
cement the social bond, but equally a bungled act can do more damage
than not giving at all. Thus giving and receiving are as problematic as
they are ubiquitous: 'the potlatch is a phenomenon of social structure:
the gathering together of tribes, clans, and families, even of peoples,
brings about a remarkable state of nerviness and excitement' (1990
[1925]: 38). Nor does the individual, as a self-interested agent, get lost
in Mauss's account. Even in societies lacking our highly differentiated
conception and legal framing of personhood, the honour and interests of
individual actors are just as much at stake as those of the family, clan or
tribe. So here we have, in a key text of Durkheimian sociology, an
account of a seemingly selfless act that attempts to demonstrate that all
is not as it seems; that giving is an act that asserts the superiority of the
giver and demeans the receiver, that generates more obligations than it
fulfils, and in which conflict and the assertion and counter-assertion of
power are omnipresent.

Mauss's broader point is deeply relevant to Hollis's investigations.
Homo sociologicus is not motivated by pure altruism any more than
homo economicus is by pure asocial egotism. Just as potlatch is
interpreted by Mauss as a proto-market, so the market itself remains
residually embedded in social relations no matter how vigorous its
attempts to disembed itself. For Mauss, the market conceived as mere
meeting place for economic interests or as the aggregate of their
interactions is the founding myth of economics, no more:

> Yet the whole of this very rich [modern market] economy is still
> filled with religious elements. Money still possesses its magical

power and is still linked to the clan or to the individual. The various economic activities, for example of the market, are suffused with rituals and myths. They retain a ceremonial character that is obligatory and effective. They are full of rituals and rights. (1990 [1925]: 72)

Mauss's strategy here is to subvert two central categorical distinctions: that between egotism and altruism and that between tradition and modernity. In effect he insists on the unavoidability of elements of egotism in acts of apparent altruism and on elements of *Zweckrationalität* in 'traditional' societies and *Wertrationalität* in 'modernity'.

The sharp distinctions Hollis draws between individualism and social gaming, altruism and egotism, and between the rational and the irrational in action make for good philosophy, but Mauss's refusal of these fixed distinctions, I would argue, makes for good social science. However, most social science is not 'good' in this sense because the majority of us work with the kind of clear-cut categorical distinctions that Hollis is using and thus are faced with the sorts of dilemmas that *Trust Within Reason* so elegantly sets out. We are thus lumbered with distinctions such as those between hierarchies and markets, self- and other-directed actions, interests and norms, etc. which often obscure more than they reveal and are the distant echoes of the more basic distinctions with which Hollis was concerned. Mauss thus represents something of a dissenting, but in my view fruitful, line of sociological investigation the most sophisticated development of which can be found in contemporary economic sociology, and in particular in the work of Mark Granovetter.[3] I shall briefly discuss some of these arguments because they seem to me have a strong affinity with the kind of mixed model of agency towards which *Trust Within Reason* seems to be moving, but can only be reached by softening the distinctions that frame Hollis's account.

Granovetter makes an assertion that poses a direct challenge to the seemingly mutually exclusive options between individual (under-) and social (oversocialized) models of agency. Both options, he argues, share 'a conception of action and decision carried out by atomized actors' (Granovetter 1985: 485):

This ironic merger is already visible in Hobbes's *Leviathan*, in which the unfortunate denizens of the state of nature, overwhelmed by the disorder consequent to their atomizations, cheerfully surrender all their rights to an authoritarian power and subsequently behave in a docile and honorable manner; by the artifice of a social contract, they lurch directly from an undersocialized to an oversocialized state. (1985: 485)

On those occasions on which economists do talk about social influences they, ironically, do so in the same oversocialized fashion as their sociology colleagues, namely they treat social influence as 'an external force that, like the deists' God, sets things in motion and has no further effects' (1985: 486). The central claim here is that rational action (even in the narrow sense of instrumental self interest) presupposes social relations because only these supply actors with the information they require about the behaviour of (at least reputationally known) others and form the basis of trust necessary for us to pursue our own interests in our own ways. Thus, for example, of the kind of n-person prisoner's dilemma represented by stampedes in crowded burning theatres, Granovetter observes, 'in the case of the burning house featured on the 11:00 p.m. news, we never hear that everyone stampeded out and that the family members trampled on one another. In the family, there is no Prisoner's Dilemma because each is confident that the others can be counted on' (1985: 490). This confidence is based upon past experience presupposing social relations. Such trust is both an opportunity for gain *and* malfeasance. Adam and Eve have perhaps a more intimate knowledge of each other than any other two persons imaginable to us. It is this knowledge, and the social relations on which it is based, that can propel Adam and Eve along the Enlightenment Trail but also provides them with opportunities for mutual deceit and betrayal.

For our purposes, the key point is that the social bond is not some altruistic norm-driven alternative to the pursuit of rational individual self-interest: 'social relations, rather than institutional arrangements or generalized morality, are mainly responsible for the production of trust in economic life' (1985: 491). The social bond, on such a sociological account, is not a normative vice which holds us in the grip of altruism, but a mechanism for overcoming the kinds of action coordination problems represented by the prisoner's dilemma, the common good, the coin game, etc. Social relations supply actors with the kinds of informal information that make the actions of others more predictable, and thus enable us to pursue our rational self-interests without having to make impossibly complex calculations about how other agents may act. Social life reduces rather than increases complexity. Via social networks, we receive, for example, information about the reliability of others whom we do not personally know (we all have 'reputations'); we know from their (formal and informal) affiliations what kinds of values and codes of conduct those individuals have signed up to, etc. Thus, it is the fact that 'business relations are mixed up with social ones' (1985: 495) that makes business possible. Such relations make it, for example, more difficult to switch the disposition to fair play on and off (Hollis 1998: 97) without incurring damage to future opportunities in a context in which reputational information flows. Hollis's striking phrase, 'embedded but not lost in the games of social life', precisely captures the view of institutional economic sociology for which, however, strict methodologically individualism does not supply a sound basis for understanding how real individuals rationally pursue their interest, but which, in contrast to the kind of functionalist sociology which Hollis clearly (and rightly) finds repugnant, does not reject the principles of a rational actor model either. The social here is not to be evoked to demonstrate the irrational ('cultural') nature of action, but quite the opposite: to demonstrate the rationality of social actions even where they do *appear* to be lost in the games of social life:

> while the assumption of rational action must always be problematic, it is a good working hypothesis that should not easily be abandoned. What looks to the analyst like nonrational behavior may be quite sensible when situational constraints, especially those of embeddedness, are fully appreciated. When the social situation of those in nonprofessional labor markets is fully analysed, their behavior looks less like the automatic application of 'cultural' rules and more like a reasonable response to their present situation. (Granovetter 1985: 506)

Given that, as Timothy O'Hagan notes, 'Hollis implicitly rejects any absolute opposition between empirical questions and questions of reason' (O'Hagan 2000: 6–7), the thought that social relations are a source of empirical information that assists rational decision making should have been less disturbing to him than the oversocialised reduction of agency to an instance of the social totality. Granovetter's aim is to prise the principle of rational action away from methodological individualism by showing that social factors facilitate rather than bind rationality. On this view, Adam and Eve can only overcome their co-ordination problems on the basis of the information that they have about each other, either directly or via socially transmitted reputational information; a view that Hollis's account of the fate of Adam and Eve on the Enlightenment Trail might be taken to support. Since non-hypothetical agents *are* embedded in social networks, such information is normally available to them. Hollis in turn, might have found the thought that it is weak ties rather than strong ones that are the most effective means of transmitting such information quite agreeable (Granovetter 1973).

One final, but important, implication of such economic sociology is that the danger of the clan-like behaviour which so concerned Hollis does not emerge with community as such, but *within* particular types of community, namely those drawn too strongly towards the pole of solidarity. Too much 'social capital' can be as inhibiting as too little (Woolcock 1998). Granovetter notes, for example, that organizations which offer secure tenure can also provide fertile conditions for stable alliances (and/or festering long-term resentments and enmities). These are among the 'dark forces' of which Hollis speaks. Too much embeddedness means too little autonomy, damaging not only the opportunities open to individuals, but to whole communities (Portes & Sensenbrenner 1993). However, such options as individualism vs egotism or embeddedness vs autonomy do not represent a choice *between* community and non-community, but *for* communities. To quote Mary Douglas again, 'the themes [e.g. of individualism and solidarity] recur because they correspond to forms of social life that recur' (Douglas 1987: 7).

Conclusion

Hollis reads the sociological model of action as though the distinction between the sacred and the profane had been abolished and in effect all had become sacred. This eliding of the distinction bypasses one of the most important contributions of Durkheimian sociology: the distinction between the sacred and profane does not merely divide social acts and social space (e.g. ritualistic from mundane action) it runs right through the self. On the Durkheimian account, both Adam and Eve will vacillate between self- and other-regarding actions because they are the embodiment of the social *and* globules of self-regarding desire at one and the same time; both saint and sinner. How far the saint-sinner will stumble along the Enlightenment Trail is neither predictable nor aided alone by Reason's lodestar. It is the outcome of a struggle not merely between Adam and Eve, or between self- and other-regarding action as mutually exclusive options, but within the selves of Adam and Eve. Hollis takes the sociological tradition to be making a kind of temporal claim: 'social *before* they are individual, and plural *before* they are singular' (1998: 106, emphasis added). Even in the anti-utilitarian Durkheimian tradition, the more interesting claim is not that the one came before, or has priority over, the other, but rather that the social and the individual, the singular and the plural, are in a constant tension within social institutions, within the interactions of actors, and, perhaps most importantly, within each self. Without the social bond Adam and Eve remain vulnerable to the centipede's sting. With only the social bond they have no interest in moving along the trail. The task of sociology is not to resolve their dilemma, but to analyse the *social* preconditions of their possible success or failure.

This was not Martin Hollis's concern, but it is one which might have had a greater bearing on the outcome of his own journey than it in fact did. At the end of his discussion of the games of social life, two paths open up. In one direction we could start to speak about the degree of rational reflection which is possible within forms of life, about the degrees of openness or closedness of human communities and about the unstable balance between self- and other-regarding action (this is the broadly sociological path taken by Simmel, Mauss, Granovetter and even, at times, Durkheim), or we could return to game theory, now, hopefully, further enriched by the sociological detour. Martin Hollis choose the second path. The discussion of social life in *Trust Within Reason* is in the end reminiscent of a line from Georg Büchner's play *Woyzeck*: 'Jeder Mensch ist ein Abgrund; es schwindelt einem, wenn man hinabsieht' [Everyone is an abyss. It makes you dizzy when you look in]. Martin Hollis looked into forms of life and drew back from the precipice. But perhaps it is not the abyss he feared. Perhaps it is more congenial and indeed close to his own hint at the end of the book that mixed motives require mixed accounts.

ACKNOWLEDGEMENTS

I would like to thank the various members of the reading groups organized by the philosophers in the School of Economic and Social Studies for making life at UEA considerably more agreeable and stimulating than it would otherwise have been. Within and beyond that context, Martin Hollis acted as both a challenging and integrative figure in a way that we shall all gratefully remember.

NOTES

1. Simmel's account of secret societies is a classical sociological study of a type of community which destroys both individuality and ultimately itself through its hostility towards outsiders (Simmel 1950 [1909]). There is a remarkable similarity here to Hollis's concerns with the clan-like tendencies of community.
2. There is some indication that this reading does Titmuss a disservice and that he is fully aware of the elements of obligation implicit in the act of giving and of the fact that givers and receivers were both 'knight' and 'knave'. Take for example the following comment: 'no such gift is or can be utterly detached, disinterested or impersonal. Each carries messages and motives in its own language' (1970: 210).
3. Curiously, Granovetter makes no reference to Mauss in his now classical article, 'Economic action and social structure', but his main contention that 'the level of embeddedness of economic behaviour is lower in nonmarket societies than claimed by susbtantivists and development theorists, and has changed less with "modernization" than they believe, but I argue also that this level has always been and continues to be more substantial than is allowed for by formalists and economists' (1985:

REFERENCES

Douglas, M. 1987. *How Institutions Think*, London: Routledge.
Durkheim, E. 1984 [1893]. *The Division of Labour in Society*. Trans. W.D. Halls, London: Macmillan.
1995 [1912]. *The Elementary Forms of Religious Life*. Trans. Karen Fields. London: Routledge.
Granovetter, M. 1973. 'The strength of weak ties'. *American Journal of Sociology*, 78/6, 1360–80.
1985. 'Economic action and social structure: the problem of embeddedness'. *American Journal of Sociology*, 91/3, 481–510.
Hollis, M. 1998. *Trust Within Reason*. Cambridge: Cambridge University Press.
Mauss, M. 1990 [1925]. *The Gift: The Form and Reason for Exchange in Archaic Societies*. Trans. W.D. Halls. London: Routledge.
O'Hagan, T. 2000. 'The dilemma of the Enlightenment'. O'Hagan & Goodenough 2000: 5–11.
O'Hagan, T. & J. Goodenough , eds. *Essays Concerning 'Trust Within Reason' in Honour of Martin Hollis 1938–1998*. Norwich: UEA Papers in Philosophy, New Series 10.

Portes, A. & J. Sensenbrenner. 1993. 'Embeddness and immigration: notes on the social determinants of economic action'. *American Journal of Sociology*, 98/6, 1320–50.
Simmel, G. 1950 [1909]. 'The secret and the secret society'. Wolff 1950: 307–78.
Titmuss, R.M. 1970. *The Gift Relationship*. London: Allen & Unwin.
Wittgenstein, L. 1953. *Philosophical Investigations*. Oxford: Blackwell.
Woolcock, M. 1998. 'Social capital and economic development: towards a theoretical synthesis and framework'. *Theory and Society* 27, 151–208.
Wolff, K.H., ed. *The Sociology of Georg Simmel*. New York: The Free Press.
Wrong, D. 1961. 'The oversocialized conception of man in modern sociology'. *American Sociological Review*, 26/2, 193–3.

11

Rational Choice and Trust

KEITH DOWDING

Martin Hollis grappled with the nature of 'rationality' and models of man throughout his work.[1] He did not like instrumental accounts, particularly those provided by rational choice theory, believing that a deeper account of rationality was required in order to make sense of human behaviour. In his last book, *Trust Within Reason* (Hollis 1998), he argued that trust cannot be explained within an egocentric account of rational action. It opens with his account of the Enlightenment Trail, a form of centipede game, with two hikers (Adam and Eve) who do not get beyond the first pub, as backward induction leads to suboptimality at the Rational Choice rather than The Triumph of Reason, a pub both much prefer. Despite its counter-intuitive and suboptimal outcome, the centipede game does not show that there is anything wrong with rational choice.[2] Rather the problem is with the game. If Adam and Eve were to be allowed to walk together regularly, then they could come to an agreement sometimes to stop at Adam's favourite pub and sometimes at Eve's. Then again, if the Enlightenment Trail can only be hiked once by strangers, but side-payments are allowed, then perhaps they could agree that the one who chose the pub would buy the drinks. Either way, drinks could be drunk at the Extra Trick or The Triumph of Reason. It is not backward induction that is the difficulty here nor 'rationality' in rational choice theory, but the problem posed by the centipede game.

I think one of the problems with single-shot games like Hollis's Enlightenment Trail is that the suboptimal outcomes which may rationally accrue do not conform to what our intuitions tell us we would do if we were faced with a problem 'like that'. While we may face problems such as 'which pub are we going to visit on our walk today', rarely, if ever, does real life resemble the centipede game. Our intuitions are not well fitted to single-shot games because we do not often play them in life, and even when we do – for example in the laboratory – our reactions are contaminated by our intuitions about similar games which we play repeatedly. For example, in the famous Prisoners' Dilemma the suboptimal defect (or hawk) strategy strictly dominates the co-operative (or dove) strategy in the one-shot game. Both players end up with their third-most-preferred payoff rather than their second-most-preferred had they both chosen their dominated strategy. The intuition of most people when first faced with this game is that there must be a way out, since the rational outcome seems so crazy. But the suboptimal outcome is not crazy; it is what rational players must end up with, for that is what rationality and their payoff functions *mean* (Dowding, 2002). This certainly does not conform to what we think real prisoners would do in a situation as described to elucidate the mathematics of the game.[3] First, because we would expect real prisoners both to have had a history together and expect to have a future together. Second, even if the prisoners do not expect to have a future together, each may expect a future with others who may get to hear about their actions in this game. Outside of laboratory conditions where the experimenters promise that all actions will remain secret, rarely do real people face situations which conform to the maths of single-shot games.[4]

The Prisoners' Dilemma has taken on such an important position in rational choice that critics often think the correct analysis of the single-shot PD means rational choice writers believe co-operation is impossible for rational actors. They do not. Iterating the game allows for other outcomes. The 'folk theorem' of PD-like games proves, roughly speaking, that in an infinite sequence of iterations, with certain assumptions about future-discounting, any finite sequence of choices, from both defecting, to one defecting and one co-operating, to both co-operating, is rational. Contrary to the popular myth that rational choice suggests co-operation is impossible, rational choice actually suggests anything can happen.[5]

Of course, its critics may then argue that rational choice, which usually places great store in its ability to produce testable predictions, has lost the plot by predicting anything can happen. More helpfully, however, we can interpret this result as suggesting we need to look at the *institutions* which foster co-operation and non-co-operation in order to explain why co-operation occurs to different degrees in different contexts, rather than expecting a generalization from a simple game to be applicable to all collective action problems. Institutions can be thought of as governance structures which direct individual effort to collective benefit.[6] They may be created deliberately with formal rules underpinned by specified sanctions, legislatures and bureaux for example, or they may develop unintentionally as norms and conventions with unspecified sanctions.[7] Promising is an institution, and so is trust. Game-theorists tend to see such institutions as the equilibria of a game, where an equilibrium, roughly speaking, is a pattern of behaviour from which it is not individually rational for players to depart.[8] Can rational choice theory explain trust as an institution in these terms?

To take a step back for a moment, we may ask why there is a felt need to explain trust at all.[9] Why is there a felt need to explain 'trust' rather than 'distrust'?[10] Should we not look for general explanations of human behaviour, which will include trust, and distrust, co-operative and non-co-operative behaviour, rather than try to explain particular facets of human action each as a special case? Rational choice theorists have the aim of such generalized explanation. Indeed rational choice theory does not explain why people trust each other: rather it explains why people learn to trust, to varying degrees and in certain contexts, some subsets of others; while learning to distrust, to varying degrees and in certain contexts, other subsets. This learning process takes place through repeated interaction, and by seeing others' interactions. Networks of knowledge about others' likely behaviour in response to their environment including our actions leads to that aspect of social capital we call 'trust'. When we meet a stranger we may have expectations about that person's behaviour based on our interactions with people 'like her'. (We do the same with dogs.) Thus it seems explaining co-operation and non-co-operation, trust and distrust, is all one. Neither is a special case, despite the ubiquity of the self-interest assumption. However, this answer does not satisfy Hollis, for it is only half the story of trust. It only explains trust as confidence in another's behaviour. If I trust you to do x, it is because I have confidence based on your past behaviour that you will do x. But trust is also about acting trustworthily. How does my confidence in you *motivate* you to do x?

This is an important aspect of trust, for we are so motivated. Why try to keep a promise when one knows that no one else can ever possibly find out whether one did so? Probably all academics have faced the situation when after many hours of marking, they realize they could not say what the script they have just marked actually argues, or even what questions have been answered. Their mind has been elsewhere. What should they do? Leave their mark, knowing there is a second marker who can cover for the first's lack of attention, or put the script back on the pile of unmarked scripts and go away and have a cup of coffee before continuing? Perhaps some academics have succumbed to the temptation to leave the mark as is, relying on the second marker for integrity, but probably most put the script back on their pile to be done another day. Why? The candidate will never know, and the second marker will not guess, for there are always a few disputes in every set of exam scripts no matter how close their marks are on average. We are motivated to keep promises, and to do our job properly, because others expect it of us.[11] How can a rational choice account deal with this? There are two answers, one very simple and one very complex.

The first rational choice answer is that utility maximization in rational choice theory is analytic. A player's payoffs in a game are deduced from her preferences over possible outcomes: that is, a utility function is constructed from a person's preferences; their preferences are not caused by the utilities they gain from the possible outcomes. This *means* anything can be bunged into a utility function, so my choice to re-mark the script *entails* that my utility is greater through that action. More simply put, self-interested utility maximization is a special assumption of rational choice, and there is no reason why we should not build duty, guilt and other concerns into the manner in which we order our preferences over possible 'states of the world', including the state 're-mark the script in conditions x' over 'do not re-mark the script in conditions x'. However, non-formal writers find this answer very unsatisfactory because it does not *explain* the motivation. It merely redescribes it in a manner which makes the mathematics of choice more tractable. Furthermore, and in the context of Martin Hollis's critique of rational choice, it simply dances around the problem identified with the self-interest assumption. Despite self-interest being a special assumption of rational choice it is one that is generally assumed in models in order to give them predictive bite and non-triviality.[12] So we need a deeper defence and for that we need to provide some micro foundations for some of the *types* of preferences we have. This is the second, very complex answer that I can only touch upon here. But in order to introduce this second answer I want to draw a distinction between two different sorts of rational choice explanation. One I will call 'reasons for action' (RFA) explanation, the other 'evolutionary explanation'.

RFA explanation takes the intentional stance (Dennettt 1987, 1991). It suggests that the most *efficient* way of explaining human action is to assume individuals act for a set of reasons. These are usually explained in terms of Humean motivation as a set of beliefs and desires (Davidson 1980; Dowding 1991: ch.1), though one may wish to understand reasons simply in terms of sets of motivating beliefs (Dancy 2000).[13] Martin Hollis attacks this form of explanation which sees reasons as causes; indeed there are problems with seeing reasons as causes (Hollis 1997: ch.6). But following Dennett I do not think we need to get into this matter. The intentional stance is useful because it is efficient. By assuming individuals act for reasons, we can predict their behaviour more easily than by other means. Even if we had a special machine which could analyse at a distance the brain states of others (whether by neurons firing or chemical reactions) and then produce a prediction of what that person is about to do, it would not be as efficient a predictor as our understanding of that person's beliefs. Certainly it would not be as good a predictor of the person's likely action in situations far in the future or that the person has never faced. Understanding their beliefs about the world and then working out what we would do in a strange situation given those beliefs would be a superior form of prediction, if only because we are more similar machines to the individual than any mechanical device ever could be, and if we 'programme' ourselves to think like that person, following the principles of charity or humanity,[14] we can predict more easily than any other such device.

RFA explanation also assumes people act 'as if' they had the representation we give to them in our formal models. For example, we can explain geometrically what Jimmy White is attempting to do when he hits the cue ball hard with plenty of side spin, potting the red to go round three sides of the table to nestle up behind the black. Jimmy White cannot do the geometry – he did not learn to read until he was in his twenties – but he plays snooker as though he understands the geometry of potting. Similarly when we make expected utility calculations to explain a person's actions we are not claiming the person actually made the calculations: simply that we can explain their actions 'as if' they did.

Such RFA explanation need not only apply to individuals. We can apply it to organizations or animals. It may seem odd to think that an animal or an organization can have 'intentions', but if you think that a dog can bark up the wrong tree then you are taking up the intentional stance; likewise if you think an organization has acted against its own interests. With the latter we usually believe that we can unpick the claims in terms of actions and interests of its members, but often this unpicking is unnecessary for the explanations we seek to the particular questions we have asked.

The attack upon rational choice's inability to explain 'trust' is that RFA explanation which predicts trusting behaviour through motivation 'explained' by a utility function is trivial. Attempting to make such an explanation non-trivial by the usual route of using the self-interest assumption fails. While we may be able to explain conditional co-operation through reciprocity in iterated games, we are unable to explain how we are motivated to act trustworthily when we know we are being trusted even when we know we cannot be found out. This leads us to look for the explanation of such motivation in the second form of rational choice modelling, evolutionary explanation.

It may seem odd to claim there is a non-RFA evolutionary form of rational choice explanation, especially since the modelling I am going to discuss does not involve assumptions about individual rationality nor about choice. The justification for claiming this is a rational choice explanation is simply that it uses much the same (indeed sometimes exactly the same) models as RFA explanation. Perhaps more correctly we can say that the same mathematical models can be interpreted either in RFA terms or evolutionary terms. For this reason the distinction between the two is often misunderstood.

The use of game theory in evolutionary explanation is well known. A key concept is an evolutionarily stable strategy (ESS), which is a strategy such that if all the members of a population adopt it, no other strategy can invade it (Maynard Smith 1982). This includes a strategy which is a mixed strategy. What Maynard Smith calls a 'genetically polymorphic population' may be in an evolutionarily stable state, even if none of its members adopt an ESS. In other words the population acts globally as though its members were playing mixed strategies although in fact each plays a pure strategy, but the dynamics are such that the mixture of pure strategies is evolutionarily stable. We may note here that a full understanding of such population dynamics has led some to accept the existence of group selection (Sober 1993: ch.4), or perhaps rather better it is to see groups as the best vehicles for genetic selection. While there may be no individual differences between animals, groups within a population may have different characteristics. For example, the relationships between the members of the groups may vary in terms of the way the group is organized: one group may have a hierarchical structure, another may be anarchistic.[15] Or where a population of animals is made up of a mix of hawks and doves, the mix differs in different groups. Either way, one group may have evolutionary advantage over another, allowing those groups with the fitter group characteristics to be selected. This is applicable to Hollis's discussion of the relative worth of different types of football team – his Marketeers, Konigsberg United and the Musketeers – as analogous to types of society (Hollis 1998: 106–10). The strongest society may well be one where some people are trustworthy and some are not. The ESS is a mixed strategy globally represented as a mix of individually pure strategies.

To explain this a little more in the context of human populations I will give an example from experimental game theory. Ostrom, Gardner and Walker (1994) report experimental results from a common-pool resource investment game. Subjects could invest in one of two markets. The first yielded constant returns, the second yielded returns dependent upon other investments. The second was a common-pool resource which yielded an output dependent upon the total number of tokens invested by the group, with a fixed return on each unit of output. Each player knew how many people were investing and how many tokens each had, and their endowments were the same. They did not know how many investment rounds there would be, though they knew the experiment would not last more than two hours. They had all played similar games before. Their experimental evidence strongly supports the hypothesis of suboptimal appropriation in a Common Pool Dilemma as predicted by non-co-operative game theory. However, the experiment did not lead directly to suboptimality but to a 'pulsing' effect. Ostrom et al. report:

> At the aggregate level, results initially appear to approximate a Nash equilibrium in a limited access CPR. But, instead of a pattern that settles down at the predicted equilibrium, we observe a general pattern across experiments where net yield decays toward 0 then rebounds as subjects reduce the level of investment in the common-pool resource. Investigating across two parametizations, we find that at the aggregate level, our results lend strong support to the aggregate Nash equilibrium prediction for the low-endowment setting. In the high-endowment setting, however, aggregate behaviour is far from Nash in the early rounds but begins to approach Nash in later rounds. At the individual decision level,

however, we do not find behaviour consistent with the Nash prediction. (Ostrom et al. 1994: 121).

In other words, globally the population dynamics approach the game-theoretic equilibrium, but the players do not individually play equilibrium strategies. The game thus reveals correct predictions for the global patterns, but the assumption of individual rationality which underlies the game-theoretic predictions do not accurately portray the reasoning of the real players. They used 'rule of thumb' reasoning such as 'invest some tokens in Market 2 when yields seems high, reduce investment when yields go down'. This leads to the global pulsing not predicted by conventional game theory; but overall the movement is towards the equilibrium it does predict.[16] Here, the individual motivation to maximize individual yield, characterized by their rule of thumb reasoning, is enough to lead players eventually to the Nash equilibrium. Some player who could second guess the rule of thumb and realize the game was heading towards the Nash equilibrium could conceivably have done better. If this sub-game perfect Nash equilibrium strategy had been adopted by some it would have yielded a better result for its players. Individuals who learned this new rule would have done better. Evolution however, only chooses the fittest in a given environment, and in this experimental environment, these rules of thumb did well enough.

What is important in evolutionary game theory is that the animals are not the players, but rather the programmes coded in their genes (Binmore 1992: ch.9). These 'replicators' determine strategies in a game and replicate themselves in proportion to their success (Dawkins 1978; see also Monod 1972: ch.1). For animals this seems uncontroversial but translating this to human behaviour is controversial and its interpretation needs great care. We accept animals behave instinctually (even as we take up the intentional stance) but like to believe that our assumption of 'acting for reason' means something more in a human context. It does, but only because our language enables us to rationalize our own actions as we carry them out. Thinking strategically is a conscious thinking through of reasons for acting in a given manner. When we act strategically, in true game-theoretic style, it is because our genes include a programme allowing us to do this. This is not to say that what we think in any given situation is encoded into genes, but rather our ability to think is so encoded. Why has evolution chosen to encode the ability to think and work out behaviour rather than to encode directly into genes behaviour mapped onto any possible situation than might arise? For reasons of efficiency. Robert Axelrod explains why it is not possible to encode reactions to any possible historical set of iterations even in a simple game like Prisoners' Dilemma (Axelrod 1997). Say one wanted to write all possible strategies (play C or play D) given the moves of both players in three previous iterations. Since there are four outcomes in each iteration, there are $4 \times 4 \times 4 = 64$ different histories for the three previous moves. To determine the choice of C or D on the next move could be specified by a list of 64 Cs and Ds. Each could be represented on a gene, and one gene could represent what to do if the history had been a run of three mutual defections. The initial premises about the three hypothetical moves that preceded the start of the game will require six more genes. We then have 70 genes on the chromosome. This string of 70 Cs and Ds would specify what the player would do in every possible prior history and serve as the chromosome for reproduction and mutation. But a huge number of strategies can be represented here. For the 64 histories, we have $2^{70} \approx 10^{21}$ strings of CD mixes. 'An exhaustive search for good strategies in this huge collection of strategies is clearly out of the question. If a computer had examined these strategies at the rate of 100 per second since the beginning of the universe, less than 1 percent would have been checked by now' Axelrod 1997: 18). Thus an ability to think is preferable to trying to encode behaviour directly onto genes and hence the development of brains. This 'phenotypic plasticity' allows for a greater variety of behaviours, development and evolutionary progress. The more developed the brain, the more clearly it can plan into the future using what has actually occurred in the past and not what could have occurred. However, even here, when faced with complex situations, and situations for which history has only partially prepared us we look for simplifying devices to aid us. We look for patterns in the data and we operate through sets of rules. More generally we can see 'rules of thumb', conventions, 'codes of conduct', ideologies and ideas as replicators. Dawkins calls such replicators 'memes'(Dawkins 1978: ch.11; 1986). How can we explain my being motivated to act trustworthily through an evolutionary account such as this? The idea is that we underpin the trivial rational choice explanation – in the example above, my decision to remark the exam script, since 'duty' has a place in my utility function – with an explanation of how it got there. It got there through a replicator.

The replicator in this case is an idea which has been promulgated through repetition in which duty matters. This is sometimes described as the internalization of a norm (Scott 1971). The idea of duty mattering to me can be seen in several senses. It might matter because of a 'feeling' or a 'sense'. That is, I 'feel' bad if I do not carry out my duty. In this sense the 'feeling' is instinctual. It might be thought of as a Humean desire. It might be thought that running such an idea takes 'duty' out of duty, since it would seem that I act thus for non-rational reasons. My motivation is a genetically programmed reaction to the situation I face. In this case, any attempt on my part to explain why I act thus out of duty is just a rationalization of my actions caused by genetic programming. However, this conclusion is not necessary for two reasons. First, we have to examine why I should have such a feeling. I can only have such a feeling because I think there is a duty to mark the exam scripts properly. I have this duty because I have decided so, no matter whether I decided that through *a priori* analytic philosophizing, or whether I learned it through socializing my synthetic experiences, probably heavily influenced by my parents and early peers, or a mixture of both. At the very least the genotype encoded in our genetic structure leads to such feelings, given our rationalizations about the situations in which we find ourselves, to the extent that when faced with the dilemma of the unconsciously marked script, the dominant phenotype is 're-mark the script'.[17] So I still have to understand that the correct thing to do is to re-mark the script in order to have the Humean desire to motivate the action. I am still a reasoning creature. This possibility is appealing. It provides a Humean motivational desire which is genetically coded, but leaves our moral behaviour as reasoned. The desire itself is likely to be pre-reasoning behaviour and to be phenomologically represented in those parts of our brain that are pre-mammal. Our 'moral sense' has developed with moral reasoning, but any 'feelings' associated with it will have developed from pre-moral reasoning desires. Indeed if we can differentiate Humean desire from belief as components in our reasons for action, then we may be able to empirically corroborate their difference phenomenologically as physical activities in different parts of the brain. Here we may hypothesize that the Humean desire is present in the pre-mammalian brain with reasoned belief appearing in evolutionarily younger parts of the brain.

However, this is not the only possibility. The picture of rational choice that I have been trying to defend is compatible with a view which sees beliefs as motivating without any associated 'desire'. We simply drop any thought of requiring a motivation beyond thinking that 'x is the right thing to do' given our moral beliefs. But this does not take us beyond any form of evolutionary selection. It takes us into memetic selection. This is the level of cultural transmission of the types of beliefs and ideas that people create and learn from each other.[18] Societies with some types of moral behaviour will do better than others in given environments. The transmission of these institutional 'replicators' can still be represented as the equilibria of games. Phenotypic plasticity allows for this learning facilitated by our ability to communicate through our highly developed languages.

In this manner our 'trivial' RFA models of human action can be underpinned by evolutionary models to explain the 'preferences', 'judgements' or utilities associated with different courses of action to produce fully-fledged explanations of human behaviour. What precisely one is trying to explain, will determine which type of rational choice explanation one utilizes. We can therefore see that fully-fledged models are able to explain why people are motivated to act trustworthily within the broader frameworks of rational choice theory.

ACKNOWLEDGEMENTS

This paper was first given at a panel in memory of Martin Hollis, at the Political Thought Conference, St Catherine's College January 8th 1999. I must thank the other panellists, especially Frank Hahn, and the audience, for stimulating discussion. I would also like to thank Oliver Curry, Jonathan Dancy and Anne Gelling for their comments on the version prepared for publication.

NOTES

1. See his early books (Hollis &Nell 1975, Hollis 1977).
2. Martin Hollis criticizes backward induction through the centipede game at greater length in Hollis 1998, ch.3 and in Hollis 1991. Morrow gives a simple explanation of the centipede game with a straightforward defence of backwards induction against the seemingly counter-intuitive outcome of the game through its use Morrow 1994: 156–8). The game first appears in Rosenthal 1981. See also Binmore 1987a, 1987b, 1997: 113–17, and McKelvey & Palfrey 1992 for experimental evidence.
3. The game itself was first created in the early 1950s by Merrill Flood and Melvin Dresher at the RAND Corporation, and the story associated with it told by Albert Tucker, a RAND consultant (Poundstone 1992: 8).
4. The difficulty of directly translating real situations to such simple games is why they are sometimes called 'toy games'. But the purpose of a toy game is to remove all the

jumble which exists in real problems in order to *train* our intuitions in strategic situations.

5. Called the 'folk theorem' because it was well known amongst game theorists before anyone published it: see Aumann & Maschler 1995. The simplest proof is probably Binmore 1992: ch.8.

6. See the discussion in Shepsle & Bonchek 1997: ch.11. The theory of institutional change suggests that institutions exist for collective (though not necessarily optimal) benefit, but the collective action problem and transactions cost entail that institutional change may be slow, meaning that institutions may not always function in the collective interest.

7. The empirical examples of norms and conventions discussed in Ostrom 1990, 1992, Keohane & Ostrom 1994, and Ostrom et al. 1994 are all underpinned by sanctions, though experimentally some norms of cooperation can develop where there are no sanctions (Ostrom et al. 1994: ch.8). Interestingly, whilst net yield is lower in these games of co-operation where there is no sanctioning, subjects overuse the sanctioning mechanism. In games where there is no communication net yield minus the costs of sanctions is lower than with no sanctions. When communication between subjects is allowed and they choose sanctions, net yield shoots up.

8. Nash equilibrium arises when each player's strategy choice is a best reply to the strategy choices of the other players. Refinements of Nash equilibrium include sub-game perfect equilibrium (Selton 1975) which occurs when each player's strategy choice is a Nash equilibrium in each sub-game of the game. It will occur when each player's strategy choice includes steering when other players make mistakes, for example. See Heap & Varoufakis 1995 for a nice historical account of the development of equilibrium concepts designed to counter problems in assumptions about players' knowledge and rationality.

9. Of course Martin Hollis has not been alone in trying to explain trust in recent years; see for example, Gambetta 1988, Coleman 1990, Braithwaite & Levi 1998.

10. A sociological reason might be the increasing dominance of rational choice explanation in the academy with its officially special but in practice general assumption of self-interest. If people are self-interested then how do they get to trust one another?

11. Experimental evidence suggests the motivation to keep promises is stronger than any shared norm of cooperation itself. See Orbell et al. 1988.

12. It is possible to build non-trivial predictive models with much broader individual motivations than self-interest, but they need to be constructed and tested with care. In this sense, the self-interest assumption is an example of model-builders' laziness, albeit justifiable (efficient) laziness.

13. The reason one may wish to understand beliefs as motivators is to defend a form of moral realism. The point is it makes no difference to RFA explanation.

14. Davidson 1980 for the principle of charity, Grandy 1973 for humanity.

15. The genetic characteristics of the animals do not differ, but their pheonotypical behaviour will. Their behaviour will differ because of the different relationships they each bear to one another. The phenotype associated with genotype gets switched on differently because of the different environment – the group the animal is in – each individual faces.

16. Not predicted by game theory with complete information. In fact pulsing behaviour may be predicted by evolutionary game theory using other assumptions, which can also represent many different types of path selection which may not be optimal. See Binmore 1992: ch.9.

17. In standard biological terms genetically encoded replicators are genotypes which are expressed in the animals' set of observable attributes or phenotypes.

18. Whether meme replication is another form of natural selection than gene selection is controversial. One way of thinking of the issue is that the phenotype of an animal is a conditional based on the genotype and the environment. How the animal actually behaves depends upon the phenotype (understood conditionally) and the environment. Culturally transmitted behaviour – part of the phenotype – switches itself on. Two genetically identical populations may have different behaviour in exactly the same environment apart from the behaviour culturally transmitted. It is the memes which replicate themselves and so explain the behaviour *given* the genotype. Whether this deserves to be called a different evolutionary process is not clear. In this story there is no gene selection and the genotype supports both behaviours. The meme is as much a part of the environment as it is the phenotype. See Dawkins 1982 for a discussion of how phenotypes become part of the environment in which gene replication occurs.

REFERENCES

Aumann, R. & M. Maschler. 1995. *Repeated Games with Incomplete Information*. Cambridge, MA: MIT Press.
Axelrod, R. 1987. *The Complexity of Cooperation*. Princeton, NJ: Princeton University Press.
Binmore, K. 1987a. 'Modelling rational players I', *Economics and Philosophy*, 3, 179–214.
  1987b. 'Modelling rational players II', *Economics and Philosophy*, 4, 9–55.
  1992. *Fun and Games: A Text on Game Theory*. Lexington, MA: D.C. Heath and Co.
  1997. *Just Playing: Game Theory and the Social Contract Volume 2*. Cambridge, MA: MIT Press.
Braithwaite, V. & M. Levi, eds. 1998. *Trust and Governance*. New York: Russell Sage Foundation.
Coleman, J. 1990. *Foundations of Social Theory*, Cambridge, MA: Belknap Harvard.
Dancy, J.P. 2000. *Practical Reality*. Oxford: Blackwell.
Davidson, D. 1980. *Essays on Actions and Events*. Oxford: Clarendon Press.
Dawkins, R. 1976. *The Selfish Gene*. Oxford: Oxford University Press.
  1986. *The Blind Watchmaker*. Harmondsworth: Penguin.
Dennett, D. 1987. *The Intentional Stance*. Cambridge, MA: MIT Press.
  1991. *Consciousness Explained*. Harmondsworth: Penguin.
Dowding, K. 1991. *Rational Choice and Political Power*. Aldershot: Edward Elgar.
  2002. 'Revealed preference and external reference'. *Rationality and Society*, 14/3, 259–84.
Gambetta, D., ed. 1988. *Trust: Making and Breaking Cooperative Relationships*. Oxford: Blackwell.
Grandy, R. 1973. 'Reference, meaning and belief'. *Journal of Philosophy*, 70, 439–52.
Heap, S.P.H. & Y. Varoufakis. 1995. *Game Theory: A Critical Introduction*. London: Routledge.
Hollis, M. 1977. *Models of Man*. Cambridge: Cambridge University Press.
  1987. *The Cunning of Reason*. Cambridge: Cambridge University Press.
  1991. 'Penny pinching and backward induction'. *Journal of Philosophy*, 88, 473–88.
  1998. *Trust Within Reason*. Cambridge: Cambridge University Press.
Hollis, M. & E. Nell. 1975. *Rational Economic Man*. Cambridge: Cambridge University Press.
Keohane, R. & E. Ostrom, eds. 1994. 'Local commons and global interdependence: heterogeneity and cooperation in two domains: special issue'. *Journal of Theoretical*

Politics, 6.

McKelvey, R & T. Palfrey. 1992. 'An Experimental Study of the Centipede Game'. *Econometrica*, 60, 803–36.

Maynard Smith, John. 1982. *Evolution and the Theory of Games*. Cambridge: Cambridge University Press.

Monod, J. 1972. *Chance and Necessity*. New York: Knopf.

Morrow, J.D. 1994. *Game Theory for Political Scientists*. Princeton, NJ: Princeton University Press.

Orbell, J. et al. 1988. 'Explaining discussion-induced co-operation', *Journal of Personality and Social Psychology*, 54, 811–19.

Ostrom, E. 1990. *Governing the Commons: The Evolution of Institutions for Collective Action*. Cambridge: Cambridge University Press.

ed. 1992. 'Institutions and common-pool resources: special issue'. *Journal of Theoretical Politics*, 4.

Ostrom, E.R. et al. 1994. *Rules, Games, and Common-Pool Resources*. Ann Arbor: University of Michigan Press.

Poundstone, W. 1992. *Prisoner's Dilemma*. New York: Doubleday.

Rosenthal, R. 1981. 'Games of perfect information, predatory pricing, and chain-store paradox', *Journal of Economic Theory*, 25, 92–100.

Scott, J.F. 1971. *Internalization of Norms*. Englewood Cliffs, NJ: Prentice-Hall.

Selton, R. 1975. 'Re-examination of the perfectlessness concept for equilibrium in extensive games', *International Journal of Game Theory*, 4, 22–5.

Shepsle, K.A. & M.S. Bonchek. 1997. *Analyzing Politics: Rationality, Behavior and Institutions*. New York: W.W. Norton.

Sober, E. 1993. *Philosophy of Biology*. Oxford: Oxford University Press.

12

The Rule of Law and the Rule of Persons

RICHARD BELLAMY

Martin Hollis acknowledged a far wider role for the political arts than many philosophers. He appreciated how in practical life 'the best' was frequently 'the enemy of the good', with compromise no bad thing (Bellamy & Hollis 1998). A paragon of civic virtue, he also thought societies functioned well only when people manifested a solidarity with others and were prepared to make sacrifices for the common good. Thus, he saw democratic politics as a useful way of tailoring moral principles to the requirements of particular circumstances, and of generating the collective agreements needed to support those public goods on which personal well-being often depends. Yet, he believed democracy had to be infused with a high degree of morality to achieve these results. Otherwise, he feared majorities could turn tyrannous and individuals be apt to free-ride or selectively defect whenever their civic obligations appeared onerous. Purely political accounts of justice as the product of a democratic procedure risked confusing might with right, with the concern and respect due to all individuals to pursue their own good in their own way descending into the unedifying (and ultimately self-defeating) spectacle of each for him (or her) self (Bellamy & Hollis 1995).

One way of characterising Hollis's position on politics, as on other topics, is as an attempt to reconcile a Hobbesian view of human nature with a Kantian view of ethics (in essence the task of Hollis 1998). He could never quite convince himself that self-interest might be brought to generate morality, dismissing appeals to super-enlightened self-interest as mere sleight of hand (Hollis 1998: 29–37). Yet, he regarded a pure Kantianism as too abstract and detached from the intricate web of people's particular attachments and modes of reasoning (Hollis 1998:

ch.5). He was attracted to Rousseau as a possible solution. Neatly poised between Hobbes and Kant, with an added dose of communitarianism, potentially Rousseau provides good reasons for individuals to commit to the common good (Hollis 1998: 150–54). Political participation offers a paradoxical, if necessary, guarantee of individual liberty, and a means of adjusting the General Will to the wills of a localised set of citizens. But Hollis reckoned that without an unlikely 'remarkable change in man' (Rousseau 1973: Book 1, Ch.VIII, 177) people would still need to be 'forced to be free', (Rousseau 1973: Book 1, Ch.VII, 177) with all the disturbing connotations that provocative phrase conjures up (Hollis 1998: 151).

Attempts to relate 'the Rule of Law' to 'the rule of persons' capture much of the reasoning and many of tensions involved in Hollis' desire to combine politics and ethics. In standard versions, the Rule of Law offers an alternative to the arbitrary rule of a person or persons. But how (if at all) the law makes such non-arbitrary rule possible, and what gains are achieved in the process, are deeply disputed matters. Frequently, the Rule of Law seems overly formalistic, sacrificing good judgement to procedural correctness and failing to answer the concerns of those to whom it is applied. What makes law substantively valuable appears to require more than simply following the rules. Meanwhile, a paradox lies at the heart of the argument – for law has to be made and implemented by one or more persons, raising the original dilemma afresh. What follows explores these issues via a study of five imaginary worlds offering different accounts of the Rule of Law. However, I begin with a sixth world which oscillates between a tyranny of laws, anarchy and personal tyranny in order to tease out the basic concept underlying these various conceptions.

Gormenghast: The Idea and Value of the Rule of Law

As readers of Mervyn Peake's novels will know, Gormenghast is a rule-governed society. Though the rule book is known, settled and prospective, however, it is also oppressive in its detailed direction of all aspects of the Castle's life: from the colour of the eggs to be eaten by the Earl on different days of the week, to the endless ceremonies that shape the activities of his subjects – be they woodcarvers, poets or school teachers. The duties of each station in life are carefully prescribed. Judges and officials have no discretion, they must adhere to the letter of the law and rigorously apply it. Those (such as the young Earl) who fail to abide by the law are either locked up until they agree to do so or banished. Little wonder that on claiming his title at the age of 21, young Titus Groan decides to rip up the rule book altogether. Henceforth, he suggests, his subjects can rely on what are surely common intuitions about equity and justice and come to him to resolve the very few conflicts that might occur. After a few weeks, however, consternation begins to arise among the people. Though the good folk of Gormenghast possess a saintly rectitude, a remarkable solidarity of spirit and a commitment to shared values, limited resources and knowledge produce co-ordination problems of both a trivial and a more serious nature. For example, a lack of settled etiquette over matters such as parking and which side of the road to drive on, leads to traffic congestion. Ownership and use rights of private and public property are uncertain, so no one knows what is rightfully theirs to exchange or employ. The Castle authorities are unsure how or when to step in and settle disputes, since their powers and their limits are also unclear. In many cases, local conventions emerge or exist to sort matters out, such as 'first come first served'. But while certain customs are morally indifferent, others are not and many are far from innocuous in their effects if not their intention. Finders may keep but the losers weep, and there is a perceived need for mechanisms for revision and reform that are congruent with the justified expectations of the various parties. Moreover, the Castle is large enough for a variety of incompatible conventions to appear that inhibit interaction and co-operation among its constituent communities. Titus does his best to sort things out, resolving disputes as they occur. But the Earl's court is soon overwhelmed. Meanwhile, the watch and the people ask for guidance as to how he might resolve future disputes so that they can avoid putting themselves in the wrong. He publishes the Collected Rulings of Titus Groan, but these often turn out to depend on obscure reasonings, to be inconsistent and to bear little or no relation to the decisions his poor minions were obliged to take on the ground. The tyranny of arbitrary rules appears to have given way to the even more arbitrary personal rule of Titus. Signs of revolt appear and support grows for a return to the old code.

Titus's difficulties mirror some of those bedevilling Lon Fuller's hapless King Rex (Fuller 1969: 33–8). However, Fuller's allegory concerns the futility of trying to rule without rules, or at least without rules that people could follow. Titus' problems also include the perversity that can arise when ruling with rules. His various experiments raise the question of whether one can link individual autonomy and legal authority in ways that avoid the Scylla of lawless anarchy and the Charybidis of legalistic despotism, without falling victim to personal tyranny. Theories of the Rule of Law aim to steer a course between these three dangers.

The standard idea of the Rule of Law can be summarised as follows: laws exist so that decisions are not made on an *ad hoc* basis (Raz 1979). To achieve this purpose, both the law and the legal system must have a certain form. With regard to the *form of the law*, laws should be general and apply equally to all (while taking into account relevant differences), be prospective (only invoking retroactivity as a curative measure), public (albeit often through publicly funded experts), clear (avoiding vague terminology open to wide discretionary interpretation) and relatively stable (but not so as to ossify). So far as the *form of the legal system* is concerned, laws should be consistent, feasible, and congruent with official action. Most importantly, the promulgation, execution and ability to contest the laws should be guided by general, equal, public, clear and relatively stable rules.

The form taken by the law, on the one hand, and by the legal system, on the other, are related, and both are central to the Rule of Law. Most theorists accept that the majority of laws will be aimed at meeting particular purposes, even if usually they can be framed in general terms, thereby falling equitably on all, be settled, well-known and clear. However, what prevents such laws being the purely personal orders of officials or rulers derives as much (if not more) from the manner in which they are enacted, implemented and systemised than from the form they take. Indeed, it is this latter feature that gets around the paradox that laws are necessarily made and enforced by persons by insisting that they do so in legal ways that are consistent and impartial.

The advantages of such a law-governed regime are supposed to be three-fold. First, there is a mitigation (but as we shall see, not the complete debarring) of the use of arbitrary power, understood as power employed with indifference to or wilfully against the public purposes for which it has been established and in a manner that undermines the coherence and consistency of the legal system. However, such public purposes need not be very nice, though some commentators (notably Fuller 1969) have supposed they would have to be. Second, there will be a stabilising of those social relationships that might collapse, develop in erratic and unpredictable ways, or not exist without the law to secure them. Different types of rule achieve these goals in different ways. For example, some rules express governing social values, e.g. aspects of marriage law; others regulate behaviour in desirable ways, e.g. much criminal law; still others constitute certain valuable practices, e.g. making wills; many rules embody conventions that resolve co-ordination problems, e.g. driving on the left; and rules can also promote the consistency needed to achieve certain purposes, e.g. rules restricting government spending so as to reduce inflation. Finally, these two benefits in their turn help foster individual autonomy by inhibiting malicious and unpredictable interferences by public authorities and others, providing a reasonably stable environment that removes high levels of uncertainty and the frustration of expectations, and by opening up otherwise unavailable valuable options. All three factors, but especially the first two, are preconditions for agents even bothering to conceive and pursue the various projects that make up an autonomous life.

It is doubtful that any regime can do without a degree of legality in the formal sense. Within a state of any size, even despotism cannot rely solely on the ad hoc and particular commands of the ruler. No despot could literally run and decide everything. His orders will have to formalised in some way so that officials can be authorised to apply them in consistent ways to those cases he has not ruled on personally. The fact that despotisms not only can but also need to employ certain formal elements of the Rule of Law has led some commentators to suggest that the doctrine must be given a more substantive content and be identified with certain principles (Craig 1997), notably human rights (Dworkin 1978: chs 2 and 3; 1995: 2). As they point out, though rule according to known laws passed and administered by legally recognised agents and agencies may be better than ad hoc rule by private individuals or bodies (Dicey 1959: 189–91), it need not be that just. Indeed, such formalism may simply stabilise an unjust regime and render it more efficient. A regular system of injustice may give citizens forewarning of how to avoid falling foul of wicked laws if they can (Rawls 1971: 59), but it also removes discretion for honourable officials and judges to quietly bend those laws to avoid their direst consequences (Waldron 1989: 82). However, identifying legality with substantive justice has problems of its own. People often disagree about the substantive nature of the just and good yet accept the legality of the decision-making process employed to decide between them because of its procedural fairness. Within liberal democracies, for example, citizens usually defer to decisions they dissent from if they have been made and implemented according to a fair and legal democratic process (see Bellamy 1999: ch. 7; 2001 for a discussion). Moreover, even laws that are substantively just will need to be framed and deployed in ways that respect the formal qualities of the Rule of Law. Otherwise, they too will appear to depend over much on the discretion and existence of supposedly wise and good rulers. In other words, we will have replaced the Rule of Law by the rule of (putatively just) persons.

This brings me to the quandary I wish to explore in this article. The formal attributes of the Rule of Law seem to be necessary qualities for any functioning legal system operating through knowable and recognisable laws. It is less clear, however, that one could either rule in such a formal way or that, if one could, it would necessarily lead to the values of equality and the preservation of autonomy standardly associated with the doctrine. In other words, I wish to question whether the Rule of Law is a form of ruling or government in any meaningful sense. If it is not, so that we must rely instead on the rule of persons to provide the benefits of equity and stability associated with the Rule of Law, then the doctrine cannot be used as a criterion for good governance, as is often supposed. Instead, we must look to other mechanisms to ensure persons rule in the spirit of the Rule of Law. The next section explores this argument by considering five worlds of the Rule of Law. We start in Bureaucratia and the attempt to simply govern through formally promulgated rules. Although this system has certain advantages, it also appears hopelessly inefficient and often unjust. That leads us to Monarchia and the suggestion that the Rule of Law must always depend on the rule of a person or persons. However, even despotic rule appears to require forms of legality whereby we recognise the despot's right to rule. Communitaria suggests that rules of recognition and social co-ordination arise from folk-ways and customs. But the resources of tradition and convention may not be just and are unlikely to be available within modern large-scale and pluralist societies, which lack the shared values to which they appeal. Libertaria tries to overcome these difficulties by formalising such a conventional system. Yet this project proves a failure. Finally, Respublica grasps the nettle of the dependency of the Rule of Law on the rule of persons by elaborating a system of government that both authorises and constrains the making of laws in ways that are non-arbitrary and non-dominating. In sum, it refines the rule of persons to produce a due process that preserves the substance and the forms of the Rule of Law.

Five Worlds of the Rule of Law

Bureaucratia

Bureaucratia was established in the wake of Napoleon's defeat when it adopted Bentham's Constitutional Code, which was subsequently revised by Max Weber, Hans Kelsen and Herbert Hart. In Weber's terminology, Bureaucratia is a legal-rational order. Its procedures are formalised and open and its laws general, clear, equal, prospective and so on. On the surface, therefore, Bureaucratia appears a well organised and efficient society, enjoying all the advantages of formal rule governedness. Yet it is also a rigid and inflexible country, lacking the dynamism of many of its neighbours. It appears that rules as such generate not just advantages but also advantages.

The advantages of a regime of devoted rule followers can be summarised in the following six points (adapted from the illuminating discussion in Sunstein 1996: 110–15). First, rules eliminate the costs of having to reinvent the wheel every time you take a decision. Case-by-case decision making imposes informational, political and psychological costs. Conscientious officials will feel it necessary to laboriously explore every possibility. This can be extremely expensive in terms of the time and effort required to gather the necessary information. Where decisions involve making potentially contentious choices there can also be high political costs in reaching agreements: informed debate also requires time and effort and can provoke divisions as well. Rules that enable thousands of decisions to be made at once avoid these inconveniences, allowing people to divert their energies to other matters. Though the costs of formulating and getting agreement on the rule may be greater than would arise in any single case, a general decision that puts these problems to one side can work out cheaper overall. Savings also result from the ways rules guard against myopia, carelessness, bias or weakness of will – all of which might arise regardless of the generally good intentions of those involved in particular cases. To take an everyday example, we all benefit from traffic regulations, such as speed limits and restrictions on overtaking, because they save us the trouble of making tricky decisions about how fast we can go and the risks of passing a car on winding roads, guarding against even good drivers making bad judgements when they are tired or in a rush.

Second, and relatedly, agreement on either meta-rules about how we make rules or a general rule may be possible even when there is disagreement over what the right decision in any particular case might be. Parties often accept a rule as binding even if they disagree over why it is so. Likewise, people can often judge a rule as reasonable without entering into meta-ethical debates over its ultimate rightness or wrongness. In fact, the presence of rules can diminish the occasion for disagreement by reducing the need to invoke the strong commitments that divide us. For example, procedural grounds can lead us all to accept majority rule as equally binding and a reasonable way to break deadlock, without our having to engage in a high-level debate over whether majority preference satisfaction is the right result. Similarly, we may be able to accept the rule of first come first served as a fair way of distributing a particular benefit in circumstances where there would be profound disagreement about the appropriate rank ordering of different claimants.

Third, as we saw, rules produce a rough and ready form of equality. They rule out discretion and discrimination by officials through being impersonal and 'blind'. Of course, treating everyone in the same way in one respect invariably highlights their differences in other respects. But this result is often desirable. For example, the rules surrounding races are designed to find out who can run the fastest by ensuring all run the same distance and start at the same time.

Fourth, rules not only constrain decision-makers in particular cases in ways that are often beneficial, but can also embolden them to take courageous or contentious decisions. The existence of a rule can help officials stand up to the rich and powerful. Extrapolation from rules can also allow decisions to be made in areas where no substantive agreement exists but a collective policy is necessary nonetheless. In each case, the decision-makers need not pit their personal view or will against those of others but can rely on the impersonal authority of a general rule. For similar reasons, the impersonality of rules can also reduce the loss of face or humiliation felt by those against whom they are applied. They need not feel the victims (or fawning beneficiaries) of official discretion.

Fifth, rules increase visibility and accountability. They standardly impose duties on those who apply them and should have a clear frame of reference. These qualities not only increase the legitimacy of officials but also empower ordinary citizens. For they enable them to ascertain when officials overstep their power or fail to fulfil their responsibilities. Finally, as we noted, rules promote individual autonomy by providing a stable framework within which persons can plan ahead. This feature is also beneficial for legislators and officials, providing them with a similarly predictable environment within which to act.

However, Bureaucratia's rule-boundedness has disadvantages too, reminiscent of the inflexibility of Gormenghast's old regime and of the muddle that had befallen Titus's initial attempts to remedy its defects. For a start, rules alone cannot guarantee justice (Hart 1958). The formal approach does involve certain substantive features of natural justice, such as equity and impartiality, that make discrimination against individuals, if not groups, difficult. Nevertheless, these formal criteria still can be met by fairly unsavoury regimes. For example, most commentators accept South Africa under apartheid conformed to a formal definition of the Rule of Law (Dyzenhaus 1991). Regrettably, purely procedural rules for elections and forming a government cannot prevent an electorate voting right-wing extremists into power, or hinder the passing of racial laws and the efficient dispatch of the persecuted group to concentration camps. Certainly, all tyrannical regimes commit many lapses from the Rule of Law, with retrospective and secret laws being used to terrorise citizens and officials alike and keep all in a state of apprehension. However, these lapses result not from legality as such but from the objectionable purposes it serves making the resort to force necessary. To that extent, evil regimes will always involve a continuous recourse to the rule of persons in the worst sense. But they cannot function as regimes without possessing a certain procedural regularity and formality.

Rules also lead to various lesser kinds of inefficient or inappropriate decision making (Sunstein 1996: 130–35). First, rules can be motivated by good general reasons that prove inappropriate in particular circumstances. For example, certain health and safety or access requirements may be excessive with regard to certain small businesses, that would cease trading if they had to meet them, and be inadequate for other kinds of concern. A small beach café, a factory refectory and a hospital canteen may well need to meet progressively higher standards rather than being treated in exactly the same way on the grounds that food is prepared for public consumption in all three. Of course, one can seek to devise an ever more extensive array of rules to cover most cases, but then the efficiency gains of having rules begin to decline.

Second, circumstances change in ways that rule-makers can not always foresee. For example, many rules governing freedom of the press devised with newspapers and terrestrial television in mind have proven unenforceable or inadequate in the age of the Internet and satellite channels.

Third, rules can entrench certain biases and injustices. By treating all in the same way, rules can harm those who ought to be treated differently or, worse, give a certain legitimacy to practices that exploit those differences. Thus, feminists have criticised equal opportunities law for including a covert (and sometimes overt) male comparator test that overlooks relevant differences such as pregnancy or the structural factors that have relegated women to low-paid, casual employment. Instead of rethinking work and gender roles in ways that are compatible with shared child care duties, family responsibilities become a disqualification for certain jobs. In general, formal equality of treatment promotes rather than reduces substantive inequalities. As in the race example given above, that can often be the goal. But social security rules aimed at supporting the neediest, and hence at reducing inequality, have to ensure that they do not treat differently situated individuals in inappropriately similar ways.

Fourth, if rules prove insufficiently discriminating, then people will end up surreptitiously bending or selectively evading them. This may result in injustices, even if they are less than those that would follow if the rule were obeyed. Transparency of decision-making also gets lost, raising the dangers of prejudice or carelessness in particular cases which rules are supposed to avoid. For instance, both these problems arose when rules governing the death penalty appeared so draconian that juries became reluctant to prosecute. Similar problems may arise if the mechanical application of the 'three strikes and you're out' rule regularly leads to life imprisonment for criminals committing minor misdemeanours.

Fifth, the predictability and fixity of rules may promote social interaction and autonomy but they also make them easy to evade. People can learn to play the rules in ways that exchange form for substance. As tax evaders well know, rules rarely cover all eventualities, leading to loop-holes that allow people to keep to the letter of the law whilst escaping its spirit.

Sixth, rules can enhance the power of administrators in adverse ways. Thus, they can produce a certain inflexible and occasionally oppressive obtuseness amongst officials. Through either stupidity or a malicious sense of their own importance, they too can employ the letter of the law to betray its spirit in cases where flexibility would be more equitable or efficient. Complex systems of rules and procedures are also difficult to understand – making it hard for the public to challenge officialdom directly. Instead, they may need to hire experts capable of understanding and working the rules for them.

As Weber recognised, bureaucracies only prove truly efficient when capably led. Even then, some degree of individual initiative is required at lower levels. Otherwise, bureaucratic rule-bound decisions become mechanical and often unsuitable. These problems can be summarised in the thought that rules cannot encapsulate good judgement, which draws on practical experience, common sense, and is sensitive to the context and differences that make each case distinctive. The trouble is that we cannot rely on judgement being either good or consistent between judges and officials. They are no more immune than others to error, partiality and other human weaknesses. Moreover, there may be more than one good way of deciding a case – especially in circumstances where more than one rule could be applied and it is open to argument which should have precedence. Judges, for example, are often forced to balance different considerations, such as freedom of privacy and freedom of speech when regulating what newspapers may print. In many cases, it is a grey area which value is most in the public interest and so which rules are appropriate.

A possible solution to this dilemma lies in having rules that govern the setting up of agencies and the conduct of their administrators, but allowing them considerable discretion in their day-to-day working, so that decisions can be made on a case-by-case basis. In other words, one could have constitutive rules that identify who may wield power and for what purpose, treating bureaucratic rules as regulative rules of thumb. In many states, welfare payments, the allocation of public housing and of hospital resources, and the routing and pricing of air travel are among the policies carried out on this basis. Increasingly, such decisions are subject to a body of administrative law providing rules and criteria for the exercise of such discretionary power. Dicey famously argued that such special rules for officials endangered the fundamental tenet of the Rule of Law – that there be one rule for all (Dicey 1959: 193). I have noted how this notion can be illegitimately discriminatory with regard to relevant differences, such as disability or gender. Likewise, it ignores that officials necessarily exercise special powers in pursuing their tasks. While these powers allow them to perform certain acts barred to ordinary citizens, such as permitting ambulance drivers to break certain speed limits when rushing an injured person to the emergency ward, their possession also imposes more stringent responsibilities upon them.

Extending administrative law can render officialdom more accountable and predictable, therefore. However, it can also raise the original dilemma all over again by working against flexibility. Yet, making the rules regulating officials too formal risks falling into the error of the purely procedural position, whereby the law becomes no more than what those duly authorised to frame and apply it say it is.

Monarchia

The tyranny of obsessively rule-bound officials can be every bit as oppressive and malicious as the personal rule of a tyrant. Indeed, some positivists and critical legal theorists suppose that the one necessarily collapses into the other. If Bureaucratia just creates a plethora of little tyrants, it might be safer (and more consistent) to place our trust in one ruler capable of holding them all in check. This thought informs the world of Monarchia, the chief apologist of which is Hobbes for whom 'law' was but 'the word of him, that by right hath command over others' (Hobbes 1991: 80).

Hobbes adds to the earlier criticisms of rules and challenges the very coherence of the idea that the law, not persons, rule. First, he observes that the meaning of laws is rarely clear, so that 'all Laws, written and unwritten have need of Interpretation' and these interpretations are usually controversial (Hobbes 1991: 143). Second, even when the meaning of laws is clear, their bearing on particular situations is not – producing another source of controversy. For example, complex cases, such as the allocation of scarce medical resources, tend to produce a high degree of indeterminacy as to what the most relevant moral and evidential considerations are – the age of the patient, the patient's healthy or poor life style, the cost of the treatment and the likelihood of its being successful, the quality of life of the patient before and after being treated, and so on. It is often unclear which rule applies, how or why, making more than one reasonable decision possible. Thus, there is no obvious way of deciding the budgetary balance between providing cheap minor operations that relieve the slight discomfort of lots of patients and funding costly intensive care for a few people with chronic conditions. Third, even if laws could be defined in an absolutely clear manner both as to their meaning and application, self-love, partiality and passion can lead people to employ them in self-serving ways and hence into conflict with each other. Hobbes believes these difficulties arise as much with the hypothetical imperatives of the Law of Nature as human laws. Therefore, laws or rules *per se* do not provide the basis for social co-operation. Rather, a peaceful society results from having a political authority vested with the power to formulate, interpret and apply the laws and, crucially, to overrule rival views of their meaning and application. The claim that laws could be set above the sovereign person or persons empowered to enact and implement them was incoherent for Hobbes. For it could only mean to set up another power with the power to judge and enforce these laws 'which is to make a new Sovereign' leading to an infinite regress with the need of 'for the same reason a third, to punish the second; and so continually without end, to the Confusion, and Dissolution of the Commonwealth' (Hobbes 1991: 169).

Hobbes is not saying that good judgement is better than rules. He is suggesting any authoritative judge is better than a situation where all exercise their judgement. Though he assumed it was in the Sovereign's long-term interest not to despoil his or her kingdom, he thought the crucial problem of social order was to overcome the chaos of conflicting judgements and rules rather than to ensure the best judge ruled. Many (Hollis 1998: 31–3 included) think that stacks the cards too favourably towards tyranny at any price. However, it turns out there are contractual terms and conditions. In common with the positivist theory of law which he inspired, Hobbes' regress argument begs the issue of how we come to authorise and recognise the Sovereign in the first place, thereby giving him the right for his every command to be treated as law (Hampton 1994: 24–5, Hart 1994: 51–61). As Hart put it, we need 'secondary' rules of recognition to identify what counts as law as well as the 'primary' rules or laws that are created within a recognised legal system (Hart 1994: 94–5). Such secondary rules operate as constitutive rules that define the very practice of law. They are needed within Hobbes' account to identify law as the product of human will – in particular that of a duly recognised monarch.

As Hart noted, both constitutive and regulative rules only prove authoritative when accepted by officials and citizens alike (Hart 1994: 51–61, 86–91). This notion of acceptance suggests a clue as to how rules and the rulers that both decree and apply them, while being in a sense subject to them, might be made responsive to the concerns of the ruled. However, it may be cashed out in a number of ways which will be explored in the subsequent sections. Hobbes suggested that acceptance could be obtained (or hypothetically modelled) by deriving the Sovereign's authority from a contract. I remarked at that start that Hollis was unconvinced that instrumental self-interested individuals of a Hobbesian kind could overcome the dilemmas of rational choice to trust each other sufficiently so as to be able to reach such an agreement – particularly when the sovereign is not a party to it (Hollis 1998: 34–7). The notion of a foundational contract is also a position that fits best with the strongly substantive version of the Rule of Law. It provides definitive rules for political and social life. Critics of this thesis object that the very idea of seeking to rationally construct the basis for social interaction is flawed. Such attempts will always reflect the bias of the most powerful groups, failing to do justice either to the diversity of interests and values held by people, or the multiplicity of ways in which they interact and might evolve.

What follows does not assess this criticism directly (see Bellamy 2001 for such a critique). Instead, it analyses two alternative conceptions that are motivated by it, and which the positions examined thus far sought to displace as being too chaotic, conflicting and particularistic to serve in the modern world. In Communitaria and, in a modified form, in Libertaria, we accept the laws because they grow out of our practices and hence reflect and are tailored to our values and interests. No person or persons rule because the laws are made by an invisible hand reflecting the community as a whole – past, present and future. By contrast, in Respublica no person or persons rule over others because we all rule together. It is the process of mutually ruling that makes the laws equally acceptable to all.

Communitaria

Communitaria holds that the Rule of Law is best manifested in an evolving tradition of law. Law so conceived equates to the common sense of the community. The promulgation of the law is but the clarification of its details. The result of numerous decisions by many individuals over time, the law's impartiality arises from not being the product of any single agent or agency seeking to construct the perfect legal code. Rather, law has developed through a process of trial and error, its guardians being an independent judicial system not only imbued with a respect for legal integrity but also sharing the values and traditions of the community. Their skill derives as much from their local knowledge, particularly the similarity of their assumptions and reasoning to those of the litigants, as from any formal training.

This conception of the Rule of Law takes the games analogy seriously, likening the law to what Wittgenstein called a 'form of life' (Wittgenstein

1953: II. 226, Tully 1995: 103–14, Hollis 1994: 154-7). In this account, law consists of a set of practices and conventions that frame our actions. We apply the rules to particular cases much as we make moves in chess or respond to tackles in football – by learning 'how to go on', how to act within the spirit of the game. Within this conception, constitutive and regulative rules interact, with the former being in large part an assemblage of the latter that is constantly enriched by further plays. Nor are these rules purely formal generalities. Rather, they spring from particular substantive purposes and their various interactions. The result of human action, they follow no overall design. Nor could a fundamental plan be distilled from them. Laws are historically and culturally specific. They reflect particular intersubjective understandings. Whilst different legal systems may share various similarities with each other, there are no universal normative features they necessarily must possess to be law.

This system appears to have several advantages over that prevailing in Bureaucratia. First , Bureaucratia's rules have a tendency to become mechanical. By contrast, Communitaria's law is flexible, evolving along with changing circumstances as judges, like the people themselves, adapt existing practices to meet new situations. Second, Bureaucratia favours technocracy. It is law made by officials and so tends to be remote from the way citizens reason. As a result, they have to hire experts to go to law, which can make litigation both costly and complex. However, Communitaria's law is attuned to the values and reasoning of ordinary people, and so is less austere and distant from their concerns and they have less need to rely on expensive specialists to understand and engage with it. Third, these implicit judgements and values provide better guidance than the official rules of Bureaucratia for the application of law to specific circumstances. The use of precedent and analogy rather than abstract reason gives judges and legislators access to the implicit and inexpressible knowledge embedded in local custom and convention. Finally, discretion is nonetheless held in check through decisions (and the promulgation of law) being little more than the concretising, refining and developing of established practices and traditions. The common law courts become in this way the guardians against indiscriminate incursions by legislators and administrators.

Communitaria sounds a cosy place. Yet, it is commonly argued (e.g. Raz 1994: 372-3), this approach only works within relatively homogenous, small-scale societies, where little changes and people can rely on 'how we do things here' as a guide to action. Even then, as

Gormenghast reveals, conventions cannot always avoid becoming ossified, senseless and restrictive rules of etiquette. If laws are no more than the rules of so many games, it is unclear what prevents tradition losing its point. Customs can be colourful but they may also be tedious and positively reactionary. That danger seems particularly great in advanced industrial societies, where market pressures produce a high degree of technological innovation as well as considerable social and geographical mobility. At the same time, enhanced functional differentiation, combined with greater ethnic, religious and cultural pluralism, undermines the relative homogeneity on which communitarian law relies. There are no longer enough shared practices and understandings to sustain the communal approach. Even if conventions could be updated sufficiently rapidly to meet the pace of change and the growing diversity, this updating would have to be so radical as to make talk of their still being continuous and coherent traditions meaningless. Meanwhile, there is an increasing need for rules to mediate between different subcultures, such as different religious, ethnic or ideological groups, and various subsystems, such as the spheres of work and family. Both groups and spheres can prioritise different values and commitments, producing conflicts over the justice of various ways of organising the economy, personal relationships, civil liberties and so on. Leaving such adjudication to putative, but no longer existing, common practices or the judiciary risks law becoming the expression of an elite or hegemonic group, insensitive to difference and hence oppressive.

The critiques of Bentham, Weber and Hobbes enter here, represented by the worlds of Bureaucratia and Monarchia. Increasingly, individuals operate in comparative isolation within a world of strangers. Modern societies, it is claimed, require impersonal rules of a formally bureaucratic kind that ensure fair dealings in complex and fluctuating situations with anonymous others who possess very different experiences, interests and values (e.g. Weber 1994: 147–9). They also need 'a very able Architect' to replace the 'crasie building' produced by people's 'irregular justling' with general rules based on clear definitions and authoritative interpretations all can accept. Geometry, not 'Tennis-play', provides the model for state-craft (Hobbes 1991: 167, 107 as cited in Tully 1995: 113–14). However, as we have seen, bureaucratic and executive rule risks being mechanical and despotic, imposing a uniformity of behaviour far more rigorous, and hence potentially more coercive, than the alleged need to conform to eccentric customs. Indeed, certain theorists associate the inefficiencies and oppression of the command economies of the former Soviet bloc with just this approach. Thus, Libertaria, examined next, portrays a world in which the market operates as a global community order, albeit one requiring a degree of formality and generality to be rendered just. Meanwhile, the final section explores the Republican attempt to democratise the dialogical style of applying, interpreting and meditating between rules characteristic of common law reasoning.

Libertaria

Nestling in the foothills of Mont Pelerin, Libertaria has adopted the constitutional scheme of the late F.A. Hayek (1960, 1973–79). Hayek's theory developed through a critique of the legal positivist tradition from Hobbes to Kelsen (1973-79: I, 74). His main fear was that the power of despotic monarchs had passed to sovereign legislatures. The resulting elective dictatorships possessed the spurious legitimacy provided by democracy, but were every bit as tyrannous (1973-79: III, 101–2). Moreover, the belief that they might be contractually constrained suffered from the same rationalistic fallacy as the aspiration of governments to rationally direct societies. Contracts simply tried to state at an abstract level the rational principles and purposes governments should serve (1973–79: I, 9–11). As we shall see below, Hayek believed all forms of what he termed 'constructivist rationalism' were impossible and pernicious. His own notion of the Rule of Law has been appositely described as a common law *Rechtsstaat*. This thesis combined a somewhat bureaucratic reading of Kant, as a purely formal universalism, with aspects of the common law tradition. The aim was to draw on the immanent reason found within human practices to fashion clear rules that could bind governments and co-ordinate social activity in ways that maximised the individual's freedom from interference.

Hayek's theory turned on a fundamental contrast he made between 'spontaneous' and 'constructed' social and political orders. In a spontaneous order the rules and institutions regulating human conduct develop unconsciously through a process of trial and error. They arise from our efforts to adapt to and modify our environment, with the most successful prevailing as various human practices interact with each other. By contrast, the theory of constructed order sees social and political rules and institutions as the potential products of a designing intelligence. Hayek related these two types of order to a further distinction he made between 'law' and 'legislation' – both terms of art in his theory (Hayek 1973–79: I, ch.2). 'Legislation' was law in the legal positivist sense of commands by a ruler aimed at directing specific individuals to a rank-ordered set of goals. Legislation so interpreted belonged to a constructed order. 'Law' reflected the conventions emerging unconsciously from the multifarious practices of agents within a spontaneous order. However, he contended these conventions became stable and widely followed through being rendered universal, general, equal, clear and prospective. For example, an informal practice of queuing could be turned into the formal rule 'first come, first served'. Hayek thought the recognition of property rights and the notion of promising needed for the making and keeping of contracts were formalised conventions of this sort. He believed only rules aimed at preventing interferences with others were capable of meeting such criteria. Thus the chief quality of law as opposed to legislation lay in its being directed neither at particular persons nor the achievement of certain purposes. If legislation consisted of ordering people about, law protected individual autonomy by limiting intervention by both governments and fellow citizens.

'Legislation' was suited to organisations, such as armies, with clear and limited tasks. However, Hayek doubted it could efficiently or justly be employed to govern a society of any complexity. Hayek's argument grew out of an analysis of the flaws of planned economies of the former Soviet type. These systems failed either to get supply to match demand or to innovate. Not only are people's wants highly diverse, they also change in unexpected ways. Moreover, part of that change results from entrepreneurs offering new products in ways that alter consumption patterns. Unless a planner is benevolent, having the public rather than his own interests at heart; omniscient, knowing both what people want now and what they might want in the future; and omnipotent, so able to meet these wants efficiently, the system was doomed to inefficiency. Worse, it would be oppressive too, since it would curtail the freedom of producers to experiment and of consumers to choose. He thought the success of markets lay in their capacity to co-ordinate the free actions of numerous strangers via the price mechanism. Price was what brought supply into line with demand, while the desire for profit led entrepreneurs to innovate, so as to produce goods more cheaply than rivals, or to invent new products. Markets needed regulating to preserve open competition, maintain freedom of contract, guard against fraud and the like. But such regulation involved 'law', not 'legislation'. In other words, it was not directed at achieving certain goals but rather at facilitating the ability of autonomous individuals to plan for themselves by providing an environment in which they could trust others to honour their bargains and not to coerce them.

Hayek generalised these criticisms of planned economies into a critique of all attempts to interfere with the market in the name of social justice (Hayek 1973–79, II). Such policies were fatally flawed, representing a slippery slope towards a Soviet-style system. For they all assumed that some agency could acquire the knowledge and ability to provide people with what they needed. Yet, that information and capacity could only be acquired and appropriately exercised by a person or institution with God-like powers. Thus, the crucial issue was to prevent governments subverting 'law' via 'legislation'. The latter might be suited to running the state bureaucracy but not for co-ordinating society as a whole. Since he did not believe 'law' could be defined *a priori*, he allotted this task to a carefully selected second chamber (Hayek 1973–79:III, ch.13).. Their role was two-fold. First, they had to prevent the passing of certain sorts of economic and social legislation that he believed could not pass his formal tests, such as attempts to fix prices or redistributive measures aimed at achieving a fairer pattern of income. Second, they had to adapt existing 'law' to evolving conditions, operating like common lawyers and arguing by analogy from precedents while ensuring the coherence and consistency of the system as a whole. The result was supposed to be an organic constitution.

Though subtler and more complex than certain critics suppose, Hayek's argument is nonetheless vulnerable to numerous objections (Bellamy 1999: ch.1). Three are particularly pertinent in this context. First, is the issue of whether one can expect Hayek's market traders to either make or keep to the rules. As rationally self-interested agents, it looks rational to defect in the Prisoner's Dilemma and to free ride in the Free-Rider problem, which is its n-player version. If so, it looks as if the theory has to recommend a battery of sanctions of all sorts, which are too cumbersome and costly to convince and whose administration raises the original crux all over again. The need for co-ordination may favour the emergence of certain practices, but it does not prevent the mutually beneficial equilibrium being one that involves considerable unfairness to one or other parties, as in Battle of the Sexes. In sum, rational choice leaves a gap between the good of each and the good of all that is unlikely to be filled spontaneously. Without a social contract of the kind he decried, it is uncertain that the particular contracts of individuals will be fairly negotiated or kept.

Second, the formal criteria Hayek employs to identify law will not necessarily operate as comprehensively as he assumes against redistributive schemes and economic planning. After all, 'all persons earning above £100,000 pay supertax' is a general, equal rule. Likewise, stable prices and plans announced well in advance may also be consistent with a purely formal view of the Rule of Law, for there are no particular purposes that cannot be framed within some general description that applies to them alone or be derived from some suitably designed general rule. The point in such cases is whether these policies are socially or economically sound. Far from being incompatible with the pursuit of social purposes, rules generally help promote them by moving officials and citizens consistently towards that objective without the need for continuous commands. Indeed, law and legislation tend to be intertwined, with government regulations invariably sharing these dual features. For if, as Hayek insists, it would be impossible to direct centrally all the activities of a complex society, it appears equally problematic to employ solely abstract procedural norms possessing no determinate content. For example, Hayek suggests that 'measures designed to control the access to different trades and occupations, the terms of sale, and the amounts to be produced and sold' all 'involve arbitrary discrimination against persons' and so offend the Rule of Law as he conceives it (Hayek 1960: 227–8). But he cannot really mean that we should not ensure that doctors and lawyers are properly qualified before being allowed to practice, or that pilots should not pass eye tests, and so on. Regulations must not only possess elements of generality and procedural correctness to ensure fairness, allow individuals to plan, and secure the benefits of social co-operation. They also need to be determined by substantive purposes and a degree of expediency governed by local conditions. Indeed, much social and economic legislation could be interpreted as evolving responses to the experience of certain consistent market failures, such as unemployment or an unwillingness to supply certain sorts of public good.

Finally, Hayek's difficulties and confusions come to a head in his view of the relation of law to liberty. His central contention is that 'when we obey laws, in the sense of general abstract rules laid down irrespective of their application to us, we are not subject to another's will and are therefore free' (Hayek 1960: 153–4). At times, he appears to suggest that so long as everyone is similarly affected by a rule, it is not aimed at anyone personally, and infraction is avoidable, then no coercion is involved. Lawgivers do not know the particular cases where their rules will be applied and the judge is simply applying that law. As a result, the law is like a natural obstacle. But this to leads to absurdities. As Hamowy (1978: 87–97) has observed, by these criteria a gangster-ridden neighbourhood – being like a plague-infested swamp, neither aimed at me personally nor unavoidable – represents no limit on my freedom. To avoid this problem, Hayek found himself having to give more substantive content to the generality of the law and its relation to liberty. We saw above how the purely formal Rule of Law provides no criteria regarding which rules should apply to what sorts of activity. Hayek partially acknowledged this difficulty in accepting that it can be misguided to apply the same rules to everyone in all circumstances. Law frequently discriminates on grounds of age or sex, for example. The key is to discover when such discrimination is reasonable or not. His response to this problem was extremely suggestive: 'Such distinctions will not be arbitrary', he wrote, 'will not subject one group to the will of others, *if they are equally recognised as justified by those inside and those outside the group*' (Hayek 1960: 154, emphasis added). The appeal here is to the test of the Rule of Law being less its formal qualities than its capacity to evince reciprocity and hence obtain mutual assent from citizens. Law is linked to equality not in the formal sense of being the same for all but in the more demanding sense of showing equal concern and respect to all, of taking everyone into account. This idea involves both formal and substantive aspects that cut across the divide between law and legislation. Rather, the distinction invoked is closer to that between law that results from a particular will and law that reflects the general will. However, that notion is distinctly political and usually associated with Rousseau and the republican tradition.

Respublica

That a political system should constitute 'an empire of laws and not of men' (Harrington 1992: 20–1) is a key tenet of the republican tradition, at least in the neo-Roman variant of Cicero, Machiavelli and Harrington recently identified by Quentin Skinner (1998: 44–5) and Philip Pettit (1999: 172–83, and see too Viroli 1998: 121–5). Republicans contrast a law-governed polity with the domination of arbitrary rule. As we saw, the distinguishing features of arbitrary rule are the capacity to exercise discretionary power at whim and without consulting the interests of those affected. Republicanism's distinctiveness resides in noting how even an enlightened and benevolent ruler who possesses this power still dominates, even if he does not actually oppress, the ruled, for they are subjects of their ruler's will. The only alternative to the domination of personal rule is for the people to be citizens and rule themselves. Paradoxically, therefore, the rule of law depends on the democratic self-rule of persons. It can be secured only if all citizens, usually through their elected representatives, can command equal consideration in the making of collective rules, and everyone within the body politic – including those authorised to rule – is equally subject to whatever laws they impose upon themselves (Skinner 1998: 74).

Thus, the republican approach concentrates on the form of government rather than any formal qualities of the law *per se* as the key to ensuring laws are made and applied in ways that show equal concern and respect to all. From this perspective, the Rule of Law arises from a particular civic condition – one where all citizens enjoy an equal political status and have no dominion over each other. To quote Harrington again: it is only when all are equal in the making of the laws that they will be 'framed by every private man unto no other end (or they may thank themselves) than to protect the liberty of every man' (Harrington 1992: 20). Republicanism operates on the basis of what Habermas has called the radical democratic 'hunch' that 'private legal subjects cannot come to enjoy equal individual liberties if they do not *themselves*, in the common exercise of their political autonomy, achieve clarity about justified interests and standards. They themselves must agree on the relevant aspects under which equals should be treated equally and unequals unequally' (Habermas 1996: xlii). Democracy has both a negative and a positive role within this argument. Negatively, it provides a control mechanism. Government's can be held to account for neither taking people's interests seriously nor treating them with equal concern and respect. Positively, it informs people about each other's interests and values, enabling them to give these due consideration and negotiate appropriate compromises when deliberating common rules and policies. This democratic approach avoids a formulaic view that laws must be general, abstract and universalisable to preserve equality and freedom. For example, it enables special rules to be tested for their mutual acceptability by checking they are regarded as neither discriminatory by those to whom they apply nor unfair privileges by the rest.

To achieve these ends, democracy must have a certain form. Republicans advocate a 'mixed' type of government to derive the Rule of Law from the democratic rule of persons. There are two central mechanisms within this peculiarly republican regime: the 'separation of powers' and the 'balance of power' (Bellamy, 1996). The first reduces the discretionary aspect of the law, preventing it degenerating into a mere command. The second encourages the law to track the interests of those to whom it applies and gives them a sense of ownership over it. Taken together, they serve to disperse power so that the law becomes more sensitive to the diversity of ideals, interests and situations within the polity. They block the abuse of power while facilitating and legitimating its constructive and more differentiated use.

The 'separation of powers' divides the legislative from the executive and judicial functions to prevent any person or group becoming a judge in their own cause. Separating those who formulate the laws from those entrusted with their interpretation, application and enforcement brings all within the law. The legislators are constrained in their ability to decree *ad hoc* or self-serving laws by the judiciary's role in applying the law to all in an impartial and consistent manner. Meanwhile, the discretionary and interpretative powers held by the executive and judicial branches are checked because exercised under laws they do not make. However, there are two well-known problems with this thesis. The first concerns the conceptual and practical difficulty of separating functions. For example, when judges adjudicate on which rules apply in given cases, they often end up setting precedents that come to constitute new rules. Similarly, officials frequently create rules in the course of implementing a law. Meanwhile, legislators are inevitably concerned with how the laws they frame will be interpreted and applied to specific cases. Indeed, we have seen how self-serving biases can be built into the most formal and general of rules. Thus, the three functions are inter-related, with each branch of government engaged to some degree in the activities of the other. The second problem arises at this point. For the constraints imposed by what functional separation is possible will be undermined if all branches of government represent similar groups and interests. Having each function run by different people will not necessarily prevent their working for a partial interest if all belong to the same party or class. This problem has been particularly acute in systems, such as the British, where the executive controls the legislature and can exert direct and indirect influence over the judiciary through appointments or other ways.

The notion of the 'balance of power' comes in here. Republicans are not overly concerned to maintain a strict separation of powers. That each branch possesses elements of all three functions not only gets over some of the impracticalities of purely formal accounts of the Rule of Law, but also allows these branches to act as more effective checks on each other. The crucial factor is that power is dispersed between and within these branches so that each constrains the discretionary power of the other. The purpose of such mutual constraining is to ensure the law addresses the concerns of those it affects in a fair manner. So the separation of powers needs to be so organised as to produce a balance of power between the various interests and values of individuals and groups within the polity, obliging them to interact with each other in ways that promote equal concern and respect.[1] For example, federalism has been a standard device of this kind. It operates to produce a balance between various sorts of local and national concerns, reinforcing the separation of powers by ensuring there are rival courts, legislatures and executives that are unlikely to be dominated by any one interest. Bicameral legislatures that are elected according to different systems operate in a similar way.

The type of interaction advocated by republicans is one which obliges the different parties to 'hear the other side'. Public measures – the *res publica* – must be publically justifiable. Such public justification involves more than a lowest-common denominator test, whereby the only legitimate collective rules relate to goods that *de facto* are in everyone's rational interest to have publically provided. In this case, those able to provide for themselves could object to supporting collective arrangements and even standard public goods might be deemed unacceptable. Instead, public justification entails the giving of reasons that are shareable by others.[2] Thus, common rules should not only treat all individuals as moral equals capable of autonomous action, but also be attentive to the variety of circumstances in which they find themselves and the diverse forms of practical reasoning they adopt. Consequently, legislators must drop purely self-interested and self-referential reasoning and look for forms of argument that could be accepted by other individuals who are similarly constrained. In other words, there will be an assumption that in evaluating laws we start by taking into account the effects of their general performance for securing the various generic goods that one could expect individuals to value in the different situations they might find themselves. This assumption implies neither that all are similarly situated nor that they value the same goods. On the one hand, it would exclude any arguments that failed to heed the plight or concerns of others and could not be plausibly shared. Thus, self-serving arguments by the prosperous that there could never be grounds for mutual aid would be unlikely to pass this test. On the other hand, it merely requires that arguments be made in terms all could relate to. This requirement is consistent with groups or individuals pointing out either how their peculiar circumstances create special demands which would be felt by others in their place, or requesting their currently ignored claims be recognised on grounds of fairness by drawing parallels with certain existing entitlements of others. When incommensurable goods and values are in play, it also allows for collective agreements to take the form of a compromise involving reciprocal concessions of various kinds (Bellamy 1999, ch.4).

These constraints will often force political arguments to manifest many of the formal features of abstractness, generality and equality typically associated with the Rule of Law. However, such formalism need not be applied in the mechanical manner advocated by Hayek and others so as to prevent overtly raising substantive positions or an appreciation of the peculiar requirements of different people's particular circumstances or experiences. Rather, the law can evolve through the reciprocal recognition of precisely such considerations, with laws and regulations becoming more diverse and specialised as societies grow more differentiated and pluralist. From a republican point of view, this development need not signal a disregard for justice – quite the contrary. The central requirement is not that the law avoids any deviation from generality and abstractness but that any particular and specific provision should be justifiable in a mutually acceptable way and bear equally and consistently on all to whom it applies. It will not be possible to decide *a priori* what rules are likely to pass this test. Much will depend on the policy and the complexion of those involved. Thus, a call by Muslims for the education system to recognise their religion will play differently in a state that supports religious schools to one where it does not. In the former, a demand for equal treatment might support the establishment of Islamic schools, in the latter it might only lead to special provision within the national curriculum, such as the ability to take a state exam on Islam. What's important is that all sides listen to the other and couch the argument in public reasons each could accept. Republicans insist such reciprocal acknowledgement and negotiation rests not on the formality of the law but the republican character of law-making as a result of an appropriate mix being achieved through a suitable balance of power.

A legitimate question arises at this point as to how one can tell whether the system is appropriately mixed or not. The solution lies in making the constitutive rules of the political system as open to democratic contestation as the regulative rules are. As I noted above, the latter result from ordinary legislation, which provides the legal framework within which citizens, public agencies and officials operate, while the former regulate the system whereby these laws are made. Clearly, the constitutive rules will influence the likely content of the regulative rules. Unsurprisingly, therefore, criticism of the injustice of the second are often linked to demands for altering the first to change biases in the legislative process. Workers and women, for example, linked their campaigns against various discriminatory laws with campaigns for suffrage reform to give them the vote. More recently, claims for polyethnic rights by multicultural groups have likewise been connected to demands for self-government and special representation rights (Kymlicka 1995: 26–33). Clearly, there are good 'Rule of Law' like reasons for making the constitutive rules harder to change than ordinary legislation. People are made securer if there is a relatively stable institutional system, which – among other things – prevents individual rights being curtailed by the whim of the majority. However, from a republican perspective, the justification of such constitutional rules is ultimately a democratic one. So, there must be reasonably accessible and practical mechanisms for their reform and review, such as referenda, which render them open to public scrutiny and discussion.

As Skinner (1996, 1998: 10–11, 59–60) has shown, republicanism was a key alternative to both Hobbes's view of the Rule of Law and those liberal arguments, such as Hayek's, that for all their antagonism to the power Hobbes accords the sovereign ruler, nevertheless develop aspects of his anti-republican critique. This Hobbesean attack raises three common criticisms that republicans need to meet. First, Hobbes denied any connection between public and private liberty (Hobbes 1991: 110). He contended individuals have no more immunity from the laws in a republican than under a monarchical government. What guarantees individual freedom is not the source of law but its extent. Liberals have developed this thesis to argue that freedom depends on limiting interference and the silence of the law. They argue that the link between liberty and political participation rests on a false account of freedom as self-realisation, in which politics is seen as part of the human good. Such accounts risk identifying serving the state with personal freedom, a position with potentially totalitarian implications (Berlin 1969: 162–6). Skinner and Pettit have revealed this interpretation to be mistaken. As we have seen, the republican's blunt response to Hobbes is that in a monarchy - however benign – one will always be subject to the will of the ruler (Harrington 1992: 19–20). One can only be sure the law will track one's private interests by ruling oneself through participating in the public sphere. Thus, private and public freedom are intimately related. However, the reasons for political participation are largely prudential. The motivation is not a strong identification with the state *per se*, so much as the desire to preserve one's liberty from arbitrary interference by dominating princes. Consequently, the need for the 'remarkable change in man', which so worried Martin Hollis, is no greater than that required for individuals to contract to leave the Hobbesean state of nature. Indeed, it is less to the extent that republican institutions take people's tendency to partiality into account while nonetheless promoting the sort of social interaction that in time leads to an awareness of the relationship of their liberty to that of others.

Second, the view of liberty as an absence of interference rather than of domination leads to a view of rights as pre-political, with law an unfortunate if necessary intervention with natural liberty, justified only by virtue of constraining the even greater hindrances that might otherwise arise from other people or agencies. Though social liberals construe such potential interferences quite broadly, so this view need not be equated with the minimal state favoured by libertarians, the presumption is always against state action. Liberals standardly draw the institutional corollary that since rights are both the basis of and constraints upon politics, they should be protected by the judiciary. By contrast, we noted how republicans view rights as the products of law. They argue that rights and liberty do not belong to any putative natural condition that the state must attempt to preserve. They are a civic achievement, the result of living under a certain sort of popular political system. Rights are identified, enacted and defended through ordinary and constitutional politics regarding the regulative and constitutive rules of the polity. Moreover, because liberty is linked to the absence of domination and arbitrary, as opposed to all, interference, intervention in the public interest is seen as often promoting the personal liberties of citizens. For it creates new opportunities that are only available in a society, rather than merely preserving the natural liberty of the pre-social state. However, republicanism is not populism, and there are guarantees for minority rights both through the anti-majoritarian bias of the balance of power and the formal judicial review allowed by the separation of powers (Pettit 1999: 180–83). Yet, though the judiciary plays a vital role in upholding the consistent application and general coherence of the law, this function does not entail anything like the judicial activism endorsed by those who take a more rights-based view of law (e.g. Dworkin, 1978; 1995). From a republican point of view, such a policy simply produces judicial domination.

Finally, Hobbes argues that equitable treatment requires uniform rules, authoritatively defined and interpreted, and that this scheme requires that power is concentrated in the hands of a monarch or some other central body. Such concentration is also necessary to ensure that rulers act responsibly. Republicanism rejects this thesis on both prudential and substantive grounds. Prudentially, it would be unwise to trust any single agent or agency to employ their power for other than self-interested purposes unless constrained by the countervailing power of others to do so. Substantively, circumstances are so various and the forms of practical reasoning employed in different activities and by different groups so diverse, that there cannot be the sort of essential and universal rules of conduct Hobbes seeks. Acceptance of common rules cannot be hypothetically derived from pure reason on *a priori* grounds, but must be actually negotiated by each participant in the decision-making process 'hearing the other side'. The Rule of Law involves the reciprocal giving and responding to the various reasons of others, not the imposition of a common mode of reasoning on all. This sort of dialogue will only take place when power is divided. As I've argued elsewhere (Bellamy 1999: ch.5), the republican notions of dispersing and balancing power for the equitable management of social division and conflict also make it highly suited for the governance of complex and pluralist societies. It encourages greater attention to practicalities and increases commitment to obeying and enforcing the rules fairly through promoting civic participation in the setting and monitoring of standards. For the Rule of Law will only be generated if political and legal officials, policies and institutions are responsive to legislation that reflects citizens evolving experience of the effects of law. Thus, the inevitable delegation of policy-making and interpretation to administrative bodies and officials has to be met by opening up such agencies and agents to democratic accountability.

Within republicanism, therefore, the Rule of Law simply is the rule of persons. What is crucial is that it is the equal rule of all persons. But that is the product of a certain form of politics that prevents the exercise of arbitrary power – namely, a system of mixed government involving the separation of powers, a representative legislature, an independent judiciary and accessible courts, that gives wide scope for civic participation and contestation. Moreover, how far the system and its attendant rules allow power to be equitably shared will itself be at issue and a matter of political debate. The result is an evolving practice of political negotiation that embodies many of the forms of the Rule of Law, but tailors decisions to the different values, interests and circumstances of those to whom they are to apply.

Conclusion

I noted at the outset how Hollis thought Hobbes presented the chief challenge to the establishment of a society of freely co-operating individuals. Accordingly, this essay has taken inspiration from a tradition of social order Hobbes sought to displace: namely republicanism and the related humanist tradition of dialogue, linking both to certain aspects of the common law. Hollis would still have expressed Kantian worries that republican communities must nonetheless be bound by 'universal demands of the right and the good', even if the details of these universal elements remains 'deliberately incomplete', 'thus leaving a realm where construction rules' (Hollis 1998: 162–3). This concern has been addressed only implicitly above. However, the republican's response is clear: there are no universal truths of reason that stand outside any construction and can serve as a criterion. Instead, we must relate our concerns to those of others in more particular ways through an on-going process of public dialogue. Thus, the Rule of Law emerges from the exercise of practical rather than theoretical reason, the product of a politics where all oblige each other to 'hear the other side'. For arbitrary power can only be blocked through the equalisation of power, and achieving this condition is a matter not of principle but of continuous political vigilance and struggle. Indeed, it is the Hobbesian desire to overcome all struggles for power that represents the chief danger to the Rule of Law, for it leads ineluctably to the arbitrary rule of some persons over the rest.

ACKNOWLEDGEMENTS

Earlier versions of this paper were given in Reading, Exeter, Montreal and Oxford. I'm grateful to Alan Cromartie, Simon Caney, Dario Castiglione, David Held, Emilio Santoro, Jim Tully, Will Kymlicka, Philip Pettit and John Gardner for their helpful observations on those occasions, and to Andrew Mason and Preston King for their comments on a later written draft.

NOTES

1. Harrington expressed this point in terms of the fable of the girls and the cake. The best way to ensure a fair division is to ensure that the one who divides the cake takes the last slice. Thus, he advocated having two councils, one to deliberate and the other to enact policy, with the first controlled by the aristocracy and the second by the whole populace (Harrington 1992: 22–5, 64–7).

2. This formulation is a deliberate weakening of Scanlon's (1998) formula of reasons others 'cannot reasonably reject', which provides greater scope for resolving fundamental disagreements between incommensurable values and judge.

REFERENCES

Bellamy, R. 1996. 'The political form of the constitution: the separation of powers, rights and representative democracy'. *Political Studies*, 44, 436–56.
          1999. *Liberalism and Pluralism: Towards a Politics of Compromise*. London: Routledge.
          2001. ' Constitutive citizenship vs. constitutional rights: republican reflections on the EU Charter and the Human Rights Act'. Campbell & Tomkins 2001: 15–39.
Bellamy, R. & Hollis, M. 1995. 'Liberal justice: political and metaphysical', *The Philosophical Quarterly*, 45, 1-20.
          1998. 'Compromise, consensus and neutrality', *CRISPP*, 1/3, 57–78.
Berlin, I. 1969a. 'Two concepts of liberty'. Berlin 1969b.
          1969b. *Four Essays on Liberty*. Oxford: Oxford University Press.
Campbell, T. & A. Tomkins, eds. 2001. *Sceptical Approaches to Entrenched Human Rights*. Oxford: Oxford University Press.
Craig, P. 1997. 'Formal and substantive conceptions of the rule of law: an analytical framework'. *Public Law*, 467–87.
Dicey, A.V. 1959. *Introduction to the Study of the Law of the Constitution*. 10 ed. London: Macmillan.
Dyzenhaus, D. 1991. *Hard Cases in Wicked Legal Systems: South African Law in the Perspective of Legal Philosophy*. Oxford: Clarendon Press.
Dworkin, R. 1978. *Taking Rights Seriously*. 2nd ed. London: Duckworth.
          1995. 'Constitutionalism and democracy'. *European Journal of Philosophy*, 3, 2–11.
Fuller, Lon L. 1969. *The Morality of Law*. Revised ed. New Haven: Yale University Press.
Habermas, J. 1996. *Between Facts and Norms: Contributions to a Discourse Theory of Law and Democracy*. Cambridge: Polity Press, 1996.
Hampton. J. 1994. 'Democracy and the Rule of Law'. Shapiro 1994: 13–44.
Hamowy, R. 1978. 'Law and the liberal society'. *Journal of Libertarian Studies*, 2, 287–97.
Hampshire, S. 1999. *Justice is Conflict*. London: Duckworth.

Harrington, J. 1992. *The Commonwealth of Oceana and A System of Politics*. Ed. J.G.A. Pocock. Cambridge: Cambridge University Press.

Hart, H.L.A. 1958. 'Positivism and the separation of law and morals'. *Harvard Law Review*, 71, 593–629.

1994. *The Concept of Law*. 2nd ed. Oxford: Clarendon Press.

Hayek, F.A. 1960. *The Constitution of Liberty*. London: Routledge.

1973–79. *Law, Legislation and Liberty*. 3 vols. London: Routledge.

Hobbes, T. 1991. *Leviathan*. Ed. Richard Tuck. Cambridge: Cambridge University Press.

Hollis, M. 1994. *The Philosophy of Social Science*. Cambridge: Cambridge University Press.

1998. *Trust Within Reason*. Cambridge: Cambridge University Press.

Pettit, P. 1999. *Republicanism: A Theory of Freedom and Government*. 2nd edition. Oxford: Clarendon Press.

Rawls, J. 1971. *A Theory of Justice*. Oxford: Oxford University Press.

Raz, J. 1979a. 'The Rule of Law and its virtue'. Raz. 1979b: 210–229.

1979b. *Authority of Law: Essays on Law and Morality*. Oxford: Clarendon Press.

1994a. 'The politics of the Rule of Law'. Raz 1994b: 370–78.

1994b. *Ethics in the Public Domain: Essays in the Morality of Law and Politics*. Oxford: Clarendon Press.

Rousseau, J.J. 1973. *The Social Contract and Discourses*. Ed. and trans. G.D.H. Cole. London: Dent.

Scanlon, T.M. 1998. *What We Owe to Each Other*. Cambridge MA: Harvard University Press.

Shapiro, I., ed. 1994. *The Rule of Law*. Nomos 36. New York: New York University Press.

Skinner, Q .1996. *Reason and Rhetoric in the Philosophy of Hobbes*. Cambridge: Cambridge University Press.

1998. *Liberty before Liberalism*. Cambridge: Cambridge University Press.

Sunstein, C. 1996. *Legal Reasoning and Political Conflict*. Oxford: Oxford University Press.

Tully, J. 1995. *Strange Multiplicity: Constitutionalism in an Age of Diversity*. Cambridge: Cambridge University Press.

Viroli, M. 1998. *Machiavelli*. Oxford: Oxford University Press.

Waldron, J. 1989. 'The Rule of Law in contemporary liberal theory'. *Ratio Juris*. 2/1, 79–96.

Wittgenstein, L. 1953. *Philosophical Investigations*. Oxford: Blackwell, 1953.

Abstracts

Trusting in Reason
PRESTON KING

The claims of reason, whether descriptive or prescriptive, should be viewed as universal. There are different ways and methods designed to enable a grasp of rationality, but there is no coherent way of designing escape from rationality. Ethics no more collapses into science than science collapses into ethics. Hence the logic of 'is' and 'ought' diverge, but without prejudice to the rationality of either. Moral theory as distinct from scientific theory is often perceived to be irrational (hence emotivists, naturalists and relativists). An important dimension of this supposed irrationality lies in the characterisation of universalism as anti-pluralist, and of pluralism as relativism. One good reason why this characterisation fails is because the contradictory of pluralism is absolutism, not universalism, and because pluralism contains significant claims that prove both coherent and apt, morally and politically.

Liberalism for the Liberals, Cannibalism for the Cannibals
STEVEN LUKES

The aphoristic title suggests a parallel between liberalism and a culturally embedded, exotic and utterly repellent practice. Is liberalism, understood as the political morality that underpins and justifies liberal practices and institutions, culturally embedded? If so, are the reasons we can offer in its defence similarly embedded and thus uncompelling to non-liberals? Are its core values defensible only by 'internal or consensual reasoning'? Arguments by Walzer, Tully and Parekh in support of this claim are examined and doubts are raised about too holistic a notion of culture. The arguments of the early Rawls and Barry against the claim and for the view that liberalism is culture-free are next examined and criticised. Hollis's idea that liberalism 'has to remain a fighting creed with universalist pretensions' is considered and compared with Barry's less nuanced view and the question of how to defend liberalism is confronted directly. Must its defence rely upon reasoning internal to a liberal outlook? A distinction is drawn between first-order beliefs about substantive issues and their background assumptions, on the one hand, and beliefs about how to argue and justify your political morality on the other. The question whether the latter can be dissociated from liberal background assumptions is raised. A second distinction is drawn between the standpoint of an anthropological observer and a participant in political discourse. From the latter's perspective, it is suggested, liberal practices and institutions may be defensible from non-liberal background assumptions. Finally, the empirical issue of whether liberalism is culture-centric is raised and the suggestion is made that to contrast it with cannibalism is to rely on an illusory notion of 'the exotic' and of the extent of moral diversity.

Hollis, Rousseau and Gyges' Ring
TIMOTHY O'HAGAN

In *Trust Within Reason*, Martin Hollis made his last attempt to present and defend a form of reasoning that would be superior to instrumental, means-end rationality, as propounded by the most sophisticated economists and philosophers in game-theory tradition. Throughout the book he engaged with those writers, in order to show that their model of rationality was conceptually flawed and morally dangerous. By adopting a superior model, that of expressive rationality, he argued, people could both understand the real dynamics of group action, and also come to engage in groups held together by ties of trust. Hollis wanted expressive rationality to be the key to what he called 'fighting liberalism'. The problem for that ideology would be to satisfy the demands of both 'communitarians', who seek to construct the self through social interaction, and 'universalists', for whom all such constructions must be judged by the transcendent standards of reason. This essay shows the importance of Jean-Jacques Rousseau in understanding that problem.

Trust and Political Constitutions
ALBERT WEALE

Trust Within Reason can be read as a work within political philosophy advocating an alternative to the dominant individualist paradigm of choice in terms of instrumental rationality. Its central analytical device, the model of The Enlightenment Trail, can be viewed as a game governed by a particular form of political constitution, namely one in which veto power is lodged in actors at different stages of decision making. Such constitutions are familiar, are associated with mistrust among key political actors and have certain pathologies. One way of overcoming these pathologies is to appeal to a political culture of trust rather than mistrust, and to identify the rationality that is essential to the practice of citizenship. This is the Rousseauian turn in the work of Martin Hollis. But the Rousseauian turn is beset with its own difficulties. Moreover, there is a need to balance the conformist aspects of citizenship with its dissenting aspects. Such a balancing cannot be accomplished by appeal to reason, no matter how stretched the concept becomes.

Trust, Choice and Routines: Putting the Consumer on Trial
ROBERTA SASSATELLI

This paper starts from Martin Hollis' framing of the problem of trust in *Trust Within Reason* and shows how his picture may be developed and challenged by shaping the agent of trust in the guise of a consumer. With the successful imperialism of neo-classical economics, the social actor is increasingly portrayed as a consumer. Sociological and anthropological studies however have shown that even consumers are not easily portrayed as individualistic, instrumentally rational and forward-looking agents. The paper thus sets out to explore how we can best conceptualise consumer choices, and with it, how we can re-think the notion of trust. Paired with different notions of consumer choice, trust may be seen as a self-fulfilling prophecy, as a complexity-reduction device and, finally, as calculated attachment. The paper ends by considering that even market relations are imbued with trust and that consumers rely on trust as much as construct trust relations through their consumer practices.

Whose Dirty Hands?: How to Prevent Buck-Passing
BARBARA GOODWIN

In any organisation, omissions or mistakes by an employee can harm customers, members of the public or other stakeholders. When disaster occurs, there is a rush to find someone responsible and people may pass the buck to avoid blame. I propose that organisations should prevent such repudiation of responsibility by adopting a model for the allocation of responsibility based, in some respects, on laws which operate on a principle of strict liability and do not require intention to be proved. I examine three models – responsibility at the top, equal responsibility and proportionate responsibility – and evaluate their efficacy at preventing avoidance of blame, and their practicability. All are problematic but employees perceive the proportionate responsibility model as the fairest. I conclude that individuals, in their public (organisational) lives, can educate themselves to feel responsibility according to the allocation model adopted by their employer, and that this internalisation safeguards against buck-passing.

Many (Dirty) Hands Make Light Work:
Martin Hollis's Account of Social Action
STEVE SMITH

Martin Hollis had a particular and powerful account of social action, an account that provided the foundation for his writings. But this is an account that is usually assumed in his work, and, for all his writing on social science, has to be brought together from a variety of sources. This paper traces the development of this account by looking at his major statements on social action. The key features of this account are an opposition to naturalism and to holism (either explanatory or understanding), and a belief in reason, agency, and ultimately the self. This is established by looking in particular at his three main books on the topic, *Models of Man*, *The Cunning of Reason*, and *The Philosophy of Social Science*. Hollis develops a notion of the social individual that is opposed to both behaviouralist attempts to explain from without, and to Winchian relativism. The paper also discusses Hollis's well-known two-by-two matrix of social theory, in which he crosses explanation and understanding with holism and individualism. Having outlined the development of his account of social action, the paper offers a critique of his position, arguing that he had a very thin conception of social structure; that he overestimated the extent to which actors have agency; that his argument relied on a Humean notion of causation which was no longer accepted in the natural sciences; that his notion of science was likewise a very partial one, namely positivist; that his belief in a common human core rationality was questionable; that he never really made good on his promise to combine holism and individualism; that his form of argumentation often relied on artificial alternatives; and that his matrix was itself open to a series of challenges. The paper concludes by noting both the tremendous power of his conception of social action and therefore the importance of developing a critique of it.

The Bond of Society: Reason or Sentiment?
ROBERT SUGDEN

This paper compares two opposing positions on the methodology of social science: the rationalist position for which Hollis was a consistent advocate, and an empiricist position deriving from Hume. The discussion focuses on Hollis's account of the 'liberal community', in which the 'bond of society' is ultimately construed in terms of rationality rather than, as in a Humean account, in terms of common sentiments. For Hollis, there is a fundamental distinction between rational and non-rational action; social science should seek to understand human action, and understanding is possible only on the basis of *a priori* postulates about human rationality. The paper argues that, in the absence of empirical criteria for identifying rational action, the distinction between rational and irrational action serves no useful purpose in social science. For anyone to begin to understand another society, some 'bridgehead' is required, but the bridgehead could be common sentiments rather than common rationality.

Collective Reasoning: A Critique of Martin Hollis's Position
NICHOLAS BARDSLEY

Martin Hollis was intrigued by conceptual problems posed by rational choice theory, the formal account of rationality commonly used in economics. In his final work, *Trust Within Reason*, these prompted a radical revision to the analysis of practical reason: that reasons for action can be collective. This is motivated by the need for a rationalisation of sensible play in 'co-ordination games', where rational choice theory is indeterminate. Economists are likely to resist the notion of collective reasoning, most obviously because of commitments to methodological individualism. I argue that this conflict is only apparent, since all that is involved is a particular way of reasoning on the part of individuals. However, philosophical analyses of collective agency cited by Hollis in support of such reasoning are problematic. There is also a substantial problem for those, like Hollis, who desire arbitration between collective and individual perspectives. Though Hollis is rightfully enthusiastic about collective reasoning, his approach is incomplete since this problem implies that he lacks an account of spontaneous co-operation.

A Quick Peek into the Abyss:
The Game of Social Life in Martin Hollis's *Trust Within Reason*
ALAN SCOTT

This article examines Martin Hollis's treatment of social action in his final book, *Trust Within Reason*. While sharing Hollis's suspicion of over-socialized models of action, the article questions the equation of sociological analysis with such a view. It argues that, even within the Durkheimian tradition, we can find a more differentiated account of action somewhere between *homo economicus* and *homo sociologicus* that is in fact closer to the mixed model at which *Trust Within Reason* itself hints. Marcel Mauss's classical *The Gift* and Mark Granovetter's economic sociology are taken as examples of this more complex account in which self and other regarding action, and community and association are not counter posed as straightforward alternatives. On such a view, in Mary Douglas's words, 'the themes [of individualism and solidarity] recur because they correspond to forms of social life that recur'.

Rational Choice and Trust
KEITH DOWDING

Martin Hollis was a great critic of the way in which rational choice theory handled human rationality. Taking as its cue Hollis's argument in his *Trust Within Reason* that rational choice cannot explain why rational individuals will trust others and act trustworthily, the paper shows how an account of trust may be developed within a rational choice framework. First, rational choice can handle the notion of trust trivially as an argument within a utility function. Secondly, an evolutionary account using rational choice methods, where the maximisers are genes, can explain how the argument gets into the utility function.

The Rule of Law and the Rule of Persons
RICHARD BELLAMY

This essay defends the Rule of Law as set of formal attributes that any regular system of law must possess. However, it disputes the view that the Rule of Law could itself be a form of rule and hence offer criteria of good governance. Consequently, the qualities of fairness and equity associated with the Rule of Law must be seen as the product of a certain sort of rule of persons. The argument progresses through an investigation of five worlds of the Rule of Law: Bureaucratica, Monarchia, Communitaria, Libertaria and Respublica. The first, third and fourth attempt to rule through law alone, the second to see the Rule of Law as a form of personal rule. All fail, with the solution provided by the fifth. By ensuring all persons rule each over the others, Respublica offers a form of good governance that produces the forms and substance of the Rule of Law.

Notes on Contributors

Nicholas Bardsley took a doctoral thesis at the University of East Anglia on the economics of nonselfish behaviour. He works at the Centre for Research into Experimental Economics and Political Decision (CREED) at the University of Amsterdam. His interests include experimental economics and issues at the interface of economics and philosophy. He is currently working on an analysis of collective intention and an experimental study of co-ordination problems.

Richard Bellamy is Professor of Government at the University of Reading. Between 1992 and 1996 he was Professor of Politics at the University of East Anglia. He is currently researching issues of European Citizenship and Constitutionalism. Recent publications include *Liberalism and Pluralism: Towards a Politics of Compromise* (Routledge 1999); *Rethinking Liberalism* (Continuum 2000) and (as co-editor with Alex Warleigh) *Citizenship and Governance in the European Union* (Continuum 2001).

Keith Dowding is Professor of Political Science at the London School of Economics and Political Science. He has published a number of books, most recently *Challenges to Democracy* (edited with James Hughes and Helen Margetts) (Palgrave 2001) as well as numerous articles in the fields of political philosophy, political theory, social choice, urban politics, public administration and British politics. He is co-editor of the *Journal of Theoretical Politics*.

Barbara Goodwin works on social justice, ideologies and utopianism. She recently published *Ethics at Work* (Kluwer 2000), a study of ethics and responsibility at work. Other recent publications include an edited volume, *The Philosophy of Utopia* (Frank Cass 2001) and the fourth edition of *Using Political Ideas* (John Wiley 1997). She is the Professor of Politics at the University of East Anglia, Norwich.

Preston King is Distinguished Professor of Political Philosophy at Emory University and Morehouse College and Honorary Professor of Philosophy at the University of East Anglia (Norwich). He is the author of, among others, *Thinking Past a Problem, Toleration* and *The Ideology of Order*, and Founding Editor of *Critical Review of International Social and Political Philosophy*.

Steven Lukes is Professor of Sociology at New York University and Visiting Centennial Professor at the London School of Economics. he is the author of *Emile Durkheim: His Life and Work, Individualism, Power: A Radical View, Marxism and Morality, Moral Conflict and Politics* and a philosophical fable, *The Curious Enlightenment of Professor Caritat*, and co-editor of the *Archives européenes de sociologie*.

Timothy O'Hagan is Senior Lecturer and current Head of Department in Philosophy at the University of East Anglia, Norwich. He is the author of *Rousseau* (Routledge 1999).

Roberta Sassatelli is Lecturer in Sociology at the University of East Anglia, Norwich. She has published widely on social and cultural theory, consumer organisations, consumer culture, fitness culture, gender and the body. She is author of *Anatomia della Palestra* (il Mulino 2000). She is currently Visiting Professor at the University of Bologna and is completing a monograph on contemporary consumer practices.

Alan Scott is Professor of Sociology at the University of Innsbruck, Austria. His research interests are in political sociology and social theory. Recent publications include 'Capitalism, Weber and democracy', *Max Weber Studies* (2000) and (with Roberta Sassatelli) 'Novel foods, new markets and trust regimes', *European Societies* (2001). He is co-editor (with Kate Nash) of *The Blackwell Companion to Political Sociology* (Blackwell 2001).

Steve Smith is Vice Chancellor at the University of Exeter. He has written extensively in the area of international relations theory, with his most recent publication being the second edition of *The Globalization of World Politics* (edited with John Baylis, OUP 2001). He is editor of the Cambridge University Press series, 'Studies in International Relations'.

Robert Sugden is Leverhulme Research Professor at the University of East Anglia, Norwich. His research uses a combination of theoretical, experimental and philosophical methods to investigate issues in welfare economics, social choice, choice under uncertainty, the foundations of decision and game theory, the methodology of economics, and the evolution of social conventions.

Albert Weale has been Professor of Government at the University of Essex since 1992. Between 1985 and 1992 he was a colleague of Martin Hollis at the University of East Anglia and co-author, with others, of *The Theory of Choice* (Blackwell 1992). He is the author of a number of works in political theory, most recently *Democracy* (Palgrave 1999).

Index

11 September 2001, 143

Aborigines, 126, 161
absolutism, 21–7, 28, 31, 32
Adam and Eve, 71–2, 80–81, 85, 86,
    194, 198, 201, 203, 204, 207
Adam, 135, 156, 162
Alaska, 12
Althusser, Louis, 197
altruism, x, 15, 70, 88, 152, 198–201
Amnesty International, 46
anthropology, 36, 39, 43, 50, 52, 85,
    87, 91, 126, 127, 137, 161–2, 166
Antigone, 136
apartheid, 229
aphorism, 35
Aristotle, 16
authoritarianism, vii
Autonomous Man, 128, 129, 130,
    131, 132
Axelrod, Robert, 215
Azande, 126, 127, 138, 139, 143

Bacharach, Michael, 154, 173, 183
Bahn, Paul, 39
balance of power, 243, 245
Banks, Joseph, 167
Baptists, 31
Bardsley, Nicholas, x
Barings Bank, 108, 118
Barry, Brian, 41, 45, 47, 48, 75
Bauman, Zygmunt, 197

behaviouralism, 65, 124
Bellamy, Richard, x, xi, 82
Benedict, Ruth, 38
Benhabib, Seyla, 43
Bentham, Jeremy, 227, 236
Berkeley, Bishop, 11
Berlin, Isaiah, 52
Bevel, Reverend, 4, 5
Bhaskar, Roy, 145
Bible, 6
Bill of Rights, 49
biotechnology, 85
Bittner, Rüdiger, 197
black canoe, 41, 47
blood donation, 60, 70, 88, 152, 154,
    188, 198
Bohr, Niels, 142
Bratman, Michael, 179
Britain, 32
Buchanan, James, 74
Büchner, Georg, 204
buck-passing, x, 106, 115
Buddhism, 51
Burke, Edmund, 59

Calhoun, John, 74
Campbells, 106
Canada, 27
cannibalism, 36–9, 51, 169
capital punishment, 79–80
Cartesianism, 129, 187
categorical imperative, 60

causation, 113, 116, 118, 121, 128, 129, 130, 132, 133, 135, 139, 140, 142, 144, 180, 181, 210, 211
censorship, 48
chess, 157–8
Chicago, 4
China, viii
choice, 94–6
Christianity, 37
Cicero, 241
citizenship, ix, 39, 46, 51, 77, 78, 80, 81, 82, 83
coffee, 210
coherence theories, 3
Coleman, James, 90
collective action, 78, 101, 159, 177, 178, 179, 180, 181, 186, 209, 218
collective agency, 177, 178, 179, 187, 189
collective beliefs, 182–3, 184
collective intentions, 177, 179, 180, 184
collective rationality, 172, 176, 177, 183, 184, 185, 187, 188, 189
Columbus, Christopher, 36
Common Agricultural Policy, 74
common knowledge of collective rationality, 184, 187, 188
common knowledge of rationality, 173, 187, 188
communitarianism, ix, 65, 67, 68, 80, 222, 234–7
compassion, 61
complementarity, 142
compromise, 82, 221, 242, 245
Condorcet, Marquis de, 57, 58, 83
Confucian ethics, 51
conscious collective, 193
consequentialism, x, 87, 176, 177, 190
constitutions, 39, 49,51, 62, 69–83, 227, 237, 239, 246, 249
consumerism, ix
consumers, x, 84–5, 89, 90–101, 134, 238
contractualism, x, 87, 89, 194

Cook, Captain James, 143, 166–7
Co-operatives, 116, 120
co-ordination games, 172, 173, 174, 184, 194
corn laws, 75
correspondence theories, 3
cosmopolitanism, 63–4
counterfactuals, 112–13, 172
counterfinality, 171, 172, 188
CRISPP, vii
Crusoe, Robinson, 18, 37
culture, 15, 43, 45, 49, 63, 65, 67, 77, 82, 91, 100, 103, 121, 129, 133; alien, 36, 126–8, 143, 161, 162, 164, 165, 166, 167; embedding in, 40, 42, 45, 48; holistic model of, 43, 49; liberalism and, 42, 43, 45, 46, 48–9, 51

Dahl, Robert, 82
de Gaulle, Charles, 76
Defoe, Daniel, 37
deism, 201
Dennett, Daniel, 211
Derrida, Jacques, 145
description, 2, 8–9, 13, 14, 15, 16, 17, 144, 180
despotism, 16, 36
determinism, 129, 130
Dicey, Albert V., 231
Diesing, Paul, 178
dirty hands, x, 106, 110, 119
disincentives, 73–4
Douglas, Mary, 91, 92, 198, 203
Dowding, Keith, xi
Dresher, Melvin, 217
Durkheim, Emile, xi, 69, 136, 197, 198, 199, 203

economics, x, 87, 90, 132, 134, 135, 136, 142, 146, 149, 150, 171, 188, 190, 199
Einstein, Albert, 8
embeddedness, 41, 52, 99, 203, 205
Emory University, 12
empiricism, x, 150, 162

empowerment, 117
Encyclopédie, 37
Enlightenment Football League, 153,
  155, 194–5, 198, 213
Enlightenment Trail, 66, 67, 71–2,
  85, 194, 196, 201, 203, 204, 207
Enlightenment, 48, 56, 57, 82, 128,
  129, 140, 146, 162, 196
ethics, ix, 5, 7, 19, 33, 37, 41, 51,
  69, 79, 82, 84, 109, 117, 119, 187,
  221, 222, 228; science and, 1, 2,
  6–8, 12, 14–18, 33, 34
European Union, 73, 74, 76
Evans-Pritchard, Edward Evan, 126,
  127, 138
evolutionarily stable strategy, 212,
  213
evolutionary biology, 17
explanation, vii, 2, 60, 91, 124, 125,
  159–34, 137, 139–41, 143, 145,
  156–60, 163, 164, 177, 78,
  209–12, 215, 217, 218
Exxon Valdez, 12

facts, 9–11, 15
falsifiability, 3
fatherland, 62–4
federation, 27
feminism, 143, 230
Feyerabend, Paul, 4, 133
Flood, Merrill, 217
Florence, 35
Foucault, Michel, 145
foundationalism, viii, 22
France, 32
Frankfurt School, 99
freedom, 29, 45, 46, 49, 58, 63, 67,
  77, 78, 80, 82, 141, 146, 238, 241,
  242, 246, 247
free-rider problem, 239
French, Peter, 179
Freud, Sigmund, 5
Friday, 18, 37
Fuller, Lon, 223

Gadamer, Hans-Georg, 51

game theory, 85, 135, 158, 171, 179,
  190, 209, 212, 213, 214, 218
Gardner, Roy, 213
Garfinkel, Harold, 93, 94
genes, 19, 215, 216, 218, 219
Germany, 27
Geuss, Raymond, 40, 49
Giddens, Anthony, 145
Gilbert, Margaret, 154, 178, 179,
  182, 183, 185, 187
Gillray, James, 37
Ginsberg, Morris, 52
Glaucon, 55–6
Glencoe massacre, 106
Glover, Jonathan, 107
Goodwin, Barbara, x
Gormenghast, 222, 223, 229, 236
Granovetter, Mark, 200, 201, 202,
  204, 205
Great Turtle Island, 41
Gross, John, 35
Gyge's ring, 55–6

Haida, 41
Hamowy, Ronald, 241
Hampton, Jean, 164
Harrington, James, 241, 253
Hart, Herbert. L.A., 64, 227, 233
Hayek, Friedrich A., 177, 237–41,
  246
Hegel, Georg W.F., 134
Heisenberg, Werner, 142
Herald of Free Enterprise IV, 106,
  109, 122
hermaneutics, 132, 139, 140, 142,
  143
hi-lo game, 173–4, 175, 176, 177,
  183, 184, 185, 187, 189, 190
Hirschman, Albert, 90, 97, 98,
  100–101
Hitler, Adolph, 9
Hobbes, Thomas, 16, 69, 77, 86,
  122, 132, 171, 200, 221, 222, 232,
  233, 234, 236, 237, 246, 247, 249
Hodgson, David H., 154
holism, 125, 137, 138, 139, 140,

141, 145, 146, 197
Hollis, Martin, vii–x, xii, 1, 36, 45, 124–5, 149, 150; and 'dirty hands', 106–8; and liberalism, 64–7, 150–53, 159, 160; and matrix of social theory, 124, 125, 137–9, 144–6; and political philosophy, 69, 77, 78, 221–2, 233, 249; and rationality, 5, 46, 56–60, 74, 77, 79–83, 85–90, 99, 101–2, 127, 130–37, 138, 139, 143, 150–68, 171–2, 174–7, 179, 182, 186, 187–9, 194–200,, 202, 207–11, 213, 221, 233–4, 235; and science/ethics divide, 2; and social action, 123, 125–46, and social sciences, 65, 156–62, 160–61, 168, 171; (works) 'A remarkable change in man', 58; 'Dirty Hands', 106; *Explaining and Understanding International Relations* (with Steve Smith), 124; *Friends, Romans and Consumers*, 90; 'Honour among thieves', 58; *Invitation to Philosophy*, vii; 'Is universalism ethnocentric?', 35; *Models of Man*, vii, 66, 125, 128, 132, 157, 171; 'Reason and ritual', 126; *Reason in Action*, vii *The Cunning of Reason*, 123, 132–3, 136, 156, 157; 'The epistemological unity of mankind', 127–8; *The Philosophy of Social Science*, vii, 125, 137, 143–4; *Trust within Reason*, vii, 56, 58, 59, 60, 64, 69, 70, 71, 72, 75. 77, 78, 83, 84, 85, 87, 88, 101, 149, 150, 151, 153, 160, 161, 169, 172, 186, 188, 189, 193, 194, 197, 200, 204, 207
Hollywood, 11
homo economicus, 90, 144, 193, 199
homo sociologicus, 144, 193, 194, 198, 199
House of Lords, 75
human nature, 15, 16, 17, 19, 49, 66, 77, 78, 80, 128, 132, 168, 221
humanism, 50, 157, 162, 168

Hume, David, 56, 86, 87, 88, 129, 132, 134, 142–3, 168, 211, 216
Hurley, Susan, 154, 186, 187

identification, 61–3, 80, 92, 95, 153, 156, 160, 194, 247
individualism, vii–viii, ix, x, 50, 69, 71, 78, 79, 80, 125, 135, 137, 138, 139, 140, 145, 172, 177, 178, 186, 194, 197, 200, 202, 203
Inquisition, 11
international relations, 124, 137
Internet, 229
Iraq, 12, 17, 108
Islam, 245

Johnson, Lyndon, 75
joint decision traps, 75
Juliet, 11
justice, 1, 3, 16, 33, 40, 44, 47, 51, 56, 58, 60, 82, 86, 87, 108, 221, 223, 225, 229, 230, 234, 239, 245, 246

Kant, Immanuel, 8, 56–7, 58, 59, 60, 79, 87, 89, 92, 120, 153, 194, 197, 221, 222, 249
Kelsen, Hans, 227, 237
Kennedy, John Fitzgerald, 75
Kilimanjaro, 8, 9
King Rex, 223
Knave, 88
Kraus, Karl, 35
Kuhn, Thomas, 133
Kurds, 12
Kymlicka, Will, 43

La Mettrie, Julien Offray de la, 129
Lakatos, Imre, 3, 133
Leeson, Nick, 118
Lesser Antilles, 36
Leviathan, 86, 132, 200
liability, 111, 114, 115, 117, 119, 120, 122
liberalism, 32, 35–54, 64, 66, 67, 68, 159, 160, 168

liberty, 29, 30, 77, 78, 222, 240, 241, 246, 247
Lock, Stock and Barrel, 150–53
loyalty, 97, 98
Luhmann, Niklas, 94, 95
Lukes, Steven, x, 18
Luxembourg compromise, 76
Lyotard, Jean-François, 145

MacDonalds, 106
Machiavelli, Niccolo, 241
MacIntyre, Alasdair, 16
Madison, James, 74
Mafia, 154, 163, 169, 196
Malachowski, Alan, 191
Malesherbes, M. de, 35
Mali, 19
Mangabeta, 39
Manicheanism, 11
Marre, James, 39
Marx, Karl, 6, 197
Mauss, Marcel, xi, 199, 200, 204, 205
maximalism, 39–40, 45, 46, 48
Maynard Smith, John, 212
McLean, Iain, 75
memes, 215, 219
mens rea, 111, 113, 117
mental processing, 155
meta-beliefs, 50
meta-principles, 50
Methodists, 31
Mexico City, 8
Midgley, Mary, 43
Miller, Kaarlo, 179
Mills, John Stuart, 41–2, 49, 178
minimalism, 39–40, 45, 46
Modest Proposal, 38
monarchy, 232–4
monetary system, 99–100
monism, 19, 25, 27, 29
Montaigne, Michel de, 36–7, 53
moral philosophy, 16, 18, 55, 67
motorist, 60, 70
Muslims, 245

Nagel, Thomas, 154
Napoleon, 227
Nash equilibria, 173, 213, 214, 218
Natural Right, 50
naturalism, 57, 58–60, 63, 82, 123, 124, 129, 130, 130, 138, 140, 142, 145, 146, 167
Nietzsche, Friedrich, 36, 95
non-hierarchical organisations, 116
Northern Ireland, 82

O'Hagan, Timothy, x, 202
Oakeshott, Michael, ix, 2
Obeyesekere, Gananth, 143
Ostrom, Elinor, 213
Other Minds problem, 131, 137, 140, 161–2, 164–6
Oxford, viii

Papua New Guinea, 7
Parekh, Bhikhu, 41, 49
Parfit, Derek, 191
Parsons, Talcott, 93
Peake, Mervyn, 222
persecution, 48
Petit Souper à la Pariesienne, 38
Pettir, Philip, 241, 247
philosophy, 12, 85, 92, 128, 149, 200, economics and, 188; history of, 89, 123; moral, 16, 18, 55, 67; of mind, 143, 147; of science, 64–7, 142, 143; of social science, 69, 123, 124, 137–40, 142, 146, 200; political, 15, 16, 18, 69, 70, 71; science and, 2, 128; social, 15, 17, 18
Pico della Mirandola, Giovanni, 135, 156
Plastic Man, 128, 129, 130, 132
Plato, 55–6
pluralism, 19–27, 28, 29, 30, 31, 32
political philosophy, 15, 16, 18, 69, 70, 71
political science, 64, 128, 132, 142, 146
Popper, Karl, 3, 133

positivism, 124, 129, 140, 142, 232
potlatch, 199
prescription, 2, 8–9, 13, 14, 15, 16
prisoner's dilemma, 171, 190, 201, 208, 215, 239
Przeworski, Adam, 138
psychology, 155, 157, 158
public goods, 41, 70, 99, 149, 221, 244

quantum physics, 142
Queen Charlotte Islands, 41
Quine, Willard V., 133

RAND Corporation, 217
rational choice theory, ix, x, xi, 102, 135, 142, 149, 150, 154, 155, 156, 171, 174, 186, 190, 207, 208, 209, 210
rationalism, expressive, x
Rawls, John, 43–5, 48, 49, 67
Rawson, Claude, 39, 51–2
reason, affective, 133; collective, 150–56, 176–88; descriptive, 1–2, 7–8, 18, 33; disinterested, 56–8; economic models of, 134, 136, 149, 151–2, 212; emotion and, 4–5; expressive, x, 58–60, 65, 103, 133–4, 160, 172, 174–5, 176, 200; ideal, 134, 135, 153; instrumental, 56–9, 69, 71 75, 76, 78, 79, 81, 83, 87, 95, 99, 133–4, 151 153, 171, 172, 174–5, 176, 195, 200, 207; prescriptive, 1–2, 7–8, 18, 33; traditional, 133; universality of, 1–2, 5, 21, 33, 34, 35, 45, 125–7, 130–32, 143, 159–70, 189, 190, 195, 207
reasonableness, 44
Rechtsstaat, 237
reciprocity, x, 60, 69–70, 79, 80, 81, 88, 97, 150, 151, 152, 199, 212, 241
Regan, Donald, 154, 176, 181–2, 186
relativism, vii, ix, s, 1, 7, 21–7, 28, 29, 30, 36, 40, 45, 66, 125, 132,

137, 138, 141, 143, 145
relativity, 142
Renfrew, Colin, 39
replicators, 214, 215, 216, 217, 218, 219
republicanism, 241–9
reputation, 56, 202
responsibility, x, 92, 106–21, 179, 196
Rhodesia, 10
rights, 39, 47, 49, 50, 51, 101, 13, 185, 223, 247, 248; civil, 74, 75; consumer, 85, 103, 104; group, 45, 246, 248; human, 46, 80, 225; individual, 42, 246; property, 238; workers', 98
Rite of Spring, 179
ritual beliefs, 126, 127
roles, 13, 101, 106, 130, 121, 135, 136, 138, 141, 144, 145, 160, 195, 198, 230
Romeo, 11
Rouget's vote, 138, 142
Rousseau, Jean-Jacques, x, 56–64, 66, 71, 77–82, 136, 185, 222, 241; Discourse on the Origin of Inequality among Men, 61, 63, 77; Social Contract, 58, 59, 61
Rule of Law, 221–49
rule-based society, 227–32

Sahlins, Marshall, 143
Salisbury, Lord, 10
Sanscoulottes, 38
Sartre, Jean-Paul, 136, 187
Sassatelli, Roberta, x, xi
Scanlon, Thomas M., 253
scapegoating, 115
Schelling, Thomas, 173
Schopenhauer, Arthur, 36
science, 3, 4, 34, 41, 64, 128, 129, 132, 133, 134, 142–5, 157, 158, 163; ethics and, 1, 2, 6–8, 12, 14–18, 33, 34; philosophy and, 2, 128; philosophy of, 64–7, 142, 143
scientific realism, 145

Scientologists, 31
Scott Report, 108
Scott, Alan, xi
Searle, John, 16, 178, 179, 180, 181, 191
Second Word War, 85
Sen, Amartya, 177
separation of powers, 74, 243, 248
September 11 see 11 September 2001
Sidgwick, Henry, 69
Simmel, George, 91, 94, 99, 197, 204, 205, 246, 247
Skinner, Quentin, 241
Skinner. B.F., 65
Smith, Adam, 56, 87, 156
Smith, Steve, x
social action, viii, 95,,96, 123, 125, 131, 133, 135, 137, 139, 140, 141, 144, 145–6, 202
social science methodology, x, xi
social sciences, empiricist, 150, 164, 168; Hollis's conception of, 64, 156–62, 168, 171; philosophy of, 69, 123, 124, 137–40, 142, 146, 200; rationalism and, 32, 33–4, 150, 160, 161, 162, 168, 171; scope and methodology, x, xi, 164, 171
social theory, 125
socialisation, 56
sociology, xi, 43, 49, 52, 85, 91, 96, 132, 144, 146, 164, 171, 193, 197, 198, 199, 200, 201, 202, 203
Socrates, 55–6
Solander, Daniel, 167
solidarism, ix, x, xi
Sophocles, 136, 137
South Africa, 229
Stevenson, C.L., 14
Stravinsky, Igor, 179
Strawson, Peter F., 128, 139
structuralism, 91, 141, 171
structuration theory, 145
Sugden, Robert, x, 154, 172, 176, 182, 183, 184
supply and demand, vii, 134

Swift, Jonathan, 38
Switzerland, 27
sympathy, 86

Tahiti, 7
Taylor, Charles, 45, 51
team reasoning, 152–3, 154, 155
Television Licensing Authority, 115
territoriality, 17
Teune, Henry, 138
Thatcherism, 90
Theravada Buddhism, 51
Tierra del Fuego, 166–7
Titmuss, Richard, 70, 88, 198, 205
Titus Groan, 223, 229
Todorov, Tsvetan, 37
toleration, 30
totalitarianism, 80
Toynbee, Arnold, 6
trust, ix, xi, 57, 59, 75–83, 85–102, 150, 172, 175, 186, 188, 189, 194, 196, 201, 207, 212, 213, 217, 234, 239, 248
truth, 1, 3, 6, 7, 8, 18, 28, 37, 40, 57, 66, 83, 126, 127, 158, 162, 1164, 169, 191, 249
Tsebelis, George, 75
Tucker, Albert, 217
Tullock, Gordon, 74
Tully, James, 41, 43, 47
Tuomela, Raimo, 179
Twain, Mark, 45
tyranny, 74, 22, 229, 232, 237

uncertainty principle, 142
understanding, vii, 2, 124, 125, 128, 131, 133, 134, 137, 139, 140, 145, 211, 212
United Kingdom, 109, 111, 114, 188
United States, 25, 27
universalism, 3, 5, 19–27, 29, 30, 35, 37, 45, 50, 52, 53, 60–64, 84, 102, 160, 194, 197, 237
University of East Anglia, 123, 149, 154, 191, 197
utilitarianism, 87, 116, 154, 176,

190, 194
utility function, 90, 215
utility theory, 174

Vauvenargues, Luc de Clapiers, 35
Veblen, Thorstein, 198
Verstehen, 80
veto points, 75, 76, 81
Vietnam, 4
Virginia School, 74
Voltaire, Francois-Marie Arouet, 36
voting paradox, 174, 181

Walker, James, 213
Walzer, Michael, 40, 43, 45, 48
Weale, Albert, x
Weber, Max, 64, 65, 133, 134, 197,

227, 231, 236
welfare state, 70
Wellington, Duke of, 75
White, Jimmy, 211
Winch, Peter, 128, 133, 138, 140,
    143
witchcraft, 11, 126, 127, 138, 139,
    143
Wittgenstein, Ludwig, 195, 196, 234
Woyzeck, 204
Wrong, Dennis, 193

Yoruba, 126
Young, Andrew, 4

Zanzibar, 19

*For Product Safety Concerns and Information please contact
our EU representative GPSR@taylorandfrancis.com Taylor & Francis
Verlag GmbH, Kaufingerstraße 24, 80331 München, Germany*

T - #0106 - 270225 - C0 - 216/148/15 - PB - 9780714684000 - Gloss Lamination